CASE FILES
FOR BASIC
TRIAL ADVOCACY

CASE FILES FOR BASIC TRIAL ADVOCACY

by the authors of THE ART & SCIENCE OF TRIAL ADVOCACY

H. Mitchell Caldwell
Professor of Law
Pepperdine University School of Law

Carol A. Chase
Professor of Law
Pepperdine University School of Law

Naomi Harlin Goodno
Associate Professor of Law
Pepperdine University School of Law

L. Timothy Perrin
Vice Dean and Professor of Law
Pepperdine University School of Law

CAROLINA ACADEMIC PRESS

Durham, North Carolina

ISBN 978-1-4224-7092-3
eISBN 978-0-32717-599-5

This publication is designed to provide accurate and authoritative information in regard to the subject matter covered. It is sold with the understanding that the publisher is not engaged in rendering legal, accounting, or other professional services. If legal advice or other expert assistance is required, the services of a competent professional should be sought.

Carolina Academic Press, LLC
700 Kent Street
Durham, North Carolina 27701
Telephone (919) 489-7486
Fax (919) 493-5668
www.caplaw.com

Printed in the United States of America
2016 Printing

ACKNOWLEDGEMENTS

We owe a debt of gratitude to law students Christina Gaudern and Adam Looney, who provided tremendous input and support for this endeavor. Their unflagging enthusiasm and good nature helped carry this project through to completion. We thank Pepperdine University School of Law students in trial practice classes who helped test these case files. We also thank and acknowledge the Labor Law Division of the American Bar Association for allowing us to modify two of their interschool trial competition problems: *Driver and Phlame v. The Bombero Fire Department* (herein re-named *William Striver and Frances Gomez v. Rancho Fire Department*) and *Price v. GEM Corporation*.

AUTHORS' NOTE

We envision the first eight case files as being particularly well-suited for use during the basic student trial advocacy exercises. These case files include a variety of civil and criminal fact patterns that provide students the opportunity to try their hand at opening statements and closing arguments, as well as at direct and cross-examinations. These case files tend to be a manageable length for weekly or bi-weekly assignments.

Case files nine through twelve are more intricate and complicated, both factually and legally, and would serve well for full trials at the end of the course.

TABLE OF CONTENTS

Chapter 1

United States of America

v.

William Stevens

(bank robbery)

UNITED STATES DISTRICT COURT

FOR THE CENTRAL DISTRICT OF GOLDEN

	)	
UNITED STATES OF AMERICA	)	
	)	
v.	)	Case No. CR 43-502
	)	
WILLIAM STEVENS,	)	
Defendant.	)	
	)	

UNITED STATES DISTRICT COURT

FOR THE CENTRAL DISTRICT OF GOLDEN

October C.Y.-2 Grand Jury

UNITED STATES OF AMERICA	)	Case No. CR 43-502
	)	
v.	)	I N D I C T M E N T
	)	
WILLIAM STEVENS,	)	[18 U.S.C. § 2113(d): Armed Bank
Defendant.	)	Robbery]

The Grand Jury charges:

COUNT ONE

[18 U.S.C. § 2113(d)]

On or about July 14, C.Y.-2, in Lead County, within the Central District of

Golden, defendant WILLIAM STEVENS, armed with a firearm and by force, violence,

and intimidation, knowingly took from the person and presence of another approximately

$742 belonging to and in the care, custody, control, management, and possession of First

Federal Bank in Universal City, Golden, a bank the deposits of which were then insured

by the Federal Deposit Insurance Corporation.

A TRUE BILL

Randall Jefferson

Foreman of the Grand Jury

BONNIE ANDERSON
United States Attorney

ROBERT CHARLES
Assistant United States Attorney
Chief, Criminal Division

JOHN PORTER
Assistant United States Attorney
Acting Chief, Criminal Complaint

Witness List

Witnesses for the State:

1. Victoria/Victor Thomas * *

2. Agent Samuel/Samantha Mines * *

Witnesses for Defendant:

1. William Stevens *

2. Al/Alicia Silver * *

Each side must call both witnesses listed for their respective side in any order.

*   This witness must be a male.

* *   This witness may be either gender.

Stipulations

1. Federal Rules of Criminal Procedure and Federal Rules of Evidence apply.

2. Each witness who gave a statement did agree under oath at the outset of the statement to give a full and complete description of what occurred and to correct the statement for inaccuracies and completeness before signing it.

3. All witnesses called to testify who have identified Defendant or identified tangible evidence can, if asked, identify the same at trial.

4. All exhibits in the file are authentic and, unless otherwise noted, are the original of that document.

5. All witness statements were given under oath.

6. Other than what appears in the witness statements there is nothing exceptional or unusual about the background of any of the witnesses that would bolster or detract from their credibility.

7. All dates are denoted by C.Y. (current year) and C.Y.-1 indicating, for example, that the date is the current year minus one.

8. All pretrial motions shall be oral.

9. No party may "invent" witnesses or evidence not specifically mentioned in this problem.

10. "Beyond the record" is not a proper objection. Rather, attorneys shall use cross-examination as a means of challenging a witness whose testimony strays beyond the facts contained in the witness's statement or deposition.

11. William Stevens has entered a plea of not guilty and has requested a trial by jury.

12. For purposes of opening statements and closing arguments, the witness statements of Hattie Davis, Ellen Ferrell, and Stella Stevens accurately reflect their trial testimony.

13. The trial court has denied a motion to dismiss the indictment.

14. Both parties have agreed that the distance between St. Peter and Universal City is twenty-five miles. Travel time on the roadways between St. Peter and Universal City is approximately thirty minutes at times other than rush hour. Rush hour is between 7 a.m. and 9 a.m. and between 5 p.m. and 7 p.m. on weekdays. The robbery took place on a weekday afternoon.

15. First Federal Bank in Universal City is federally insured by the FDIC.

16. It is stipulated that the State of Golden State driver's license is Defendant's driver's license and that all information on the license is correct. It is further stipulated that the photograph and information is that of Defendant.

17. Section 2113(d) of the United States Code of Criminal Procedure defines bank robbery as using force and violence, or intimidation to take, or attempt to take, from the person or presence of another any property or money or any other thing of value belonging to, or in the care, custody or control of, any bank, credit union or savings and loan.

18. The prosecution and defense may call only the two witnesses listed on their respective witness list. Each party may call an additional witness by deposition or witness statement. Any such testimony is subject to objections pursuant to the Federal Rules of Evidence. If a witness is called by deposition or witness statement, the opposing party may cross-examine that witness by deposition or witness statement. The parties have agreed to waive Confrontational Clause objections for only this witness.

Witness Statement of Victoria/Victor Thomas

Date: August 1, C.Y.-1

My name is Victoria/Victor Thomas and I reside at 1523 Malcolm Avenue, Universal City, Golden. I am presently employed as a senior teller for the First Federal Bank in Universal City, and have been employed there since C.Y.-5.

On July 14, C.Y.-1, I was working as a teller at the First Federal Bank in Universal City. My teller window is the closest teller window to the bank entrance, which is on the north side of the building. At approximately 1:50 p.m. on July 14, C.Y.-1, just as I returned from my lunch break, I noticed a man enter the bank. I did not have a customer at my window at that time, and I was able to get a good look at him. He was a male [describe in general terms the physical description of the witness portraying Defendant]. He wore his hair in corn-row braids, but what I remember most is that he had really unusual eyes. They were large and looked kind of "glassy." The man hesitated briefly after he entered the bank, and seemed to be fumbling with something in his jacket. He then yelled, "Everyone on the floor, everyone on the floor." I saw that he had a gun in his right hand. There was one customer, Hatti Davis, at a window to my left, and when she tried to move toward the door, the man told her to get down or he would "blow your damn head off."

I saw the customer and everyone else get down on the floor, and I did too. The man jumped over the counter yelling that he would shoot anyone who moved. He ordered everyone to lie face down and said he would shoot anyone who looked at him or moved.

I laid on my stomach and tried not to move. My heart was pounding and I was afraid that he would shoot me. Out of the corner of my eye I saw his shoes were very close to where I was laying. I heard him open a drawer above me, which I assumed was my cash drawer. He then moved away, and I heard another drawer open. There were only two tellers working at this time, and only two cash drawers were in use. I heard him try to open another drawer, but he could not do so. He swore and then ran out of the bank. Nobody moved for a minute or two and then I heard Ellen Ferrell, the branch manager, tell us that she had activated the silent alarm. I got up and watched Ellen lock the doors. She told us not to touch anything until the police had arrived.

We all stood together in the branch lobby area while we waited for the police to arrive. Hatti Davis, the customer who had tried to leave, was crying, so I went over to try to calm her down. After she settled down a bit, I told her that we would need to be prepared to give a detailed description of the robber to the FBI, and we began to compare notes on what the robber had looked like. Both of us were struck by his unusual eyes.

When the FBI Agent (Agent Mines) arrived, he/she spoke with us individually. When it was my turn I described the robber's appearance and especially his strange eyes. Then Agent Mines and I walked to my teller station. My cash drawer was still open. Agent Mines asked me if I noticed anything unusual. I looked in the drawer and, in addition to the fact that the money was gone, I noticed that a small plastic card was in my drawer. I mentioned this to the Agent, who turned the card over. It was a driver's license. When I looked at the photo on the license I said, "That's him. That's the guy who robbed me." Even though the photograph did not show the robber wearing corn-row braids, it was definitely the same person. The photo had those same eerie, big, glassy eyes. I couldn't take my eyes away from the photograph.

Two weeks after the robbery, on July 29, C.Y.-1, I was asked to attend a live line-up. I was able to immediately pick out the guy who robbed me. He was in the number 5 position of 6 men. Even though his hair was not braided in corn-rows, his distinctive eyes caught my attention. I am absolutely positive that the guy I picked out of the line up was the robber.

I have reviewed my witness statement. This is a complete and accurate account.

V. Thomas
Victoria/Victor Thomas

Witness Statement of Special Agent Samuel/Samantha Mines

Date: August 1, C.Y.-1

My name is Samuel/Samantha Mines and I am a Special Agent with the FBI who works in the bank robbery division of the FBI. I have been a Special Agent for four years and was a uniformed police officer for Lead County for ten years prior to that.

On July 14, C.Y.-1, at approximately 2:15 p.m., I responded to the First Federal Bank in Universal City. We had received a signal from the silent alarm at the bank and believed that there might be a situation in progress there. I was accompanied by two uniformed policemen who were in a separate marked police cruiser. When we arrived, the doors to the bank were locked, but the branch manager unlocked the door to admit us. While the patrol officers walked the bank looking for evidence and dusted the counters for fingerprints, I interviewed the victim teller, Thomas. Thomas described the robber as a male [describe in general terms the physical description of the witness portraying Defendant], who wore his hair in corn-rows. He/She also described his eyes as large and "glassy."

When I walked over to Thomas' teller window, I noticed that his/her teller drawer was open. There were a few slips of paper and a plastic card lying face down, but there was no money in the drawer. I called Thomas over and asked him/her to examine the drawer and tell me if anything seemed out of place. He/She said, "Well, all the money is gone. And I don't remember seeing that card before."

I pulled crime scene gloves on and carefully turned the plastic card over. As I did so, Thomas exclaimed, "Oh my God. That's the robber!" The plastic card was a driver's license issued by the State of Golden to William Stevens. As Thomas stared at the photograph, I pointed out to him/her that the person pictured did not have a corn-row hairstyle. He/She was adamant that it was the same person and said he/she would recognize those eyes anywhere.

I ran a check on William Stevens using his driver's license number. He has had three prior convictions. The first, which was 10 years old, was a misdemeanor drug possession conviction. The second was a felony possession with intent to distribute methamphetamine, for which he was convicted 7 years ago and served two years in prison. The third was a bank robbery conviction 5 years ago. He was released from prison two weeks prior to the robbery of the First Federal Bank on July 14.

Based on the information obtained at the bank, I presented an affidavit in support of a complaint for bank robbery. A warrant was issued and the following day we attempted unsuccessfully to arrest the defendant at the address listed on the warrant. There did not appear to be anyone at home. We waited two more days before returning to that address and continued our attempt to locate Stevens. When we returned to the listed residence on July 17, C.Y.-1, we were able to affect the arrest.

The Assistant United States Attorney had us do a line-up a few days later, after they had interviewed Stevens. Defense counsel was present, as were witnesses Thomas, Ellen Ferrell, and Hatti Davis. Thomas and Davis positively identified Stevens as the robber. Ferrell said that Stevens resembled the robber but could not be certain that he was the same person. The license was not tested for fingerprints because two eyewitnesses gave a positive identification of Stevens.

I have reviewed my witness statement. This is a complete and accurate account.

S. Mines

Samuel (Samantha) Mines

GOLDEN

DRIVERS LICENSE

G5674320

WILLIAM EDWARD STEVENS
1900 SPARKS AVE.
THOUSAND OAKS, GOLDEN 90392

CLASS: C

SEX: M   EYES: XXX
HEIGHT: X' X"   HAIR: XXX
WEIGHT: XXX   DOB: 2/29/1963

EXPIRES: 2/29/C.Y.-2

UNITED STATES DISTRICT COURT

FOR THE CENTRAL DISTRICT OF GOLDEN

UNITED STATES OF AMERICA v. WILLIAM STEVENS	))))))	Criminal No. 099-J32

CERTIFIED JUDGMENT OF CONVICTION AND COMMITMENT ORDER

On April 3, C.Y. – 6, Assistant United States Attorney being present and Defendant having appeared in person with counsel, being the date fixed by the Court for pronouncement of judgment and sentence upon a verdict of Guilty of the offense of bank robbery in violation of 18 U.S.C. § 2113(d), Defendant was sentenced to the Correctional Facility for a period of 5 years commencing at 12:00 o'clock noon on April 7, C.Y. – 6.

IT IS FURTHER ORDERED, that the Clerk of this Court deliver a certified copy of this Judgment and Commitment to the Sheriff or other appropriate officer as a commitment of Defendant.

IT IS SO ORDERED.

B. Young
_____
Betty Young
United States District Court Judge

Date: April 3, C.Y.–6

IN THE CIRCUIT COURT OF THE THIRTEENTH JUDICIAL CIRCUIT

IN AND FOR LEAD COUNTY, STATE OF GOLDEN

CRIMINAL DIVISION

STATE OF GOLDEN	)	
	)	
	)	Criminal No. 054-K49
v.	)	
	)	
WILLIAM STEVENS	)	

CERTIFIED JUDGMENT OF CONVICTION

On November 10, C.Y. – 8, Assistant United States Attorney being present and Defendant having appeared in person with counsel, being the date fixed by the Court for pronouncement of judgment and sentence upon a verdict of Guilty of the offense of possession of illegal drugs with intent to distribute in violation of Penal Code § 450.21, Defendant was sentenced to the Golden State Correctional Facility for a period of 2 years commencing at 12:00 o'clock noon on November 15, C.Y. – 8.

IT IS FURTHER ORDERED, that the Clerk of this Court deliver a certified copy of this Judgment and Commitment to the Sheriff or other appropriate officer as a commitment of Defendant.

IT IS SO ORDERED.

Gary Good
_____
Judge Gary Good

Date: November 10, C.Y. –8, State of Golden

IN THE CIRCUIT COURT OF THE THIRTEENTH JUDICIAL CIRCUIT

IN AND FOR LEAD COUNTY, STATE OF GOLDEN

CRIMINAL DIVISION

STATE OF GOLDEN	)	
	)	
	)	Criminal No. 084-N42
v.	)	
	)	
WILLIAM STEVENS	)	

CERTIFIED JUDGMENT OF CONVICTION

On August 20, C.Y. – 11, Assistant United States Attorney being present and Defendant having appeared in person with counsel, being the date fixed by the Court for pronouncement of judgment and sentence upon a verdict of Guilty of the offense of possession of illegal substances in violation of Penal Code § 423.12, Defendant was sentenced to the Bay County Jail for a period of 6 months commencing at 12:00 o'clock noon on August 25, C.Y. – 11.

IT IS FURTHER ORDERED, that the Clerk of this Court deliver a certified copy of this Judgment and Commitment to the Sheriff or other appropriate officer as a commitment of Defendant.

IT IS SO ORDERED.

_____*P. Williams*_____

Judge P. Williams

Date: August 20, C.Y. –11, State of Golden

Witness Statement of Hatti Davis

Date: August 1, C.Y.-1

Special Agent S. Mines conducted the following interview of Hatti Davis on August 1, C.Y.-1.

My name is Hattie Davis and I am a retired middle school social studies teacher. I have lived in Universal City for thirty-five years.

On July 14, C.Y.-1, I was at the First Federal Bank in Universal City just after I met my friend, Annie Jones, for lunch. We ate at the El Adobe Cantina, and because it was Annie's birthday, we celebrated with a margarita each. I am not a drinker, and the drink made me feel a little giddy. I was glad that the bank was just a few blocks from the El Adobe, so that I could walk there rather than drive. I don't recall exactly what time I arrived at the First Federal Bank, but it was after lunch, so I will guess it was about 1:45. I went to the bank to deposit my pension check.

As I was waiting to get my deposit receipt from the teller, I heard a man yell "everyone on the floor." When I looked at him and saw that he had a gun, I tried to leave, but the man ordered me to get onto the floor, and using profane language, he threatened to shoot me.

I laid on the floor until after the man left. I don't know why, but when it was over I started to cry. One of the bank employees came over to help me calm down. Then he/she told me I needed to try to remember what the bank robber looked like. I was drawing a blank – at first I only remembered that he was [describe in general terms the physical description of the witness portraying Defendant] and that he wore his hair in little braids. After speaking with the teller, I recalled that he had large eyes. I think he/she described them as "glassy," and that is a good description of them.

About two weeks later, I received a phone call from Agent Mines asking me to attend an identification line-up, which I did. There were six men present. I was there with the two people from the bank and we were each given a card and asked to indicate if we recognized one of the men as the bank robber. At first, I could not be certain, because none of them wore braids in his hair. But I glanced over at the teller and saw that he/she had picked the second man from the right. I looked at him more carefully and agreed that he was the robber. I so indicated on my form.

I have reviewed my witness statement. This is a complete and accurate account.

Hattie Davis
Hattie Davis

Witness Statement of Ellen Ferrell

Date: August 1, C.Y.-1

Special Agent S. Mines conducted the following interview of Ellen Ferrell on August 1, C.Y.-1.

My name is Ellen Ferrell and I am the branch manager of the First Federal Bank in Universal City. I have been the branch manager for two years. Prior to that, I was an assistant manager at another branch.

On July 14, C.Y.-1, at a little before 2:00 p.m., I was just finishing my lunch break. As I opened the door of our break room to enter the lobby of the bank, I saw that there appeared to be a robbery in progress. Everyone was on the floor except for a man, whom I had not seen before. He was behind the counter at Thomas' teller window. I knew immediately that this was a robbery, and I was able to quietly close the door without having been seen by the robber. We have a silent alarm which alerts the police if we have a problem. There are alarm buttons at each teller station, as well as one near the vault, one at the manager's desk and one in the break room. I activated the alarm button and waited, listening at the door. After I heard running footsteps, I counted to ten and slowly opened the door. The man was gone, and people were starting to get up off the floor.

I locked the bank doors until the police had arrived. At the request of Agent Mines, I reviewed the records for Thomas' teller window. Based on records, it appears that $742 was taken by the robber.

Approximately two weeks later, I attended a live identification line-up. Thomas and one of our customers, H. Davis, were also there. I indicated that the second guy from the right resembled the robber, but I told Agent Mines that I could not be certain of that.

I really only had a quick glance of him through a partially opened door before I closed

the door.

I have reviewed my witness statement. This is a complete and accurate account.

Ellen Ferrell
Ellen Ferrell

FIRST FEDERAL BANK IN
UNIVERSAL CITY
4386 Figueroa Avenue
Universal City, Golden 92343

Morning Teller Disbursement Report

Date & Time: _____ July 14, C.Y. – 1, 9:00 a.m. _____

Teller Name & Employee ID: _____ Victoria/Victor Thomas, ID # 375139 _____

Initial Disbursement to Teller's Drawer: ____ $1,000 cash _____

Teller Signature: _____ *V. Thomas* _____

**FIRST FEDERAL BANK IN
UNIVERSAL CITY**
4386 Figueroa Avenue
Universal City, Golden 92343

Teller Cash Disbursement Report

Date & Time: _____ July 14, C.Y.-1, 1:30 p.m. _____

Teller Name & Employee ID: _____ Victoria/Victor Thomas, ID # 375139 _____

Initial Cash Disbursement to Teller's Drawer: _____ $1,000 cash _____

Total Cash Disbursements: __$258_____

Time	Amount	Description
9:10 a.m.	- $52	Cash Check for Customer
9:21 a.m.	- $100	Withdrawal by Customer
9:55 a.m.	- $40	Withdrawal by Customer
10:03 a.m.	- $80	Cash Check for Customer
10:13 a.m.	+ $500	Cash Deposit by Customer
10:22 a.m.	+ $60	Cash Deposit by Customer
10:54 a.m.	- $300	Cash Check for Customer
11:19 a.m.	- $274	Cash Check for Customer
11:56 a.m.	- $122	Cash Check for Customer
12:14 p.m.	+ $170	Cash Deposit for Customer
12:29 p.m.	- $20	Withdrawal by Customer

Teller Signature: _____ *V. Thomas* _____

Interview of William Stevens

Date: July 20, C.Y.-1

Special Agent S. Mines conducted the following interview of William Stevens on July 20, C.Y.-1. Defense counsel, Mary Robbins, was present throughout.

Q: Please state your name.

A: William Stevens.

Q: Mr. Stevens, you have been advised that you have the right to remain silent and that anything you say can be used against you. Is that correct?

A: Yes.

Q: And do you still choose to waive that right and to submit to this interview?

A: Yes.

Q: And you were further advised that you have the right to have an attorney present. Ms. Robbins, here, is representing you in this case. Is that also correct?

A: Yes.

Q: And do you wish to proceed with this interview?

A: Yes.

Q: You are aware that you have been charged with robbing the First Federal Bank in Universal City on July 14, C.Y.-1, is that correct?

A: Yeah, I know what the charges are, but I wasn't anywhere near the bank on that day.

Q: Okay. Why don't you tell me where you were, starting with the morning of July 14, C.Y.-1?

A: I went to St. Peter to visit some friends the day before, and ended up staying overnight. I had an appointment near Universal City at about 1 o'clock p.m. on July 14,

C.Y.-1, but when I went to my car around noon, it wouldn't start. I called the Auto Club, waited about half an hour, and when the guy/girl finally got there, he/she fiddled with some things, tried using jumper cables, but he/she couldn't get the car to start. I told the guy/girl to keep working. I had to meet with my parole supervisor at 1 o'clock and those guys don't have much of a sense of humor about guys missing appointments.

Q: How long did it take him/her to get your car started?

A: The guy/girl was worthless! He/She couldn't start it. I was screwed.

Q: What happened next?

A: The guy/girl left.

Q: Did he/she give you a receipt or anything that would indicate that he/she was not able to start the car?

A: I don't remember. I was pretty angry. This was my first meeting with my parole supervisor since I had been released a couple weeks ago. I knew I was going back if I didn't show up.

Q: What did you do next?

A: The guy/girl had given me back my driver's license and my Auto Club card. A lot of good they were to me then. I just tossed them into my car. It wasn't going nowhere and I was stuck. Then, I walked to a motel a couple of blocks away. The guy there sells, um, weed. I hung out there for a couple of days.

Q: Did you obtain "weed"?

A: Yeah. And some other stuff. I figured I would be going back in, so I had better make the most of it while I could.

Q: Do you have anyone who can place you at the motel on July 14, C.Y.-1?

A: (*laughs*) You want me to rat out my connection, is that it?

Q: No. I am just trying to ascertain whether there is a way to verify your supposed alibi.

A: I've got nothing to say about the motel. But the Auto Club will have a record, right?

Q: We'll check it out. We'll check everything out. You mentioned that you were supposed to meet with a parole officer on July 14, C.Y.-1, and that it would be your first meeting since your release. Why were you in prison?

A: Bank robbery. It was about five, six years ago, I dunno. I did my time. Even had "good" time. It was a long time to rot in prison. I didn't want to go back, which is why I was so mad when my car wouldn't start.

Q: Just a couple of additional questions, Mr. Stevens. Have you ever worn your hair in corn-row braids?

A: (*laughs*) Nah. I am a real person, not some pompous celebrity.

Q: Any idea how your driver's license ended up in the teller drawer at the First Federal Bank?

A: You're the detective, so maybe you can figure it out and tell me. I know I didn't put it there. I wasn't anywhere near there. And if I was going to rob a bank, I sure wouldn't leave my driver's license there like some calling card.

Interview terminated at request of counsel.

Witness Statement of Al/Alicia Silver

Date: August 2, C.Y. -1

My name is Al/Alicia Silver. I am a tow truck driver for Harbor Towing. We are under contract to the automobile club to render roadside assistance to its members. When we receive a service call from the automobile club, we go to the location where the vehicle is located. Usually, the problem is a dead battery, and we use jumper cables to start the car. If that does not work, I see if I can isolate the problem. Sometimes it is obvious – like a broken belt. If we cannot find the problem or cannot get the car started, we offer to tow it to the nearest mechanic.

On July 14, C.Y.-1, I was at work. I had several calls that day, including the one described in the reports you showed me. I respond to a lot of requests for service each day, and I don't recall the particular details of many of them. When I looked at the report, I remembered a few things. One was that the location in St. Peter, where the car was, is a questionable area. There is a lot of police activity there, and we are told to take extra precautions in that neighborhood. I am always on my guard there.

I remember that I couldn't get the guy's car started. I didn't pay much attention to the guy, and really can't describe him. But the paperwork shows that the guy's name was William Stevens, and his driver's license was noted on the record. Wouldn't be able to recognize him if I saw him again. I don't focus much on the people. My business is to get their cars started. The paperwork indicates that I couldn't start the car and that he refused my offer to tow his car to a mechanic. The nearest bus stop I know of is about two miles from where the car stalled. I don't know what he did next, though I vaguely recall he seemed pretty irritated and he said something about missing an appointment. I didn't waste time hanging around to see what would happen next. Not in that neighborhood.

I have reviewed my witness statement. This is a complete and accurate account.

A. Silver
Al (Alicia) Silver

AUTOMOBILE CLUB SERVICE REPORT

HARBOR TOWING COMPANY

DATE: _____ July 14, C.Y. – 1 _____

ARRIVAL TIME: __ 12:24 p.m. _____

DEPARTURE TIME: _____ 12:40 p.m. _____

DESCRIPTION OF SERVICE PROVIDED: I arrived on scene, near St. Peter, to find that the member's, William Stevens, car would not start. I attempted to start the vehicle using jumper cables. After the car would not start with the aid of jumper cables, I attempted to isolate the problem. However, I was still unable to start the car. I offered to tow the member's car to the repair facility of his choice and he refused. I took some information from the member, including his driver license number, which was G5674320.

HARBOR TOWING EMPLOYEE SIGNATURE: _____ *A. Silver* _____

Witness Statement of Stella Stevens

Date: August 3, C.Y. -1

Special Agent S. Mines conducted the following interview of Stella Stevens on August 3, C.Y.-1.

My name is Stella Stevens. I am William Steven's aunt – his mother's sister. I work as a hairdresser and have done so for the past 25 years.

On July 14, C.Y.-1, at approximately 11 a.m., I was walking to the salon where I work as a hairdresser. It is in Universal City. I saw my nephew, William Stevens, talking to some men on the other side of the street. His back was to me and he did not see me, nor did I approach him. I am sure it was him, though. His hair was nearly shoulder length, and when I saw him it was not braided in corn-rows.

I have done corn-row braids on a few of my clients. It is a pretty time-consuming process. When I have done it, it takes several hours. The exact amount of time varies according to the client and whether beads or other accessories are used, but it typically takes me 3 to 4 hours to do a corn-row hairstyle.

I have reviewed my witness statement. This is a complete and accurate account.

Stella Stevens
Stella Stevens

Jury Instructions

Members of the jury, I thank you for your attention during this trial. Please pay attention to the instructions I am about to give you.

In this case, the Government has charged William Stevens with armed bank robbery under 18 U.S.C. § 2113 which provides as follows:

§ 2113 Bank Robbery

    (a) whoever, by force and violence, or by intimidation, takes, or attempts to take, from the person or presence of another any property or money or any other thing of value belonging to, or in the care, custody or control of, any bank, credit union or savings and loan association shall be imprisoned not more than twenty years.

* * *

    (d) whoever, in committing or in attempting to commit, any offence defined in subsection (a) of this section, assaults any person, or puts in jeopardy the life of any person by the use of a dangerous weapon or device, shall be imprisoned not more than twenty-five years.

Based on this statute, the crime of bank robbery, as charged, has four essential elements, which are:

1.   Defendant took money belonging to First Federal Bank in Universal City;

2.   First Federal Bank in Universal City is federally insured by the FDIC;

3.   Defendant used force and violence, or intimidation in doing so; and

4.   Defendant intentionally made a display of force that reasonably caused Victoria/Victor Thomas to fear bodily harm by using a firearm.

As used above, intimidation means doing something that would make an ordinary person fear bodily harm.

To overcome Defendant's presumption of innocence, Government has the burden of proving that:

1. The crime with which Defendant is charged was committed; and

2. Defendant is the person who committed the crime.

Defendant is not required to prove anything.

Whenever the words "reasonable doubt" are used, you must consider the following: A reasonable doubt is not a mere possible doubt, because everything relating to human affairs is open to some possible or imaginary doubt. It is that state of the case which, after the entire comparison and consideration of all the evidence, leaves the minds of the jurors in that condition that they cannot say they feel an abiding conviction of the truth of the charge. It is to the evidence introduced during this trial, and to it alone, that you are to look for that proof. A reasonable doubt as to the guilt of Defendant may arise from the evidence, a conflict in the evidence, or a lack of evidence. If you have a reasonable doubt, you should find Defendant not guilty. If you have no reasonable doubt, you should find Defendant guilty.

You must decide this case based only on the law and the evidence. It is up to you to decide what evidence is reliable. You should use your common sense in deciding which evidence is reliable and which evidence should not be relied upon in considering your verdict. You may find some of the evidence not reliable or less reliable than other evidence.

A witness is a person who has knowledge related to this case. You will have to decide whether you believe each witness and how important each witness's testimony is to the case. You may believe all, part, or none of a witness's testimony. In deciding whether to believe a witness's testimony, you may consider, among other factors, the following:

1.   Did the witness seem to have an opportunity to see and know the things about which the witness testified?

2.   Did the witness seem to have an accurate memory?

3.   Was the witness honest and straightforward in answering the attorneys' questions?

4.   Did the witness have some interest in how the case should be decided?

5.   Does the witness's testimony agree with the other testimony and other evidence in this case?

6.   Has the witness been offered or received any money, preferred treatment, or other benefit in order to get the witness to testify?

7.   Had any pressure or threat been used against the witness that affected the truth of the witness's testimony?

8.   Did the witness at some other time make a statement that is inconsistent with the testimony he or she gave in court?

9.   Was it proved that the witness had been convicted of a crime?

You may rely upon your own conclusions about the witnesses. A juror may believe or disbelieve all or any part of the evidence or the testimony of any witness.

Defendant in this case has become a witness. You should apply the same rules to consideration of his testimony that you apply to the testimony of the other witnesses.

There are some general rules that apply to your deliberations. You must follow these rules in order to return a lawful verdict:

1.   You must follow the law as it is set out in these instructions. If you fail to follow the law, your verdict will be a miscarriage of justice.

2.   This case must be decided only upon the evidence that you have heard from the answers of the witnesses and have seen in the form of exhibits and these instructions.

3.   This case must not be decided for or against anyone because you feel sorry for anyone or are angry at anyone.

4.   Remember the lawyers are not on trial. Your feelings about them should not influence your decision in this case.

5.   Your duty is to determine if Defendant has been proven guilty or not. It is the judge's job to determine the proper sentence if Defendant is found guilty.

6.   Whatever verdict you render must be unanimous; that is, each juror must agree to the same verdict. The verdict must be the verdict of each juror, as well as of the jury as a whole.

7.   It is entirely proper for a lawyer to talk to a witness about what testimony the witness would give if called to the courtroom. The witness should not be discredited for talking to a lawyer about his or her testimony.

8.   Your verdict should not be influenced by feelings of prejudice, bias, or sympathy. Your verdict must be based on the evidence and the law contained in these instructions.

Deciding a proper verdict is exclusively your job. I cannot participate in that decision in any way. Please disregard anything I may have said or done that made you think I preferred one verdict over another.

Only one verdict may be returned as to the crime charged. The verdict must be in writing and the verdict form has been prepared for you. It is as follows:

[READ VERDICT FORM]

In just a few moments, you will be taken to the jury room by the bailiff. The first thing you should do is elect a foreperson who will preside over your deliberations like the chairperson of a meeting. It is the foreperson's job to sign and date the verdict form when all of you have agreed on a verdict in this case and to bring the verdict back to the courtroom when you return.

In closing, let me remind you that it is important that you follow the law spelled out in these instructions in deciding your verdicts. Even if you do not like the laws, you must apply them. There are no other laws that apply to this case.

UNITED STATES DISTRICT COURT

CENTRAL DISTRICT OF THE STATE OF GOLDEN

UNITED STATES OF AMERICA	)	
	)	
v.	)	Case No. CR 43-502
	)	
WILLIAM STEVENS,	)	
Defendant.	)	
	)	

VERDICT

As to the charge of armed bank robbery in violation of 18 U.S.C. § 2113(d), we, the Jury, find Defendant, William Stevens:

_____   Guilty

_____   Not Guilty

So say we all.

_____
Foreperson of the Jury

_____
Date

Chapter 2

Jeffrey Kent

v.

Bonds Rentals

(negligent failure to warn)

IN THE CIRCUIT COURT OF THE THIRTEENTH JUDICIAL CIRCUIT

IN AND FOR LEAD COUNTY, STATE OF GOLDEN

CIVIL DIVISION

JEFFREY KENT, Plaintiff,	))))	
v.	))	CASE NO: CV 34-206
BONDS RENTALS, Defendant.	))))	

IN THE CIRCUIT COURT OF THE THIRTEENTH JUDICIAL CIRCUIT

IN AND FOR LEAD COUNTY, STATE OF GOLDEN

CIVIL DIVISION

JEFFREY KENT, Plaintiff,	))))	CASE NO: CV 34-206
v.	))	
BONDS RENTALS, Defendant.	))))	COMPLAINT FOR PERSONAL INJURY JURY TRIAL DEMANDED

Plaintiff, Jeffrey Kent, sues Defendant, Bonds Rentals, and alleges:

1.   Plaintiff and Defendant are residents of and/or do business in Lead County, therefore, jurisdiction is proper in this Court.

2.   On December 15, C.Y.-2, Plaintiff rented a Rock Industrial-Grade HM3920 Jackhammer (herein the "Jackhammer"), manufactured by Rock Industries, from Bonds Rentals. Plaintiff entered into an Equipment Rental Agreement with Bonds Rentals for rental of the Jackhammer.

3.   While Plaintiff was using the Jackhammer on December 15, C.Y.-2, the Jackhammer hit a rock and jumped, causing the blade to hit Plaintiff's right foot, severing three of the toes on that foot.

4.   Plaintiff was operating the Jackhammer in a reasonable and prudent manner at the time of the accident.

5.   Defendant knew or should have known that when the Jackhammer is used in a rocky area, it will be more likely to jump and potentially cause injuries.

6.   Defendant negligently failed to warn against this possible danger by not placing a warning on the Jackhammer of the potential risk.

7.   Defendant additionally negligently failed to warn against this possible danger by not placing a warning in the rental agreement to alert users of the Jackhammer to this potential risk.

8.   Defendant is liable for the injury of Plaintiff for failure to warn because Defendant knew of the potential risks that presented a substantial danger to users of the Jackhammer, but failed to warn of the potential risks, and because the failure to give sufficient warning was a substantial factor in causing Plaintiff's injury.

9.   As a result of the aforesaid injury to Plaintiff's foot, Plaintiff has suffered and will continue to suffer significant losses and prays for damages in excess of the jurisdictional requirements of this Court.

WHEREFORE, Plaintiff prays that this Honorable Court:

1.   Enter a judgment against Defendant;

2.   Award Plaintiff compensatory damages, punitive damages, and damages for pain and suffering and lost future earnings;

3.   Award Plaintiff reasonable attorney's fees and costs; and

4.   Award other such relief that this Court deems just and appropriate.

Dated: June 29, C.Y.-1   HENNIGAN, FORD & LEE, LLP

Jonathan Hennigan
BY: JONATHAN HENNIGAN
Attorneys for Plaintiff Jeffrey Kent

IN THE CIRCUIT COURT OF THE THIRTEENTH JUDICIAL CIRCUIT

IN AND FOR LEAD COUNTY, STATE OF GOLDEN

CIVIL DIVISION

JEFFREY KENT, Plaintiff, v. BONDS RENTALS, Defendant.	CASE NO: CV 34-206 ANSWER TO COMPLAINT FOR PERSONAL INJURY

Defendant, Bonds Rentals, hereby answers the Complaint of Plaintiff, Jeffrey Kent, by admitting, denying and affirmatively alleging as follows:

1.   Defendant admits jurisdiction.

2.   Defendant lacks sufficient information to respond and on this ground denies each and every allegation contained in this paragraph.

3.   Defendant lacks sufficient information to respond and on this ground denies each and every allegation contained in this paragraph.

4.   Defendant lacks sufficient information to respond and on this ground denies each and every allegation contained in this paragraph.

5.   Defendant denies each and every allegation contained in this paragraph.

6.   Defendant lacks sufficient information to respond and on this ground denies each and every allegation contained in this paragraph.

7.   Defendant lacks sufficient information to respond and on this ground denies each and every allegation contained in this paragraph.

8.   Defendant denies each and every allegation contained in this paragraph.

9.   Defendant lacks sufficient information to respond and on this ground denies each and every allegation contained in this paragraph.

Defendant, Bond Rentals, asserts the following affirmative defenses:

1.   At the time of Plaintiff's injury on December 15, C.Y.-2, Plaintiff was not wearing proper safety shoes while operating the Rock Jackhammer. Plaintiff's failure to wear such safety shoes was the proximate cause of his injury.

2.   At the time of Plaintiff's injury on December 15, C.Y.-2, Plaintiff knew he was not properly trained or experienced in the operation of the Rock Jackhammer. Plaintiff's lack of knowledge and training was the proximate cause of his injury.

3.   At the time of Plaintiff's injury on December 15, C.Y.-2, Defendant was not aware, nor could it reasonably have been aware, that there was an increased risk of injury when using the Rock Jackhammer in rocky soil. Because Defendant was not aware of the risk, it did not have a duty to warn Plaintiff against such increased risk.

WHEREFORE, Defendant prays for judgment as follows:

1.   That the Complaint be dismissed in its entirety;

2.   That judgment be granted to Defendant;

3.   For costs of suit and attorney's fees; and

4.   For such other and further relief as the Court may deem just and proper.

DATED: July 20, C.Y.-1   RIVERA & KOHN

Michael Wilson
_____
BY: MICHAEL WILSON
Attorneys for Defendant Bonds
Rentals

Witness List

Witnesses for Plaintiff:

1. Jeffrey Kent *

2. Raleigh Jenkins * *

Witnesses for Defendant:

1. Chris Bonds * *

2. Bernard/Bernardette Rock * *

Each side must call both witnesses listed for their respective party.

* This witness must be a male.

* * This witness may be either gender.

This is a bifurcated trial, only the issue of liability will be tried.

Stipulations

1. Federal Rules of Evidence apply.

2. Each witness who gave a deposition did agree under oath at the outset of his or her deposition to give a full and complete description of what occurred and to correct the deposition for inaccuracies and completeness before signing the deposition.

3. All witnesses called to testify who have in statements identified Defendant or tangible evidence can, if asked, identify the same at trial.

4. All exhibits in the file are authentic and, unless otherwise noted, are the original of that document.

5. All depositions were signed under oath.

6. Other than what appears in the witness statements or depositions, there is nothing exceptional or unusual about the background of any of the witnesses that would bolster or detract from their credibility.

7. All dates are denoted by C.Y. (current year) and C.Y.-1 indicating, for example, that the date is the current year minus one.

8. All pretrial motions shall be oral.

9. No party may "invent" witnesses or evidence not specifically mentioned in this problem.

10. "Beyond the record" is not a proper objection. Rather, attorneys shall use cross-examination as a means of challenging a witness whose testimony strays beyond the facts contained in the witness's statement or deposition.

11. This case shall be tried on *liability* only. If Plaintiff should prevail at trial, the question of damages shall be reserved for the jury in later proceedings.

12. The State of Golden is a comparative negligence state. The jury shall apportion the percentage of negligence, if any, to each party.

13. The law is accurately set forth in the jury instructions.

14. The Silverado Memorial Hospital "Patient Discharge Report" of Jeffery Kent is authenticated under Federal Rule of Evidence 902(11) and is admissible as a certified business record under Federal Rule of Evidence 803(6).

15. Neither party shall request Plaintiff, Jeffrey Kent, to exhibit the injury to his foot.

16. Plaintiff Jeffrey Kent has entered into a settlement agreement with Rock Industries, the manufacturer of the Industrial Grade HM3920 Jackhammer. The terms of that settlement agreement are confidential and not admissible at trial.

17. The plaintiff and defendant may call only the two witnesses listed on their respective witness list. Each party may call an additional witness by deposition or witness statement. Any such testimony is subject to objections pursuant to the Federal Rules of Evidence. If a witness is called by deposition or witness statement, the opposing party may cross-examine that witness by deposition or witness statement.

Deposition of Jeffrey Kent

Date: 11/10/C.Y.-1

Q: Mr. Kent, did you rent a jackhammer from Bonds Rentals?

A: Yes.

Q: When was that?

A: On December 15, C.Y.-2.

Q: What were you going to use it for?

A: To chip out an asphalt driveway.

Q: Was this driveway at your house?

A: No, it was at my mother's.

Q: How did you come to be removing your mother's driveway?

A: After my dad died, my mom moved out of their house and bought a fixer-upper. She said the old house was too big, and it reminded her too much of my dad. I've been helping her do some small projects to fix the house up. A cement driveway was the next thing on our list.

Q: Are you a professional contractor?

A: No. I'm a firefighter.

Q: Why didn't you let a professional do the work?

A: Since my dad died, Mom's money has been a little tight, and we thought that if I chipped out the old driveway and we hired someone to just pour the cement for the new driveway that it would save money.

Q: Did your mom go with you to rent the jackhammer?

A: No, she was out of town visiting my sister. I wanted to surprise her by having the driveway dug out when she got home.

Q: Had you ever used a jackhammer before?

A: I have a buddy who rented a jackhammer once. He let me try it for a few minutes. It didn't look hard to use. In fact it was kind of fun to use. Boy, was I wrong.

Q: Who manufactured that jackhammer?

A: I don't remember.

Q: Do you know if it was an industrial-grade jackhammer?

A: No, I don't think so. I don't really know the difference.

Q: I want to talk about the day you rented the machine. Who did you talk to?

A: Well, I know now that it was Chris Bonds, but I didn't know his/her name when I rented it.

Q: Tell me about your interactions with Chris Bonds.

A: He/She helped me pick out a jackhammer and then filled out an Equipment Rental Agreement and I signed it.

Q: Did he/she give you any safety instructions?

A: He/She might have said something. I don't remember. I just wanted to get home and get started. It's hard to remember, but I think he/she gave me a safety manual to read while he/she was filling out the paperwork.

Q: Did you read it?

A: I flipped through it. Like I said, I had used a jackhammer before and it didn't look like the manual was telling me anything I didn't already know.

Q: What time did you start using the jackhammer?

A: I came home, had some lunch, and changed my clothes, so probably about 2:00 that afternoon.

Q: Was it hard to operate the jackhammer?

A: No, not at all. It was just like the time my buddy let me use his.

Q: At some point, there was a problem, right?

A: Well a couple of times when I hit a particularly hard spot, I guess a hard rock, the hammer would jump. Kind of slide over the rock. It really jerked when that happened.

Q: Did that happen before you were injured?

A: Yeah, maybe a couple of times.

Q: Okay, let's talk about how you were injured. What happened?

A: It was about forty-five minutes after I got started. I think I must have hit something really hard because it really jumped and I lost control of it. I tried to hold on, but it jumped so violently, and it came down on my foot. I tried to get my foot out of the way, but it all happened too fast.

Q: What happened next?

A: I dropped the jackhammer and looked at my foot. It cut right through my shoe and I could see lots of blood. There was a big pool of blood on the ground. Thank God Raleigh, my mom's neighbor, was out watering his/her lawn and saw what happened and came to help.

Q: That was Raleigh Jenkins?

A: That's right.

Q: What happened next?

A: I was so stunned, that I just stood there. It took me a minute to realize what had happened. Then the shock wore off and my foot hurt worse than anything I had ever felt before. It was pretty bad! Everything started to spin. I was really dizzy from all the pain. Raleigh managed to sit me on the lawn and get my shoe off. He/she wrapped my foot in some towels.

Q: Did that help with the bleeding?

A: I don't think so. The blood soaked through the towels. He/she picked up the toes that had been cut off and wrapped them up in some plastic wrap and put them in a bag with ice. Then he/she helped me get into his/her car and drove me to the hospital. I felt really bad because I got blood all over his/her car. I just couldn't stop the bleeding no matter what I did. I don't think Raleigh will ever get that car totally clean.

Q: What happened once you got to the hospital?

A: The nurse in charge took one look at my foot and rushed me back to a room. A doctor came to see me and told me that three of my toes had been cut off and I needed immediate surgery to sew them back on.

Q: How did the surgery go?

A: I guess it was a success, at least at first. The doctor seemed to be happy with how it
      went. I didn't really understand everything he told me, he used a lot of doctor terms
      and I was pretty out of it.

Q: How long did it take to recover?

A: I didn't ever really recover. My foot continued to hurt really bad. After several days,
      the toes just weren't healing like they should have been, and they started to turn
      black. It sounds really gross, but the doctor told me that I had gangrene. He said that
      means the toes had died and were starting to rot. I believed it. They smelled like
      they were rotting. All three toes had to be taken off to keep the gangrene from
      spreading into my foot.

Q: So now you're missing three toes?

A: I am. The big one and the two next to it.

Q: Has that had a big impact on your life?

A: It has. Quite a bit, actually. I had to retire on disability from my job as a firefighter.
      Toes, especially your big toe, are where you get your sense of balance. Missing those
      toes has affected my balance and made me really unsteady. Can't have that when
      you're a firefighter.

Q: What do you do now for work?

A: Nothing right now. I'm still trying to figure that out. All I've ever wanted to be was
      a firefighter. Now that I can't be that anymore, I'm not sure what else to do. Plus,
      since my injury didn't happen on the job, I didn't get any worker's compensation
      benefits or anything like that. Things are not going so well right now.

Q: I want to back up a little bit. You said that the jackhammer jumped when you hit a
      rock. Now, you said that wasn't the first rock you hit while you were
      jackhammering?

A: No, that's the weird thing. Silverado is a really rocky place. The majority of the city
      is on a really big hill. Pretty much the entire city is sitting on a big hill made of
      granite. Everybody who lives in Silverado knows that we're going to find lots of
      rocks anytime we dig a hole or do something like that. I had already hit a few rocks
      with the blade and hadn't lost control of the hammer. I don't know why it jumped so
      hard the last time.

Q: You weren't doing anything differently the last time? You were paying attention just
      as much as before?

A: Of course. I know a jackhammer can be dangerous. I was being careful. As far as paying attention, I was totally focused. A jackhammer isn't something to mess around with.

Q: You also said earlier that you changed your clothes before you started working on the driveway. What did you change into?

A: I put on an old shirt, jeans, some safety goggles and some sturdy running shoes.

Q: Can you tell me about that day, December 15, C.Y.-2? What was the day like?

A: It was a great day. It was sunny and breezy. December in Silverado is usually pretty cold, but it was unusually warm that day. I got pretty hot with all the jackhammering. I looked in my mom's refrigerator and the only thing that was really cold was a beer, so I brought that outside. I sipped it while I worked, trying to keep cool.

Q: One last thing, besides changing your clothes, did you do anything else to prepare for using the jackhammer?

A: Since it had been awhile since I tried using a jackhammer, I called my buddy who let me use his jackhammer before and asked for some tips. He told me that using jackhammers were all pretty similar, and that I should be fine.

Q: You said you signed an Equipment Rental Agreement when you rented the jackhammer. I'd like to ask you a couple of questions about that. If you remember, what was in that Agreement?

A: Basic things like my name, address, how much it was going to cost, how long I was keeping it, things like that.

Q: Did the Agreement say anything about safety?

A: I think it did. There were a few spots I had to initial.

Q: Did you read the information before you initialed?

A: I'm sure I did. It was a couple of years ago so I don't remember specifics, but I am sure I read, or skimmed, it.

Q: Thank you, Mr. Kent.

I affirm under penalty of perjury that my answers are full and complete.

Jeffrey Kent
_____
Jeffrey Kent

Deposition of Raleigh Jenkins

Date: 11/16/C.Y.-1

Q: Good morning Mr./Ms. Jenkins. I'm going to ask you a few questions about what you witnessed on the afternoon of December 15, C.Y.-2.

A: Okay.

Q: Before I get to what happened, I want to ask you a few background questions. Where do you live?

A: I live in Silverado, at 4520 Walnut Street. I live across the street from Alma Kent, Jeff's mom.

Q: When you say Jeff, do you mean Jeffrey Kent, the plaintiff in this action?

A: I do.

Q: Thank you for your clarification. How long have you lived there?

A: Oh gosh, forever. Probably 45 years.

Q: Do you live there alone?

A: I do now. I got divorced a long time ago and all my kids have grown up and moved away.

Q: What do you do for a living?

A: I am a retired handyman. I spent the last few years helping to build houses.

Q: Did you ever use a jackhammer on the job?

A: Not personally, but I saw people using them.

Q: Now I'd like to turn to the afternoon of December 15, C.Y.-2. Can you tell me what you were doing that afternoon?

A: Well even though I'm older, I like to stay active. I can't just sit around with my cat Murphy on my lap watching Oprah.

Q: And so what were you doing?

A: Oh, sorry. I didn't really answer the question, did I? I was watering my lawn.

Q: So you were in the front of your house when you noticed Mr. Kent in the driveway of his mother's house?

A: I had just come back out to finish up the lawn when I noticed him with the jackhammer. I had watched him for just a second. It looked like he was using the jackhammer just like I used to see people on the job use it. Everything was just fine when all the sudden it looked like something happened with the jackhammer, it jerked, and then Jeff just started screaming. I got over to him as quick as my legs would allow.

Q: What did you see when you got to where Mr. Kent was?

A: Blood. Lots of blood. Jeff's foot was bleeding really bad.

Q: Could you tell what had happened?

A: It looked like he had cut through his shoe with the jackhammer. A piece of his shoe with toes in it was nearby.

Q: What did you do?

A: I did what I could. I went into Alma's house and got a couple of towels to try to stop the bleeding. The toes that were cut off were lying on the driveway, so I picked them up and took them in the house. I found some plastic wrap and wrapped them up and put them in a bag of ice.

Q: What did you do next?

A: I went back outside to check on Jeff and he was still really bleeding and said he was getting dizzy. I went and got my car and took him to the hospital.

Q: It is fortunate that you happened to be in a position where you could see what happened and help out.

A: I try to be observant.

Q: You do? What are you looking for?

A: I like to keep an eye on my neighbors.

Q: What are you watching for?

A: I have a couple of neighbors that I don't trust. I think one is a drug dealer. He has people coming to his house at all hours of the night. Something isn't right.

Q: How well do you know Mr. Kent and his mom?

A: Not well. She has only lived there a few years. Jeff comes by about once a week to help her out.

Q: I want to ask you a couple of questions about the view you had of Mr. Kent from your front lawn.

A: Okay.

Q: You said you were across the street?

A: Yes.

Q: About how many feet would you say you were from Mr. Kent when you saw the accident?

A: I don't know. Just across a normal street. Maybe 150 feet?

Q: Is there anything that was in the way of your view, like trees?

A: No, I have a couple of rose bushes, but they're small and didn't get in the way.

Q: I see you're wearing glasses today. Were you wearing those that day?

A: I was wearing sunglasses that day because the sun was so bright.

Q: Did you have a hard time seeing what happened?

A: No, I'm farsighted. I only need these glasses to read and see things up close. I can see fine far away.

Q: Mr./Ms. Jenkins, I want to ask you one more thing. You said you were watching Mr. Kent for a few seconds before he got hurt, right?

A: Yes.

Q: Did it look like he was using the jackhammer in a safe manner?

A: I think so. When I was on the job, I saw construction workers using them, and it looked like Jeff was using it the same way.

I affirm under penalty of perjury that my answers are full and complete.

Raleigh Jenkins
Raleigh Jenkins

Deposition of Chris Bonds

Date: 11/20/C.Y.-1

Q: Good afternoon Mr./Ms. Bonds. You work for Bonds Rentals, right?

A: Well, I own it.

Q: So what do you do?

A: The books, contracts, purchasing, payroll. Pretty much everything. I also work as a rental clerk when one of my guys is out.

Q: What are your duties when you are acting as a rental clerk?

A: I am who people talk to when they want to rent some piece of machinery.

Q: So Bonds Rentals is an equipment rental store?

A: Yes. We rent all kinds of construction equipment.

Q: Let's talk about December 15, C.Y.-2, the day Mr. Kent rented a Rock jackhammer.

A: Okay.

Q: I understand he dealt with you in renting the jackhammer, is that right?

A: Yes.

Q: Tell me what you recall.

A: It was all pretty normal. He came in and said he wanted to rent a jackhammer because he was doing some work for his mom.

Q: Did he say what type of work?

A: He said he was chipping out an old asphalt driveway.

Q: How did you decide which jackhammer would best suit his needs?

A: Well, we don't carry too many models of jackhammers so there weren't a lot to choose from. He said he wanted an industrial-grade jackhammer, so that narrowed the choices down to one.

Q: Did he say why he needed it industrial-grade?

A: He said he figured that an industrial-grade would be more powerful and would mean less work for him. He said that he was in favor of anything that meant less work.

Q: To your knowledge, had he ever used a jackhammer before?

A: He said he had. But he didn't say whether it was industrial-grade.

Q: How old was the jackhammer rented by Mr. Kent?

A: Not very old. I bought it from Rock sometime in January of C.Y.-2.

Q: Can you tell me about the process of renting a piece of equipment from Bonds Rentals?

A: Sure. When the customer comes in the rental clerk helps the customer decide what equipment would best suit their needs. Then we fill out an Equipment Rental Agreement and take a deposit.

Q: Do you do anything else?

A: Sometimes. Our company policy is that if the customer has never used a particular piece of equipment that we give them a short safety demonstration, showing them the proper way to use the equipment, and the proper safety precautions to take.

Q: Did you do this for Mr. Kent?

A: No, I didn't think it was necessary.

Q: Why not?

A: Because he said he had used a jackhammer before.

Q: To your knowledge, had he used that specific type of industrial jackhammer before?

A: He couldn't remember. He wasn't sure what the brand was, but all jackhammers are pretty similar.

Q: What types of things are included in the safety demonstration?

A: Let's see, things like how to hold the equipment properly, what types of jobs you can use it for, what sort of safety gear you need to wear, things like that.

Q: You mentioned safety gear. What kind of safety gear should one wear when operating a jackhammer?

A: Typically someone should wear a long sleeved shirt and long pants to protect their skin from flying pieces of whatever they're chipping out and steel-toed boots.

Q: Do you recall telling Mr. Kent those specific instructions?

A: For the life of me I can't specifically recall.

Q: Let's turn to another area. I understand you had a personal as well as professional relationship with Rock, the company that made the jackhammer we are talking about here, is that right?

A: Well, first off let me tell you Rock makes really good equipment, and they always do a good job of standing behind it for stuff like warranties. They have confidence in their product and so do I. Plus, since I know the president of Rock, we get a few perks.

Q: What kind of perks?

A: Well, by far the best one is that we get to see their new equipment before it is made public. Bernard/Bernardette lets me be the first one to place an order, so I always get the new and best equipment Rock makes.

Q: Are you referring to Bernard/Bernardette Rock?

A: Yes.

Q: Any other perks?

A: From time to time Bernard/Bernardette has some extra baseball tickets he/she throws my way. You know, four or five times a season. Great seats.

Q: Were you ever informed by Bernard/Bernardette Rock that the type of jackhammer Mr. Kent was using occasionally jumped or jerked?

A: You mean personally? I don't recall any such conversation.

Q: Had you been so informed, would you have done anything differently when renting that particular type of jackhammer?

A: I don't know. I would have to think about that.

Q: Well, let me ask this. If you had known, would you have informed your rental customer of that possibility?

A: Of course. It's not in anybody's interest for a customer to be injured.

Q: You are aware that Silverado and the surrounding areas are particularly rocky, aren't you?

A: Seems to me that is fairly common knowledge.

Q: Did you supply Mr. Kent with any instruction or warning beyond what is reflected in the rental agreement?

A: Like I said, I don't recall all the specifics. I usually have them look through the safety manual for equipment while I fill out the rental agreement. I do remember telling him, "This is a heavy-duty machine, so watch yourself."

Q: Did he respond to your warning?

A: You know, I'm not really sure. If I'm totally honest, he may have been a little distracted by a woman who walked in about that time. She was very distracting.

Q: Is there anything else you would like to mention?

A: Just that I'm so sorry this happened to Mr. Kent. This is something you never want to see happen to your customers.

Q: Thank you Mr./Ms. Bonds.

I have reviewed the transcript of my deposition. This is a complete and accurate account.

Chris Bonds
Chris Bonds

Deposition of Bernard/Bernardette Rock

Date: 11/23/C.Y.-1

Q: Mr./Ms. Rock, can you tell me what you do for a living?

A: I am the President of Rock Industries.

Q: What type of company is that?

A: We manufacture construction equipment. Anything from cranes to augers.

Q: Do you also manufacture jackhammers?

A: Yes, we do.

Q: Did you manufacture the jackhammer used by Mr. Kent on December 15, C.Y.-2?

A: Yes. That was our industrial-grade HM3920.

Q: Who is the average user of your product?

A: Our consumers are broken up into two groups. The first is construction workers.
       They compose a large percentage of our consumers.

Q: Who is in the second group?

A: The second group is people doing home improvement projects themselves.

Q: And these people are not professionals?

A: No, though some think they are. These are usually people who may not have any
       training or familiarity with the machines. They compose a very small percentage of
       the people using our products.

Q: Does it concern you that people who haven't been trained are using these machines
       that could be dangerous?

A: It does. My company takes safety concerns very seriously and we do everything we
       can to make sure our consumers stay safe.

Q: What types of things do you do?

A: Well, almost all of the non-professional users of our products do not buy them. Since
       they're only going to be using them once they rent instead. One thing we do is have
       places who rent our equipment sign an agreement that they will properly explain how

to use the product and give safety precautions to each and every person who rents a piece of Rock equipment. We also require that the equipment rental outlets give a safety manual to each customer for the piece of equipment they are renting. Also, if we have reports of any incidents involving our equipment, we send "incident reports" to all rental dealers who rent our equipment and to registered owners of the equipment.

Q: What assurances do you have that the equipment rental companies comply with these precautions?

A: We try to deal with only responsible and trustworthy companies.

Q: Any precautions beyond that?

A: Not specifically.

Q: Do you think a do-it-yourselfer is going to sit down and read the manual before he starts his project?

A: They should, but in case they don't, we also put warning labels on every piece of equipment.

Q: Is that company policy?

A: Yes, very strict company policy.

Q: What types of things do you warn about?

A: Common misuses of the equipment and dangers the do-it-yourselfer would probably not be aware of.

Q: Are we just talking about jackhammers here, or other types of industrial-grade equipment as well?

A: I'm talking about our whole line of industrial-grade equipment.

Q: Why would the do-it-yourselfer not be aware of those dangers?

A: He is generally not familiar with this type of equipment and may only be thinking about the really obvious dangers. We want to keep them safe, so if we think they should know about something, we stick a warning on the machine itself.

Q: Were there any warning labels on the HM3920?

A: Yes, it said, "When using wear proper safety attire. This equipment should not be used while under the influence of alcohol or any medications causing drowsiness."

Q: That was the extent of the warning?

A: We didn't feel we needed to place any other warnings on that particular piece of equipment.

Q: Whose decision was that?

A: My company has a safety panel that discusses these matters and makes recommendations.

Q: Who makes the final call?

A: As the President, I'm the ultimate decider.

Q: So there had never been a safety concern about the HM3920?

A: Not a legitimate one.

Q: Can you explain that?

A: Well sometime in December of C.Y.-3, we received a report that a construction worker using a HM3920 had it jump away from him when he used it on a particularly hard surface. No big deal. Jackhammers normally jump a little with operation.

Q: Why do you say no big deal?

A: It only happened once. Our technician tried to duplicate the claim but couldn't get it to do it again. So we figured it was a problem with the user.

Q: So once isn't enough for it to be a possible problem?

A: Well, just to be sure we sent out a notice to all registered purchasers of the HM3920 telling them of the report and of the testing we did to try to duplicate it.

Q: Did you send this notice to Bond's Rentals?

A: I don't specifically recall, but I am sure we did. We would have sent the notice to all registered purchasers of the HM3920.

Q: Were there any other incidents that you are aware of?

A: Well, about March C.Y.-2, we heard of a renter of the HM3920 who lost control of the jackhammer. It hit his foot, but he had worn steel-toed shoes, so he wasn't injured.

Q: Did Rock take any steps after learning of that incident?

A: We didn't learn any specifics, so we could not try to duplicate it. We did send a notice to all HM3920 purchasers advising users to wear proper safety gear.

Q: Did you send a notice to Bonds Rentals?

A: I am sure we would have, but don't specifically recall. As I said, we send incident reports to all purchasers of our equipment.

Q: Let's turn to Mr. Kent, the man injured when using the HM3920. Why do you believe he was injured?

A: He wasn't properly attired and I understand he may have been drinking. So who knows what he was doing? For heaven's sake, he was wearing running shoes. Who wears running shoes when they're using a jackhammer? He had no idea what he was doing.

Q: What type of shoes should he have worn?

A: Industry standard is steel-toed boots. If he had been wearing those, they would have protected his toes when they were hit by the jackhammer.

Q: Is there anything else you want to mention?

A: Just that I am sorry that this happened to Mr. Kent. If Mr. Kent had been prepared, this could have all been avoided.

Q: Thank you Mr./Ms. Rock.

I have reviewed the transcript of my deposition. This is a complete and accurate account.

B. Rock
_____
Bernard/Bernardette Rock

ROCK INDUSTRIES
2930 East Madison Avenue
Silverado, Golden 90394

INTERNAL MEMORANDUM

TO: Bernard/Bernardette Rock, President

FROM: Arthur Jensen, Equipment Testing Division

DATE: December 20, C.Y.-3

SUBJECT: Rock Industrial-Grade HM3920 Jackhammer

As you know, company policy dictates that we test every piece of equipment for which we have received an incident report.

The purpose of this Memorandum is to alert you to a recent test performed on the Rock Industrial-Grade HM3920 Jackhammer following a report of an incident that caused the jackhammer to jump unexpectedly.

I attempted to duplicate this occurrence, but without success. I repeated the test four additional times, each time utilizing a different surface. I detected no erratic movement during any of these tests.

Despite my inability to duplicate the incident through additional testing, the fact that the jackhammer jumped when it hit a rock should be noted, and a product advisory should be sent to all registered purchasers of the HM3920.

ROCK INDUSTRIES
2930 East Madison Avenue
Silverado, Golden 90394

PRODUCT NOTIFICATION

TO: Purchasers of Jackhammer HM3920

FROM: Rock Industries Safety Division

DATE: January 15, C.Y.-2

SUBJECT: Rock Industrial-Grade HM3920 Jackhammer

We have received a report of Rock Industries Jackhammer HM3920 jumping unexpectedly. Efforts by our technicians to duplicate the reported movements have been unsuccessful.

As always, appropriate safety precautions must be followed when using any jackhammer.

ROCK INDUSTRIES

2930 East Madison Avenue
Silverado, Golden 90394

PRODUCT NOTIFICATION

TO: Purchasers of Jackhammer HM3920

FROM: Rock Industries Safety Division

DATE: April 30, C.Y.-2

SUBJECT: Rock Industrial-Grade HM3920 Jackhammer

We have received a report of a user of Rock Industries Jackhammer HM3920 who lost control of the jackhammer during use. Cause was not determined. The jackhammer struck user's steel-toed boot and because of the use of this proper safety equipment, injury was averted.

As always, appropriate safety precautions must be followed when using any jackhammer.

SILVERADO MEMORIAL HOSPITAL
39 LAKE ROAD
SILVERADO, GOLDEN 93820

Patient Name: Jeffrey Kent

Date: December 28, C.Y.-2

Treating Physician: Cameron Wilson, M.D.

PATIENT DISCHARGE REPORT

The Patient was admitted in the emergency department on December 15, C.Y.-2 at 3:15 p.m. with an injury to his right foot. The big toe and the two adjacent toes had been severed by a jackhammer. The Patient brought the severed toes with him to the emergency department. The toes had been wrapped in plastic wrap and placed in a bag of ice to preserve them.

Vitals were taken, and the Patient's blood pressure was dangerously low, caused by blood loss.

An operating room was immediately scheduled and I attempted to reattach the severed toes. The surgery took 11 hours, and was initially successful.

To reattach the severed toes, I fixed the toes in place at the bone using wires and steel plates. I then sewed the muscle tissue, small blood vessels and nerves back together.

I informed the Patient that he will never regain full use of his toes. However, with intensive physiotherapy, the function of the toes will likely improve.

I also informed the Patient that, even with physiotherapy, he will still have pain in the toes and will have only limited use. I warned the Patient that one's toes play a large role in maintaining balance, and because of the compromised nature of his injured toes, he will likely be forced to relearn how to keep his balance.

The Patient was discharged on December 17, C.Y.-2 with a prescription for Vicodin and instructions to come back in ten days.

The Patient was also given strict instructions not to put any weight on his right foot, and to keep it elevated at all times until the inflammation is reduced.

Ten days later, an examination revealed that the Patient's toes were turning black and had a foul odor. Upon examination, I discovered that gangrene had set in and that the Patient's toes had died and the flesh was rotting. The toes had to be immediately removed so as to prevent the spread of the gangrene up the Patient's leg.

The Patient's recovery from that final surgery has been unremarkable.

Signed: *C. Wilson*

Cameron Wilson, M.D.

DISTRIBUTION AGREEMENT

THIS DISTRIBUTION AGREEMENT (herein the "Agreement") is made as of June 12, C.Y.-12, by and between Rock Industries (hereinafter "Rock"), a Golden State corporation and Bonds Rentals (hereinafter "Bonds"), a Golden State corporation.

WHEREAS, Rock is engaged in the marketing and sale of construction equipment (herein the "Product"); and

WHEREAS, Bonds desires to serve as a rental location for the Product in accordance with the terms and conditions of this Agreement.

NOW, THEREFORE, it is agreed as follows:

1.   Appointment. Rock hereby appoints Bonds as an authorized independent representative to purchase and rent to consumers the Product of Rock in the following geographical area: Silverado, Golden State.

2.   Term. The term of this Agreement shall be from the date set forth above until terminated by either party.

3.   Relationship Created. This Agreement shall not create a partnership, joint venture, agency, employer/employee or similar relationship between Rock and Bonds. Bonds shall be an independent contractor.

4.   Customer Safety. Bonds agrees to explain how to use each piece of equipment rented by each customer. Additionally, Bonds agrees to apprise customers of any safety concerns related to the piece of equipment rented. Such concerns may be raised by Rock or by another source.

5.   No Assignment. The rights and duties under this Agreement are personal and may not be assigned or delegated without the prior written consent of the other party.

6.   Indemnification and Hold Harmless. Rock shall indemnify and hold Bonds harmless of and from any and all liability attributable solely to the negligent, intentional, or other acts of Rock or its employees.

7.   Entire Agreement. This Agreement contains the entire agreement between the parties and any representation, promise or condition not incorporated herein shall not be binding upon either party.

8.   Termination. This Agreement may be terminated, with or without cause, by the delivery of written notice of said termination to the other party. Said termination shall be effective on the "effective date" which, for purposes of this Agreement, shall be the date thirty (30) days after receipt of said written notice by the other party.

The parties hereto have caused this Agreement to be executed as of the day and year first above written.

Rock Industries,
a Golden State corporation

By: *B. Rock*
Bernard/Bernardette Rock

Bonds Rentals,
a Golden State corporation

By: Chris Bonds
Chris Bonds

EQUIPMENT RENTAL AGREEMENT

OWNER: Bonds Rentals
3920 Mission Road
Silverado, Golden 93029

RENTER: Jeffrey Kent
4930 Lincoln Avenue
Silverado, Golden 93029

Place of Use: 4515 Walnut Street

EQUIPMENT RENTED

1. Rock Industrial-Grade HM3920
2.
3.

Rental Rate: $170 per day

Term of Rental: 2 days

SAFETY INFORMATION
***Renter MUST initial each line below.

_JK_   Equipment rented from Bonds Rentals can be dangerous and utmost care should be used when operating.

_JK_   Equipment should not be operated while under the influence of medication or alcohol.

_JK_   Proper safety attire must be worn at all times while operating the Equipment. Consult the safety manual to determine the proper safety attire required for each piece of equipment.

Jeffrey Kent
RENTER

12/15/C.Y.-2
Date

ROCK INDUSTRIAL-GRADE
HM3920 JACKHAMMER

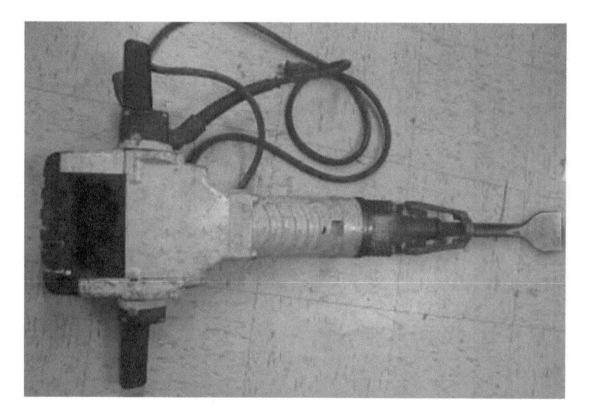

Features
- Does not need a compressor – can plug in anywhere
- Large handles reduce vibration, reducing user fatigue
- Asphalt cutter bit attached

Specifications
- Motor: 1975W
- Beats per minute: 1,500 bpm
- Length: 27-1/2 inches
- Weight: 67 lbs.

Safety Equipment
- Hard hat, safety goggles, steel-toed shoes

Warranty
- One-year limited warranty from date of purchase

HM3920 JACKHAMMER SAFETY MANUAL – PAGE 2

Jury Instructions

Members of the jury, you have now heard all the evidence and the closing argument of the attorneys. It is my duty to instruct you on the law that applies to this case. You will have a copy of my instructions with you when you go to the jury room to deliberate.

I will now tell you the law that you must follow to reach your verdict. You must follow that law exactly as I give it to you, even if you disagree with it. If the attorneys have said anything different about what the law means, you must follow what I say. In reaching your verdict, you must not speculate about what I think your verdict should be from something I may have said or done.

Pay careful attention to all the instructions that I give you. All the instructions are important because together they state the law that you will use in this case. You must consider all of the instructions together. You must decide this case based only on the law and the evidence.

A witness is a person who has knowledge related to this case. You will have to decide whether you believe each witness and how important each witness's testimony is to the case. You may believe all, part, or none of a witness's testimony. In deciding whether to believe a witness's testimony, you may consider, among other factors, the following:

1.   How well did the witness see, hear, or otherwise sense what he or she described in court?

2.   How well did the witness remember and describe what happened?

3.   How did the witness look, act, and speak while testifying?

4.   Did the witness have any reason to say something that was not true? Did the witness show any bias or prejudice? Did the witness have a personal relationship with any of the parties involved in the case? Does the witness have a personal stake in how this case is decided?

5.   What was the witness's attitude toward this case or about giving testimony?

Sometimes a witness may say something that is not consistent with something else he or she said. Sometimes different witnesses will give different versions of what happened. People often forget things or make mistakes in what they remember. Also, two people may see the same event, but remember it differently. You may consider these differences, but do not decide that testimony is untrue just because it differs from other testimony.

However, if you decide that a witness has deliberately testified untruthfully about something important, you may choose not to believe anything that witness said. On the other hand, if you think the witness testified untruthfully about some things but told the truth about others, you may accept the part you think is true and ignore the rest.

You must not be biased in favor of or against any witness because of his or her race, sex, religion, occupation, sexual orientation or national origin.

Plaintiff has the burden in this case to prove each element of his claim by a preponderance of the evidence. The term "preponderance of the evidence" means the greater weight and degree of credible evidence admitted in this case. Simply put, Plaintiff must prove it is more likely than not that each element of his claim is true.

Plaintiff claims that he was harmed because Defendant negligently failed to warn him about the jackhammer's dangers. To establish this claim, Plaintiff must prove all of the following:

1. That Rock Industries manufactured the jackhammer;

2. That Bonds Rentals rented the jackhammer to Plaintiff;

3. That the jackhammer had potential risks that were known to Bonds at the time of rental;

4. That the potential risks presented a substantial danger to users of the jackhammer;

5. That ordinary consumers would not have recognized the potential risks;

6. That Bonds Rentals failed to adequately warn of the potential risks;

7. That the jackhammer was used in a way reasonably foreseeable to Bonds Rentals;

8. That Jeffrey Kent was harmed; and

9. That lack of sufficient warnings was a substantial factor in causing Jeffrey Kent's harm.

Negligence is the doing of something which a reasonably prudent person would not do, or the failure to do something which a reasonably prudent person would do, under circumstances similar to those shown by the evidence. It is the failure to use ordinary or reasonable care. Ordinary or reasonable care is that care which persons of ordinary prudence would use.

Liability is to be apportioned among persons whose fault caused or contributed to a loss or injury, in proportion to their percentage of fault; as a result you are first required to decide whether an actor's negligence was a proximate cause of Plaintiff's loss or injury.

Proximate cause is defined as a reasonably close causal connection between the conduct and the resulting loss or injury. The law defines cause in its own particular way. A cause of injury or harm is something that is a substantial factor in bringing about an injury or harm. There may be more than one cause of an injury. When negligent conduct of two or more persons contributes concurrently as a cause of an injury, the conduct of each is a cause of the injury regardless of the extent to which each contributes to the injury.

Should you find that Defendant caused Plaintiff's injuries you will be asked to consider Defendant's contention that Plaintiff's injuries were due to Plaintiff's own negligence. This is referred to as contributory negligence. However, if you find that Plaintiff was negligent, that does not prevent Plaintiff from recovering damages if you find that Defendant's negligence also played a part in causing Plaintiff's injuries. In this situation you will be asked to assign a percentage of fault to each party and Plaintiff's damages will be reduced accordingly.

Your foreperson shall preside over your deliberations. All jurors should participate in all deliberations and vote on each issue. The votes of ten or more jurors are required to reach a verdict. If your verdict is in favor of Plaintiff, you must also answer written questions on a form that will be given to you. Ten or more jurors must agree on each answer but it need not be the same ten or more jurors. The verdict must be in writing and the verdict form has been prepared for you. It is as follows:

[READ VERDICT FORM]

In just a few moments, you will be taken to the jury room by the bailiff. The first thing you should do is elect a foreperson who will preside over your deliberations like the chairperson of a meeting. It is the foreperson's job to sign and date the verdict form when all of you have agreed on a verdict in this case and to bring the verdict back to the courtroom when you return.

In closing, let me remind you that it is important that you follow the law spelled out in these instructions in deciding your verdicts. There are no other laws that apply to this case.

IN THE CIRCUIT COURT OF THE THIRTEENTH JUDICIAL CIRCUIT

IN AND FOR LEAD COUNTY, STATE OF GOLDEN

CIVIL DIVISION

JEFFREY KENT, Plaintiff, v. BONDS RENTALS, Defendant.	)))))))))	CASE NO: CV 34-206

We, the Jury, answer the questions submitted to us as follows:

QUESTION NO. 1: By a preponderance of the evidence, do you find Defendant negligent in failing to warn?

        ANSWER: Yes _____   No _____

      If you answered the above question "No", you will not answer the remaining questions, but will simply sign the Verdict. If you have answered Question No. 1 "Yes", then you must answer Question No. 2.

QUESTION NO. 2: By a preponderance of the evidence, do you find that Defendant's negligent failure to warn was the cause of Plaintiff's injuries?

        ANSWER: _____.

QUESTION NO. 3:   By a preponderance of the evidence, do you find that Plaintiff's actions were the cause of his injuries?

        ANSWER: _____

QUESTION NO. 4: To what percentage do you attribute the fault of each party?

        PLAINTIFF: _____ %
        DEFENDANT: _____ %

_____
Date

                                        _____
                                        Foreperson

State of Golden

v.

Steven MacNamara

(domestic violence)

IN THE CIRCUIT COURT OF THE THIRTEENTH JUDICIAL CIRCUIT

IN AND FOR LEAD COUNTY, STATE OF GOLDEN

CRIMINAL DIVISION

STATE OF GOLDEN	)	
	)	
	)	
v.	)	CASE NO: CR 98-351
	)	
STEVEN MACNAMARA,	)	
Defendant.	)	
	)	

IN THE CIRCUIT COURT OF THE THIRTEENTH JUDICIAL CIRCUIT

IN AND FOR LEAD COUNTY, STATE OF GOLDEN

CRIMINAL DIVISION

THE 9TH DAY OF MARCH, C.Y.-2

STATE OF GOLDEN	)	**MISDEMEANOR COMPLAINT**
v.	)	CASE NO: CR 98-351
STEVEN MACNAMARA, Defendant.	)	

COMES NOW the undersigned and states that he is informed and believes, and upon such information and belief declares: That on or about 12/03/C.Y.-3, at and in the City of Silverado, in the County of Lead, State of Golden, a misdemeanor in violation of section 483.2 of the Golden State Penal Code was committed by the above-named defendant(s), who at the time and place last aforesaid, did willfully and unlawfully inflict a bodily injury resulting in a traumatic condition upon Brenda MacNamara, who is the spouse of the defendant.

Marshall Winters
Declarant and Complainant

Witness List

Witnesses for the State:

1. Brenda MacNamara * *

2. Officer Taylor Richardson * * *

Witnesses for Defendant:

1. Steven MacNamara *

2. Jamie Moore * * *

Each side must call both witnesses listed for their respective party in any order.

* This witness must be a male.

* * This witness must be a female.

* * * This witness may be either male or female.

Stipulations

1. Federal Rules of Criminal Procedure and Federal Rules of Evidence apply.

2. Each witness who gave an interview reviewed the officer's report of his or her interview and signed the interview verifying that it was accurate.

3. All exhibits in the file are authentic and, unless otherwise noted, are the original of that document.

4. Other than what appears in the officer's report of the interviews, there is nothing exceptional or unusual about the background of any of the witnesses that would bolster or detract from their credibility.

5. All dates are denoted by C.Y. (current year) and C.Y.-1 indicating, for example, that the date is the current year minus one.

6. All pretrial motions shall be oral.

7. No party may "invent" witnesses or evidence not specifically mentioned in this problem.

8. "Beyond the record" is not a proper objection. Rather, attorneys shall use cross-examination as a means of challenging a witness whose testimony strays beyond the facts contained in the officer's reports of the interviews.

9. The physical description of a witness should be tailored to that of the student playing the witness, except for the height, weight, and age.

10. The tape recording of the 911 call was destroyed by no fault of the Silverado Police Department. However, the transcript of the 911 call, which was prepared by Officer Richardson, survived.

11. Brenda MacNamara's "Credit Report" is authenticated under Federal Rule of
    Evidence 902(11) and is admissible as a certified business record under Federal Rule
    of Evidence 803(6).

12. Golden State Penal Code section 483.2 provides: "Any person who willfully and
    unlawfully inflicts bodily injury resulting in a traumatic condition upon a person who
    is his or her spouse is guilty of spousal abuse."

13. The prosecution and defense may call only the two witnesses listed on their
    respective witness list. Each party may call an additional witness by deposition or
    witness statement. Any such testimony is subject to objections pursuant to the
    Federal Rules of Evidence. If a witness is called by deposition or witness statement,
    the opposing party may cross-examine that witness by deposition or witness
    statement. The parties have agreed to waive Confrontational Clause objections for
    only this witness.

enter into evidence

SILVERADO POLICE DEPARTMENT REPORT

Crime/Incident	Case Number
PC 483.2 – Spousal Abuse	49302-342

Date & Time Reported	Location of Occurrence
12/3/C.Y.-3 1:20	385 North Fair Oaks, Silverado

VICTIM							
Name (Last, First, Middle)				Residence Address			
MacNamara, Brenda				385 North Fair Oaks, Silverado			
SEX	DESCENT	HAIR	EYES	HEIGHT	WEIGHT	BIRTH DATE	AGE
F	XXX	XXX	XXX	5'0"	103	C.Y.-34	34
Location of Arrest				Weapons			
385 North Fair Oaks				Shoe, Gun			
Occupation				Injuries			
Office Manager				Lump on head, bruises on arms and face			

SUSPECT							
Name (Last, First, Middle)				Residence Address			
MacNamara, Steven				385 North Fair Oaks. Silverado			
SEX	DESCENT	HAIR	EYES	HEIGHT	WEIGHT	BIRTH DATE	AGE
M	XXX	XXX	XXX	5'10"	205	C.Y.-34	34
Location of Arrest				Weapon			
385 North Fair Oaks				Fists			
Occupation				Injuries			
College Professor				Cut on head, cuts on hands			

Reporting Officer: Richardson

SILVERADO POLICE DEPARTMENT

Report Type: Investigation Narrative

Report by: Officer Taylor Richardson (initialed: *TR*)

Date: 12/3/C.Y.-3

On 12/3/C.Y.-3 at approximately 12:50 a.m., I was dispatched to a residence located at 385 N. Fair Oaks, Silverado, pursuant to a 911 call. I was advised that a woman had called reporting that she had been battered by her spouse.

Upon arrival at said location, I noted a woman, later identified as Brenda MacNamara, sitting on the front porch. I exited my vehicle and as I approached saw that she was holding a revolver. I ordered her to put down the gun and lie on the porch. She immediately complied and I confiscated the Smith & Wesson revolver. I handcuffed Mrs. MacNamara, called for backup, and asked where her husband was. She pointed into the house. I ordered her to remain on the ground and entered the residence. I found Steven MacNamara locked inside the bathroom. I ordered him out and handcuffed Mr. MacNamara and escorted him back to the front of the house. When he saw his wife, he screamed, "You are crazy, woman!"

Mrs. MacNamara screamed back, "If you ever touch me again, I'll kill you."

I put Mr. MacNamara in the back of my patrol car to separate the two of them because they would not stop screaming obscenities and threats at each other. As I leaned down to help Mr. MacNamara into the car, I smelled alcohol on his breath.

When the backup unit arrived, I obtained a statement from each of them (see attached reports). I took note of the injuries to both individuals. Mrs. MacNamara had a lump on her head and contusions on her forearms and face. She was also missing one of her front teeth and her mouth appeared swollen. A search for the tooth was conducted in the house, but it was not found. Mr. MacNamara was bleeding from what appeared to be a 2 inch gash on his scalp. I photographed and took into evidence a woman's high-heeled shoe and the revolver. I later booked them into evidence. The photograph of the woman's high-heeled shoe is attached to this report as Attachment "A," and the photograph of the revolver is attached as Attachment "B."

Mr. MacNamara was arrested for a violation of PC 483.2 and both Steven and Brenda MacNamara were transported to the Lead County Hospital for treatment. Brenda MacNamara was administered an MRI which showed no internal injuries. She said she would make an appointment with her dentist to have her mouth checked out. Steven MacNamara required four sutures to his scalp. Following treatment, Steven MacNamara was transported to the Lead County Jail and booked.

I spoke to another officer who told me that the Silverado Police Department had responded twice in the past to domestic problems between Brenda and Steven MacNamara but no arrests had been made and no reports had been prepared. Both of those calls were made by Brenda MacNamara.

I referred Steven MacNamara to the District Attorney for prosecution.

Motive, intent,
Prior inconsistent
' statement
— 803 (6) (7)
— Record of regular
Practive or
activity
— Record of public
records

SILVERADO POLICE DEPARTMENT

Report Type: Interview of Brenda MacNamara

Report by: Officer Taylor Richardson (initialed: *TR*)

Date: 12/3/C.Y.-3

Brenda MacNamara reported that she arrived home about 12:30 a.m. and was confronted by her husband. Before she left home, she had told him she would be back home by 7:30 p.m. When she arrived home, her husband immediately started yelling that he had been worried and that she should have told him she was going to be late. She said that her husband then noticed that she had driven up in a new car. He flew into an angry rage and began screaming that she was not to make large purchases without consulting him. She said that she and her husband were under severe financial strain and were continually fighting about finances.

At that point, her husband grabbed her by the wrist and told her that she would be taking the car back in the morning. She did not respond, just wrenched her wrist free and walked into the house. As Mrs. MacNamara walked past him, she thought she smelled beer. He followed her and continued to yell at her. He then grabbed her and shoved her and she struck her head on the corner of a wall and fell to the ground. After a few seconds she got up and ran into their home office. Mr. MacNamara followed her into the office and shoved her to the ground. She tried to get up, but he sat on her and pinned her arms. He continued yelling at her as he held her down. The more she struggled, the angrier he got. After a few minutes, he said, "If you don't stop struggling and start listening to me, I'm going to make you listen." Mrs. MacNamara continued to struggle and demanded to be let up. Mr. MacNamara then punched her in the mouth, knocking out one of her front teeth. She kept squirming around in an attempt to get away. She got an arm free, grabbed her shoe, and hit Mr. MacNamara with the heel. She did not know where she hit him. As soon as she hit him, Mr. MacNamara got off of her. Mrs. MacNamara then ran into the back of the house and retrieved a gun from the master bedroom closet. When her husband saw the gun he ran to the bathroom and locked himself inside. Mrs. MacNamara then went outside and called the police.

Mrs. MacNamara told me that this wasn't the first time her husband had attacked her. About three years ago, he hit her with his fists. He said he was sorry and that he would never do it again, and that he loved her very much and wanted to work on their marriage. She believed him and did not file charges.

Reviewed and verified by: *Brenda MacNamara*
Brenda MacNamara

SILVERADO POLICE DEPARTMENT

Report Type: Interview of Steven MacNamara

Report by: Officer Taylor Richardson (initialed: *TR*)

Date: 12/3/C.Y.-3

I read Mr. MacNamara his Miranda rights from my Silverado Police Department issued Miranda card. He waived his rights and agreed to speak with me.

Mr. MacNamara told me that he and his wife are having dire financial trouble because she has a significant spending problem. He related that she has "racked up" significant debt on her credit cards. He related that in an attempt to get a handle on their finances, the two made an agreement not to make any large purchases without consulting the other person.

He reported that Mrs. MacNamara arrived home at about 12:30 a.m. in a newly-purchased Mercedes-Benz C-Class automobile. He demanded to know why she bought a new car without discussing it with him. The two got into an argument. She became enraged and stormed away.

He said that his wife ran into the office and he followed. When he entered the office, she attacked him with one of her high-heeled shoes and struck him on the head. He reported that she "just lost it" and continued to try and strike him with the shoe. He was able to knock the shoe out of her hand and she came at him with her fists. He tried to restrain her but she kept flailing around and banged her head and face on a desk and then a door jam while he attempted to get her to stop. He claimed that that was when she lost one of her teeth. She got one of her hands free and started clawing and scratching at his hands, trying to get him to let her go.

Mrs. MacNamara then broke free and ran into the back of the house and got a gun. She ran back into the office, stuck the gun in Mr. MacNamara's face and said she was going to kill him because she hated him. He related he was afraid of what she was going to do, so he locked himself in the bathroom. He refused to come out until officers arrived.

When I asked if Mr. MacNamara had ever hit his wife before he adamantly denied any prior abuse.

Reviewed and verified by: *Steven MacNamara*
Steven MacNamara

ATTACHMENT "A"

ATTACHMENT "B"

enter in evidence

Transcript of 911 call from 562-445-2392 on December 3, C.Y.-3 at 00:47 hours

SILVERADO POLICE DISPATCH: Silverado Police, what is your emergency?

CALLER: My husband just hit me, I want him arrested!

DISPATCH: Your name and address?

CALLER: Brenda MacNamara. 385 North Fair Oaks in Silverado. Hurry!

DISPATCH: What is your current situation?

CALLER: What do you mean?

DISPATCH: Are you in immediate danger?

CALLER: [*unintelligible*] I've gotta protect myself. He's in the back of the house.

DISPATCH: Have any shots been fired?

CALLER: No, but you better get somebody over here, because if he comes after me I'll shoot him.

DISPATCH: Put away the firearm. We should have a unit there within minutes.

CALLER: I'm going to wait out in front of the house.

DISPATCH: I understand. Are you on a landline or a cell?

CALLER: It's my cell.

DISPATCH: Stay on the line until we arrive.

CALLER: Okay – but I'm staying in front.

DISPATCH: That's fine – but please stay on the line.

CALLER: I will.

At 00:53 hours . . .

CALLER: The officer has arrived.

DISPATCH: Good luck, Mrs. MacNamara.

SILVERADO POLICE DEPARTMENT

Report Type: Follow-Up Report

Report by: Officer Taylor Richardson (initialed: 𝒯ℛ)

Date: 12/4/C.Y.-3

On 12/4/C.Y.-3, I received a message through dispatch to call Brenda MacNamara at her residence. Mrs. MacNamara had been the victim in a domestic violence case on 12/3/C.Y.-3. I was the responding officer on that call.

At about 18:00 hours on 12/4/C.Y.-3, I placed a telephone call to Mrs. MacNamara at her residence. She answered, identified herself, and stated, without being asked, that the arrest of her husband on the previous day had all been a mistake. While she admitted that she and her husband had a heated altercation, she said that she had hurt herself while attacking him but that he never hit or attacked her. I told her that I did not believe her explanation and further I explained that if her husband is threatening her to convince her that she should not pursue charges, that she should tell me, because that is a felony. She insisted on her husband's innocence and urged me to drop the case. I explained that the matter was out of my hands and had already been referred to the district attorney.

Mrs. MacNamara cursed me and terminated the call.

SILVERADO POLICE DEPARTMENT

Report Type: Follow-Up Report

Report by: Officer Taylor Richardson (initialed: *TR*)

Date: 12/5/C.Y.-3

Once again while on patrol I received a call from dispatch that Brenda MacNamara had called and asked me to call her at her residence.

At about 16:30 hours on 12/5/C.Y.-3, I called her at her residence. She seemed very agitated. She urged that the case against her husband should go forward. I again explained that I filed my report with the district attorney, and that the matter was out of my hands. Mrs. MacNamara told me that her husband had in fact beaten her and that her previous call should be ignored.

I asked her to explain her change of mind. She related that on 12/4, after her husband was released from jail, he returned to their home and asked her, "What do I need to do for this thing to go away?"

Mrs. MacNamara said she responded by cursing at him, but that he persisted and again said, "What can I do?"

Mrs. MacNamara told him that if he would agree that she could keep the Mercedes she had bought on 12/2 and if he would make all the payments on the car, she would call and drop the charges. She related that her husband agreed and in fact her husband listened to the conversation that she had with this officer on 12/4.

Following the phone conversation between Mrs. MacNamara and this officer, Mr. MacNamara told Mrs. MacNamara that he would not make payments on the car and that as far as he was concerned the car could be repossessed. Mrs. MacNamara then related that her husband had taunted her by saying that he had "screwed-up the case so bad that it will never see the light of day."

I indicated to Mrs. MacNamara that I would immediately write up a report of this call and file it with the district attorney.

Reviewed and verified by: *Brenda MacNamara*
                           Brenda MacNamara

King of Glory Episcopal Church

19383 North Raymond Avenue, Silverado, Golden 29103

April 9, C.Y.-2

To Whom It May Concern:

Steven MacNamara asked me to write a letter in reference to my interactions with him and his wife, Brenda. I am an ordained priest. I have been friends with Steven MacNamara since we were kids. I officiated at Steven and Brenda's wedding 15 years ago, and they have been members of my congregation ever since.

For the past few years, Steven and Brenda have been having money trouble, which has caused a number of disputes between the two of them. I have heard from some of my other parishioners that on more than one occasion Steven and Brenda have gotten into heated arguments in the church parking lot. One of those parishioners told me he saw Brenda shove ⟩ *object* Steven during one of those arguments.

They began having weekly counseling sessions with me to try to solve their problems. Because of confidentiality reasons, I am not permitted to discuss what went on in those sessions. The only thing I can say is that they both had a lot of anger. Steven was usually quick to anger and more than once I had to ask Brenda to leave the room until I could get him to calm down.

The only time I saw any physical altercation between them was one day after services when the congregation was gathering over coffee in the patio. I heard Brenda mention to another parishioner that she needed a new pair of shoes. Steven was nearby, and said something to Brenda, which I did not quite hear. He then reached out and placed his hand on her shoulder and she swatted it off her. Then he said, in a rather loud voice, "You can't spend money we don't have on things you don't need." Brenda shoved him in the chest and stormed off. Later, Steven sought my help.

About two weeks before the incident now under investigation, Steven asked me to join them for dinner at their house. Brenda was in the middle of making dinner when I arrived and it was clear she was not expecting me. She was sullen and uncommunicative throughout dinner. At one point Steven broached the topic of her spending and when I turned to look at Brenda she screamed, "Now I know what this is about!" She turned and tried to leave the room and, as she passed Steven, he grabbed Brenda by the wrist and pulled her toward him. He shouted at her that he was "just trying to get her help for her spending problem" because he "wanted the marriage to work." Brenda broke out of Steven's grip and left the room.

Steven and Brenda are good, God-fearing people who I believe love each other and are trying to cope with their problems. They both have quick tempers and at times seem to lose control of their emotions.

*Jamie Moore*_____

Pastor Jamie Moore

Object unduly pre(s)usual not probative of any material fact — this idea can get in another ways — no evit of husband income

CREDIT REPORT

Personal Profile

Name: Brenda MacNamara

Address: 385 N. Fair Oaks
                     Silverado, Golden

Current Employer: Ace Construction Co.

Credit Score

525

Account History

BANANA REPUBLIC

Acct Number: XXXX XXXX XXXX 2950
Acct Type: Revolving
Acct Status: Open
Date Open: 5/1/C.Y.-5
Balance: $3,500.00
Comments: CHARGE

MACY'S   ~ 19.5

Acct Number: XXXX XXXX XXXX 5492
Acct Type: Revolving
Acct Status: Open
Date Open: 4/13/C.Y.-2
Balance: $1,523.87
Comments: CHARGE

OLD NAVY

Acct Number: XXXX XXXX XXXX 3059
Acct Type: Revolving
Acct Status: Open
Date Open: 3/18/C.Y.-9
Balance: $239.54
Comments: CHARGE

DISCOVER

Acct Number: XXXX XXXX XXXX 0274
Acct Type: Revolving
Acct Status: Open
Date Open: 11/3/C.Y.-10
Balance: $0
Comments: CREDIT CARD

VICTORIA'S SECRET

Acct Number: XXXX XXXX XXXX 8497
Acct Type: Revolving
Acct Status: Open
Date Open: 8/5/C.Y.-3
Balance: $950.00
Comments: CHARGE

AMERICAN EXPRESS

Acct Number: XXXX XXXX XXXX 9416
Acct Type: Revolving
Acct Status: Open
Date Open: 7/9/C.Y.-6
Balance: $13,403.00
Comments: CREDIT CARD

Outstanding Debt

ACME FINE USED CARS

Amount Owed:	$35,000
Date Opened:	12/02/C.Y.-3
Payment Status:	Repossessed

SILVERADO PUBLIC LIBRARY

Amount Owed:	$425.00
Date Opened:	6/15/C.Y.-6
Payment Status:	Past Due

IRS WAGE GARNISHMENT

Amount Owed:	$5,000
Date Opened:	5/12/C.Y.-3
Payment Status:	Current

45K

Jury Instructions

Members of the jury, I thank you for your attention during this trial. Please pay attention to the instructions I am about to give you.

In this case, Steven MacNamara is accused of spousal abuse.

To prove the crime of spousal abuse, the State must prove the following three elements beyond a reasonable doubt:

1. Steven MacNamara used force or violence upon Brenda MacNamara, resulting in bodily injury.
2. The use was willful and unlawful; and
3. At the time of the use of force or violence, Brenda MacNamara was Steven MacNamara's wife.

- cycle of abuse
- self defense doesn't make sense
- one heel on

The use of force or violence is not unlawful when done in lawful self-defense. The burden is on the State to prove that the use of force or violence was not in lawful self-defense. If you have a reasonable doubt that the use of force or violence was unlawful, you must find Defendant not guilty.

Steven MacNamara has entered a plea of not guilty. This means you must presume or believe that Steven MacNamara is innocent. This presumption stays with Steven MacNamara as to each material allegation in the indictment through each stage of the trial until it has been overcome by the evidence to the exclusion of and beyond a reasonable doubt.

To overcome Defendant's presumption of innocence, the State has the burden of proving that:

1. The crime with which Defendant is charged was committed; and

2. Defendant is the person who committed the crime.

Defendant is not required to prove anything.

Whenever the words "reasonable doubt" are used, you must consider the following:

A reasonable doubt is not a mere possible doubt, because everything relating to human affairs is open to some possible or imaginary doubt. It is that state of the case which, after the entire comparison and consideration of all the evidence, leaves the minds of the jurors in that condition that they cannot say they feel an abiding conviction of the truth of the charge.

It is to the evidence introduced during this trial, and to it alone, that you are to look for that proof. A reasonable doubt as to the guilt of Defendant may arise from the evidence, a conflict in the evidence, or a lack of evidence. If you have a reasonable doubt, you should find Defendant not guilty. If you have no reasonable doubt, you should find Defendant guilty.

You must decide this case based only on the law and the evidence. It is up to you to decide what evidence is reliable. You should use your common sense in deciding which evidence is reliable and which evidence should not be relied upon in considering your verdict. You may find some of the evidence not reliable or less reliable than other evidence.

A witness is a person who has knowledge related to this case. You will have to decide whether you believe each witness and how important each witness's testimony is to the case. You may believe all, part, or none of a witness's testimony. In deciding whether to believe a witness's testimony, you may consider, among other factors, the following:

     1.   Did the witness seem to have an opportunity to see and know the things about which the witness testified?

     2.   Did the witness seem to have an accurate memory?

     3.   Was the witness honest and straightforward in answering the attorneys' questions?

     4.   Did the witness have some interest in how the case should be decided?

     5.   Does the witness's testimony agree with the other testimony and other evidence in this case?

     6.   Has the witness been offered or received any money, preferred treatment, or other benefit in order to get the witness to testify?

     7.   Had any pressure or threat been used against the witness that affected the truth of the witness's testimony?

     8.   Did the witness at some other time make a statement that is inconsistent with the testimony he or she gave in court?

     9.   Was it proved that the witness had been convicted of a crime?

You may rely upon your own conclusions about the witnesses. A juror may believe or disbelieve all or any part of the evidence or the testimony of any witness.

Defendant in this case has become a witness. You should apply the same rules to consideration of his testimony that you apply to the testimony of the other witnesses.

There are some general rules that apply to your deliberations. You must follow these rules in order to return a lawful verdict:

1.   You must follow the law as it is set out in these instructions. If you fail to follow the law, your verdict will be a miscarriage of justice.

2.   This case must be decided only upon the evidence that you have heard from the answers of the witnesses and have seen in the form of exhibits and these instructions.

3.   This case must not be decided for or against anyone because you feel sorry for anyone or are angry at anyone.

4.   Remember the lawyers are not on trial. Your feelings about them should not influence your decision in this case.

5.   Your duty is to determine if Defendant has been proven guilty or not. It is the judge's job to determine the proper sentence if Defendant is found guilty.

6.   Whatever verdict you render must be unanimous; that is, each juror must agree to the same verdict. The verdict must be the verdict of each juror, as well as of the jury as a whole.

7.   It is entirely proper for a lawyer to talk to a witness about what testimony the witness would give if called to the courtroom. The witness should not be discredited for talking to a lawyer about his or her testimony.

8.   Your verdict should not be influenced by feelings of prejudice, bias, or sympathy. Your verdict must be based on the evidence and the law contained in these instructions.

Deciding a proper verdict is exclusively your job. I cannot participate in that decision in any way. Please disregard anything I may have said or done that made you think I preferred one verdict over another.

Only one verdict may be returned as to the crime charged. The verdict must be in writing and the verdict form has been prepared for you. It is as follows:

[READ VERDICT FORM]

In just a few moments, you will be taken to the jury room by the bailiff. The first thing you should do is elect a foreperson who will preside over your deliberations like the chairperson of a meeting. It is the foreperson's job to sign and date the verdict form when all of you have agreed on a verdict in this case and to bring the verdict back to the courtroom when you return.

In closing, let me remind you that it is important that you follow the law spelled out in these instructions in deciding your verdicts. Even if you do not like the laws, you must apply them. There are no other laws that apply to this case.

IN THE CIRCUIT COURT OF THE THIRTEENTH JUDICIAL CIRCUIT

IN AND FOR LEAD COUNTY, STATE OF GOLDEN

CRIMINAL DIVISION

STATE OF GOLDEN	)	
	)	
	)	
v.	)	Case No. CR 98-351
	)	
STEVEN MACNAMARA,	)	
Defendant.	)	
	)	

VERDICT

As to the charge of Spousal Abuse in violation of Golden State Penal Code

section 483.2 we, the Jury, find Defendant, Steven MacNamara:

_____   Guilty

_____   Not Guilty

So say we all.

_____

Foreperson of the Jury

_____

Date

Chapter 4

James Price

v.

GEM Corporation

(employment discrimination)

UNITED STATES DISTRICT COURT

CENTRAL DISTRICT OF THE STATE OF GOLDEN

JAMES PRICE, Plaintiff, v. GEM CORPORATION, Defendant.	)))))))))	CASE NO: 17-cv-4923[1]

---

[1] Modified from a case file originally prepared by The American Bar Association Section

of Labor & Employment Law, © 2009.

UNITED STATES DISTRICT COURT

CENTRAL DISTRICT OF THE STATE OF GOLDEN

JAMES PRICE, Plaintiff, v. GEM CORPORATION, Defendant.	))))))))))	CASE NO: 17-cv-4923 **COMPLAINT**

Plaintiff, JAMES PRICE, by his attorney, complains against Defendant, GEM CORPORATION, as follows:

1.   This is an action for damages and declaratory and injunctive relief to redress deprivations of Plaintiff's civil rights in violation of Title VII of the Civil Rights Act of 1964 ("Title VII"), *as amended*, 42 U.S.C. §§ 2000e *et seq.*

2.   Jurisdiction of this Court is invoked pursuant to Section 706 of Title VII, 42 U.S.C. § 2000e-5, and 28 U.S.C. § 1343(4).

3.   The unlawful employment practices that are the subject matter of this lawsuit occurred within this judicial district. Venue is, therefore, proper here.

4.   Plaintiff JAMES PRICE is a citizen of the United States and a resident of the State of Golden. Plaintiff was employed as a supervisor by Defendant from May 17, C.Y.-4 to May 15, C.Y.-2, and, at all times relevant herein, was an employee of Defendant within the meaning of Section 701(f) of Title VII, *as amended*, 42 U.S.C. §§ 2000e-(f).

5.   Defendant GEM CORPORATION maintains its headquarters in Springfield, State of Golden. At all times relevant herein, Defendant was Plaintiff's employer within the meaning Title VII.

6.   On June 22, C.Y.-2, Plaintiff timely filed a charge of religious discrimination with the Equal Employment Opportunity Commission ("EEOC"). On November 30, C.Y.-2, Plaintiff received his Notice of Right-to-Sue from the EEOC.

7.   Plaintiff filed this lawsuit within ninety (90) days of receipt of his Notice of Right-to-Sue referenced above. Specifically, this lawsuit was filed on December 15, C.Y.-2.

8.   GEM CORPORATION hired Terri Saks as its Vice President of Laboratory Operations on February 28, C.Y.-3. Terri Saks immediately began to supervise Plaintiff.

9.   Within months of Saks' supervision of Plaintiff, Plaintiff was treated differently in the workplace because of his religion. This discrimination included, without limitation:

> (a) Counseling Plaintiff about his religious discussions with co-workers;
>
> (b) Plaintiff's verbal warning of Defendant and Plaintiff's suspension on March 22, C.Y.-2 and May 8, C.Y.-2, respectively; and
>
> (c) Plaintiff's termination on May 15, C.Y.-2.

10.   As a result of the foregoing, Plaintiff has suffered, and continues to suffer, lost wages and pain and suffering in the form of emotional distress, anxiety, embarrassment, and humiliation.

11.   Defendant thereby violated Plaintiff's Title VII rights in a willful, intentional, and/or reckless manner.

WHEREFORE, Plaintiff prays that this Honorable Court:

A.   Enter a judgment that Defendant unlawfully discriminated against Plaintiff because of his religion in violation of Title VII;

B.   Award Plaintiff reinstatement with his employment of Defendant, back pay, and actual damages in the amount shown to be due, with pre- and post-judgment interest;

C.   Award Plaintiff compensatory damages in an appropriate sum;

D.   Award Plaintiff reasonable attorney's fees and costs; and

E.   Award other such relief that this Court deems is just and appropriate.

PLAINTIFF DEMANDS TRIAL BY JURY.

                              JAMES PRICE, Plaintiff

                              By: _____*Jim Price*_____
                                     Attorney for Plaintiff

UNITED STATES DISTRICT COURT

CENTRAL DISTRICT OF THE STATE OF GOLDEN

JAMES PRICE, Plaintiff,	))))	
v.	))	CASE NO: 17-cv-4923
GEM CORPORATION, Defendant.	))))	**ANSWER**

Defendant, GEM CORPORATION, by its attorney, respectfully submits the

following Answer and Affirmative Defenses to Plaintiff's Complaint:

1.   Defendant admits the allegations in Paragraph 1 of the Complaint.

2.   Defendant admits the allegations in Paragraph 2 of the Complaint.

3.   Defendant denies that any unlawful employment practices were committed

but admits that Plaintiff worked within this judicial district.

4.   Defendant admits the allegations in Paragraph 4 of the Complaint.

5.   Defendant admits the allegations in Paragraph 5 of the Complaint.

6.   Defendant admits that Plaintiff filed a charge of religious discrimination

with the EEOC on June 22, C.Y.-2, and that a Notice of Right-to-Sue was issued on

Plaintiff's charge. With respect to the remaining allegations of Paragraph 6, Defendant

has insufficient information to admit or deny them and demands strict proof thereof.

7.   Defendant admits that Plaintiff filed this lawsuit on December 15, C.Y.-2,

but has insufficient information to admit or deny when Plaintiff received his Notice of

Right-to-Sue and demands strict proof thereof.

8. Defendant admits the allegations in Paragraph 8 of the Complaint.

9. Defendant denies each and every allegation in Paragraph 9 of the Complaint.

10. Defendant admits that no disciplinary action was taken against Plaintiff prior to coming under supervision of Terri Saks. Defendant affirmatively states that Plaintiff was disciplined for legitimate, nondiscriminatory reasons. Defendant denies the remaining allegations in Paragraph 10 of the Complaint.

11. Defendant denies the allegations in Paragraph 11.

AFFIRMATIVE DEFENSES

12. Plaintiff fails to state a claim upon which relief may be granted against GEM CORPORATION under Title VII, *as amended*, 42 U.S.C. §§ 2000e *et seq.*

13. Any actions taken against Plaintiff, including his termination, were based on legitimate non-discriminatory reasons.

WHEREFORE, Defendants pray that this Court:

A. Dismiss Plaintiff's claims in their entirety;

B. Award reasonable costs and attorney's fees; and

C. Grant such other relief that this Court may deem just and proper.

GEM CORPORATION, Defendant

By: _____*Steve Davidson*_____
Attorneys for Defendant

Witness List

Witnesses for Plaintiff:

1. James Price *

2. Carol Connor * * *

Witnesses for Defendant:

1. Terri Saks * *

2. Jonny Joyce * * *

Each side must call both witnesses listed for their respective party.

* This witness must be a male.

* * This witness must be female.

* * * This witness may be either gender.

This is a bifurcated trial, only the issue of liability will be tried.

Stipulations

1. Federal Rules of Evidence apply.

2. Each witness who gave a deposition did agree under oath at the outset of his/her deposition to give a full and complete description of what occurred and to correct the deposition for inaccuracies and completeness before signing the deposition.

3. All exhibits in the file are authentic and, unless otherwise noted, are the original of that document.

4. All depositions were signed under oath.

5. Other than what appears in the witness statements or depositions, there is nothing exceptional or unusual about the background of any of the witnesses that would bolster or detract from their credibility.

6. All dates are denoted by C.Y. (current year) and C.Y.-1 indicating, for example, that the date is the current year minus one.

7. All pretrial motions shall be oral.

8. No party may "invent" witnesses or evidence not specifically mentioned in this problem.

9. "Beyond the record" is not a proper objection. Rather, attorneys shall use cross-examination as a means of challenging a witness whose testimony strays beyond the facts contained in the witness's statement or deposition.

10. The law is accurately set forth in the jury instructions.

11. The plaintiff and defendant may call only the two witnesses listed on their respective witness list. Each party may call an additional witness by deposition or witness statement. Any such testimony is subject to objections pursuant to the Federal Rules of Evidence. If a witness is called by deposition or witness statement, the opposing party may cross-examine that witness by deposition or witness statement.

Deposition of James Price

Date: 5/1/C.Y.-1

Q: Good morning. We met a few minutes ago. Please state your name.

A: James Price.

Q: Early on in your life what was your religious background or affiliation?

A: Judaism.

Q: When did that change from Judaism to Christianity?

A: Around C.Y.-11.

Q: At some point did you become a born-again Christian?

A: Oh, yes.

Q: Tell me when you became a born-again Christian.

A: I would say in C.Y.-11. When I entered the church, I became born-again.

Q: What does born-again mean to you?

A: Born-again means born of the Spirit.

Q: Specifically what did you do in terms of living your life for Christ?

A: Oh, they will tell you go preach, go teach, go witness, go give to the poor, go into the missionary field, go to seminary, go into the prisons, go door to door.

Q: How about in the workplace? Would you witness to people on the job?

A: Yes. It depends.

Q: As part of the Christian teaching, is it indicated that the Christian faith does not advocate homosexuality of any kind?

A: The Bible, the New Testament, states that no fornicator or whoremonger will enter into the Kingdom of God. I don't condemn people that are homosexual. I personally don't believe it is appropriate but who am I to judge anyone?

Q: And the same thing with people that fornicate, or adulterers?

A: Yes. The same answer I just gave.

Q: Is it your feeling that people should have a choice in their religion?

A: Yes.

Q: Is it part of your personal mission as a Christian to go out into the world and try to spread God's Gospel to everyone?

A: Yes, but there is a qualification. Talking to people about religion when they want to talk about religion is fine. There are a number of people that cross the line and talk about religious beliefs when people don't want to hear it. I don't do that.

Q: You were hired at GEM as a Med Tech on May 17, C.Y.-4, and you were promoted to night shift supervisor, correct?

A: Yes.

Q: And you were terminated from GEM, correct?

A: Yes.

Q: You were not laid off, is that right?

A: No. Well, terminated because of what they said, religion. I want to say something. When I worked for GEM I was expecting to – it was a good career move. I liked GEM. It was a great job. And then it changed, you know, when Terri Saks got there. It was a great job and they promised me a lot of things. They made me supervisor. Then my whole world fell apart in like what, 15 months? Terri Saks ruined my life. I knew how to run that lab. I ran that lab well. I had 30 people in that lab and I did a great job for GEM.

Q: You knew when you came on board at GEM in C.Y.-4, they could fire you at any time and you could quit at any time?

A: Yes.

Q: Did you understand that if you had a problem at GEM that you could go to several people to complain?

A: Yes.

Q: Did you ever make a complaint to anyone at GEM?

A: I complained to Terri Saks about Terri Saks.

Q: What did you complain about and when did you complain?

A: Terri? I resented her making anti-Semitic remarks to me and I complained to her. One time she said that all you Jews are the same. And I said to her, "You probably believe that the Holocaust was fake," and she said, "Yes."

Q: When did this happen?

A: While I was working there. I don't remember the exact date.

Q: Did you think about complaining to Corporate?

A: No, I figured that since we had a pretty good working relationship that we would just, you know, it was important to work around it or ignore it or accept it, whatever, to keep my job, you know?

Q: Did you actually discuss Christianity and religious beliefs with some of your coworkers when you were at Med Tech?

A: Yes.

Q: Do you recall any of your coworkers telling you that they did not want to discuss religion with you?

A: No.

Q: Do you recall in March or April of C.Y.-2 sitting down with Paula McDonald or Terri Saks to discuss complaints they received about you related to your discussions about religion with people that didn't want to hear it?

A: No.

Q: So, if both of them testify that they discussed this with you in an oral counseling session they would be lying?

A: Yes. Terri one time told me that someone was offended by something. I don't remember. And I told her that if it offended that person, I won't do it. That's the only time. I don't remember anything else.

Q: Did Albert DuFricio and Lisa Stiles both work under your supervision during the night shift?

A: Yes.

Q: Did you know they were having an affair?

A: No.

Q: Do you recall telling Lisa that she was living in sin with Albert and that she should cut it out?

A: No.

Q: Joan Caruso. Do you remember talking to her about her lifestyle as a lesbian?

A: No.

Q: You never confronted her about her homosexual relationship with Jane Christie?

A: No.

Q: Evelyn Roby, did you ever discuss religion with her?

A: Yes. Evelyn is born-again.

Q: How about Javed Quershi? Do you recall giving him a Bible?

A: Yes.

Q: Do you recall him telling you he didn't want the Bible?

A: No.

Q: In April of C.Y.-3, do you recall giving Terri Saks a Bible?

A: Yeah.

Q: Do you remember her saying she didn't want it?

A: No.

Q: You didn't insist that she keep it? She just accepted the Bible that you gave her?

A: She did. It was a leather-bound Bible. She accepted it and thanked me.

Q: Now, you mentioned early on when we were discussing Christianity and religion and so forth that you witnessed to people, but you witness to people once you have prayed and God has given you direction as to who you should witness to or not witness to. Is that a fair characterization of what we talked about?

A: Not all the time. Sometimes it's spontaneous.

Q: Alright. Do you remember in March of C.Y.-2 Terri Saks meeting with you to discuss a complaint by Jane Christie, also known as Rusty, regarding you?

A: No. That never happened. I never said or did anything that was inappropriate or unwelcome to Rusty.

Q: Did you ever go up to Jane Christie and tell her that you could cure her homosexual illness with prayer?

A: No.

Q: Did you ever talk to her about her lesbian relationship and the fact that that is not the proper way of life?

A: I just gave her a Bible and told her to read, like, Romans 1 concerning what the word of God says about it. That is all.

Q: You never said the following to Jane Christie, quote, "God told me that saving your soul was more important than my job." You never told her that?

A: I don't remember saying that.

Q: You never told her that her lifestyle was ungodly?

A: No.

Q: You never discussed it with her at all?

A: She discussed it with me after I gave her the Bible and she read about it.

Q: What did she say?

A: I don't recall. But she brought it up.

Q: Do you ever recall telling her that being a lesbian was wicked?

A: No.

Q: Did you ever allow your wife, Ginger Price, into the lab at night?

A: Yes.

Q: Wasn't that against the rules at GEM to do that?

A: Not that I knew of because it was going on ever since I had been there.

Q: Did you receive a verbal warning on or about March 22, C.Y.-2?

A: Yeah.

Q: Can you just tell us what that is all about?

A: They told me all kinds of things. But I got to tell you I never harassed anyone at
        GEM. I had many talks with Javed Quershi about religion. He talked about Islam
        and I talked about Christianity. At no point did our talks ever become
        inappropriate or harassing. I gave him a Bible and I asked him for a copy of the
        Koran. As for Rusty, she came to me and asked me to pray for her and her
        girlfriend, Joan. She asked me what the Bible says about homosexuality. I told
        her that it would upset her and she insisted on knowing. I told her that the Bible
        says homosexuals are condemned to Hell. I was careful to tell her that I was not
        judging her in any way. She told me that she understood. She was not upset at
        all. She thanked me for being honest and praying for her and Joan.

Q: On May 5, C.Y.-2, you left your shift early, correct?

A: Yes. I was suspended one day for doing something that everyone else did before I
        was the night shift supervisor. It was common practice to get your work done and
        let a senior employee, who had to be there until the test was finished, lock up.

Q: Do you recall on May 10, C.Y.-2, having a meeting with Paula McDonald and
        Terri Saks to discuss staffing issues and your suspension that we just talked
        about?

A: Right.

Q: Do you remember having a confrontation with Terri?

A: Yes.

Q: Do you remember slamming your fist down on the table and going at her?

A: It wasn't my fist. It was the palm of my hand.

Q: Did you block her way out of the room?

A: No, I didn't block the way.

Q: You just slammed your hand on the table?

A: Yes. I was angry.

Q: That is all you did?

A:　　When I slammed my hand on the desk, Terri came out from behind the desk, put her hand on my face and started shaking my face. I told Terri to take her hands off of me.

Q:　　What happened on the night of May 12, C.Y.-2, when Frances' going away party took place? What happened with Carol Conner?

A:　　Okay. My wife had come in for the party because they were having a going away potluck for Frances. The employees were preparing for it. And Frances walks in with her replacement, Carol Conner. Carol was being introduced to everyone at the party and when I met him/her, he/she had a large necklace with a crucifix. My wife said that she could see that Carol is a Christian and I asked Carol which church he/she attended. Carol replied that he/she really didn't go to church on a regular basis and he/she seemed a bit ashamed of that fact. And my wife said yeah, you know, you should go.

Q:　　And that was it?

A:　　That was it. It was very innocent. When I came to work on May 15, Terri told me that she wanted to talk to me in her office. This was not unusual. I went in Terri's office and sat down. I was given the termination paper. I was not asked any questions, which was odd. I thought people should investigate something before taking someone's job.

Q:　　Do you think Terri Saks targeted you because of your religious beliefs?

A:　　Yes.

Q:　　You think that's what developed the whole altercation between you ---

A:　　Yes, in fact, I think Terri Saks singled me out because I was religious.

Q:　　What do you mean?

A:　　Well, for example, I asked for time off. I asked for time off to go to a religious retreat and also to visit Israel. People routinely take vacation days without any problems. Terri Saks denied both of my requests.

Q:　　Can you tell me what type of damages you sustained because of alleged wrongful termination from GEM?

A:　　Well, financial damages. I had to live off my savings, which was rapidly depleted. My marriage suffered and broke up. I was evicted. I lost everything.

A:　　No further questions.

I affirm under penalty of perjury that my answers are full and complete.

Jim Price
JAMES PRICE

Deposition of Carol Connor

Date: 5/12/C.Y.-1

Q: Who are you employed by?

A: Starlight Corporation.

Q: And how long have you been with Starlight?

A: Six months.

Q: Where were you employed before Starlight?

A: GEM Corporation.

Q: When did you start with GEM?

A: May 12, C.Y.-2.

Q: When did you leave?

A: Around December 9, C.Y.-2.

Q: How long did you work there?

A: About 7 months.

Q: Can you tell us what happened the first night you were employed at GEM?

A: I came in to work for training at 6 p.m. Frances Gomez was training me. And we got a phone call from the lounge that they wanted her in there for a break or whatever. We went in. It turned out that there was a going-away party for her that night. We walked in. She introduced me to Mr. Price as the nighttime supervisor. He noticed my cross which was outside of my shirt. He said "what a nice crucifix you have on."

Q: Is it fair to say that the only person you knew in that work area was Frances?

A: Yes.

Q: But you also knew Donna Corleone?

A: Right.

Q: Because she's a friend of yours?

A: But she works days.

Q: So the only person you knew that night at the party was Frances because she had been training you?

A: Yeah.

Q: And it was her job to train you in her position because you were taking her spot, is that right?

A: Right.

Q: I interrupted you in the middle when you were talking about your crucifix. You said that Mr. Price noticed the crucifix that you had on. Is that right?

A: Right.

Q: I see you are wearing a crucifix here today. Is that the same one?

A: Yeah.

Q: Would it be fair to say that it is about two inches long and maybe an inch wide?

A: Yes.

Q: Tell us what happened once he noticed the crucifix.

A: Like I said, he said, "What a beautiful crucifix you have on." I said, "Thank you." Then he proceeded to ask, "When was the last time you went to church? Do you go to church?" And I said, "I can't remember the last time I did go."

Q: Now, let me stop you. Is this the first time you met Mr. Price?

A: Yeah.

Q: And after he asked you about the cross, what happened next?

A: He commented on the cross, and then it just started going into religion and do I go to church, and what church do I go to? I said, I can't remember the last time I did go to church. I said I go, like, on the holidays, Christmas, Easter. He said, no, you should really go, it's a fulfilling experience, I mean, like an experience, and it's good for you. I felt uncomfortable because I was the new person, I didn't know anybody in there. So I said, "Frances, I'm going to go back to work, I'll see you later." And that was it.

Q: Now, did you see Mrs. Price there?

A: Yes.

Q: Did you know that that was Mr. Price's wife when you saw her?

A: I had no idea.

Q: What did she have on?

A: A lab coat.

Q: So you thought she was another employee?

A: An employee, right.

Q: Did you speak with her at all?

A: I can't remember exactly what she said, but she was agreeing with Mr. Price.

Q: Did you tell Mr. Price that you didn't want to hear any of his conversation about church and so forth?

A: No. I didn't want to be rude. He was my supervisor.

Q: So instead of saying anything to him, you just excused yourself and went back to work?

A: Right.

Q: Okay. What time did you get off on the night of the 12th, if you can recall?

A: Ten. Ten o'clock.

Q: So your shift that night was from six until ten?

A: Right.

Q: Strictly for the purposes of training?

A: Right.

Q: Did you do anything in terms of complaining to anyone or mentioning the fact that Mr. Price said this to you between the hours of six and ten?

A: No.

Q: So you didn't say it to anybody?

A: No.

Q: Did you call anybody?

A: No.

Q: Okay. So you never complained about it during those four hours between six and ten?

A: No.

Q: When you left the lab, what did you do?

A: After a friend picked me up, I used my cell and called Donna and told her what happened. I just thought it was strange that he did not know me, and he just started preaching to me about church and God, you know. I just thought it was strange. So I called Donna as a friend and I said, you know, what's going on? You know, am I going to have to deal with this every day or whatever? She's like, no, what happened? And I went into it, and I told her. And that was it. And then the next day I came in, and he was gone.

Q: When you mentioned that you called Donna, are you referring to Donna Corleone?

A: Yes.

Q: And she is or was the daytime supervisor at GEM, is that right?

A: For Client Services.

Q: So you would report to Donna?

A: Right.

Q: Did you call her as a friend, or did you call her as your supervisor, or both?

A: Both.

Q: Did what Mr. Price said to you really upset you?

A: It didn't upset me. I just thought it was strange.

Q: So you called Donna to just tell her that you thought it was kind of strange?

A: Yeah.

Q: And the next work day on May 15th you came into work at what time?

A: Six o'clock.

Q: And what did you find out?

A: Terri Saks called me into her office.

Q: And what happened?

A: She asked me what had happened, because Donna told her what happened. And she asked me what happened, and I told her. And she just told me that they let him go, because I was not the only one that complained. And that's it, I guess.

Q: Did you tell Ms. Saks the same thing that you're telling us today?

A: Yeah.

Q: Did Donna Corleone ever mention Mr. Price to you prior to your working here?

A: No.

Q: So you had no idea who this guy was before you started working at GEM?

A.   No.

Q: Did Donna actually help you get the job at GEM? Did she tell you there was an opening?

A: Right.

Q: Was Donna's position the equivalent of, say, Mr. Price's position at night?

A: Yes. She was a supervisor, he was a supervisor. One was day shift, one was night shift.

Q: So both of them would report to Ms. Saks?

A: Right.

Q: Were you upset by Mr. Price's conversation with you?

A: No, not at all.

Q: Why don't you describe the feeling when you got into your friend's car and picked up the cell phone to call Donna.

A: Like I said, I was new here, I didn't know anybody. I felt uncomfortable going into the lounge, you know. It was just a surprise for Frances. I felt uncomfortable because I was new. And then when he came off so powerful the way he did about religion and church, I thought it was strange, that's all.

Q: You had not spoken to Ms. Saks prior to her terminating Mr. Price, is that correct?

A: No.

Q: So you didn't file a report on the incident before they terminated him?

A: No.

Q: Was anything else said by Ms. Saks to you concerning the termination of Mr. Price?

A: I don't remember.

Q: Did you say anything to Ms. Saks?

A: Yes, I said that I wasn't trying to get Mr. Price in trouble by talking to Donna and felt bad that it got him fired.

Q: Did Ms. Saks respond to that?

A: Well, she seemed really irritated and said that Mr. Price had bothered other people too about religion. She said she wanted me to file a complaint.

Q: What did you say to that?

A: I said that I didn't want to do that and what difference did it make anyway since Mr. Price had already been fired.

Q: Did Ms. Saks respond?

A: No, but I could tell that she was very annoyed with me. She said just go back to work.

Q: Did Ms. Saks say anything else?

A: She said that this is confidential, you can't discuss this, it is between us.

Q: Okay. Why did you leave GEM?

A: Well, I guess I wasn't happy there.

Q: Why not?

A: Lot's of reasons, but mainly I didn't like the way Ms. Saks dealt with people.

Q: What do you mean?

A: She was hard on people, especially people she didn't like, and just not very nice.

Q: I have no further questions.

I affirm under penalty of perjury that my answers are full and complete.

                                    _____*Carol Connor*_____
                                          CAROL CONNOR

Deposition of Terri Saks

Date: 5/5/C.Y.-1

Q: Ms. Saks, how old are you?

A: I am 43 years old.

Q: Do you have any family?

A: Yes. I have a husband, George. We have been married for 18 years. We have two kids, a boy and a girl. Justin is 14 and Katie is 12.

Q: Do you and your family profess any religious faith?

A: No.

Q: Are you an atheist?

A: No. I would consider myself agnostic.

Q: Ms. Saks, what is your occupation?

A: I am the Vice President of Laboratory Operations at GEM Corporation.

Q: When did you first start working for GEM?

A: I was hired at GEM in C.Y.-9. I left for a time and I came back in C.Y.-3.

Q: What did you do before you worked at GEM?

A: I was the Director of Laboratory Operations for Harris Industries. I worked in that position for 4 years. Before that, I was a Lab Technician at Troush Laboratory for 3 years.

Q: Did you do anything before working at Troush?

A: Before that, I didn't work outside the home.

Q: What is the extent of your formal education?

A: I graduated from Golden State University with a B.S. in Natural Science.

Q: Do you have any specialized training beyond the baccalaureate level with respect to laboratory work, blood testing, serology, or anything of that nature?

A: I am a certified Medical Technologist.

Q: Ms. Saks, what exactly does GEM do?

A: We are a laboratory testing facility. We run tests on a lot of things, but mostly we do blood work. We do all of the blood work for Mercy General Hospital.

Q: What were your duties and responsibilities as the Vice President of Laboratory Operations at GEM?

A: I would oversee the day-to-day operations of the laboratory operations. Maintain the software and hardware departments, sign-off on purchasing agreements, troubleshoot for lab technicians, just basically maintain the overall operation of the lab.

Q: Did you have the responsibility of hiring and firing employees in the laboratory?

A: It was not solely my responsibility, but I did have final authority.

Q: Were you present the night when Mr. Price had a discussion with Carol Connor at the party in the laboratory?

A: No, I was not there.

Q: Didn't you terminate Mr. Price because he commented about Mr./Ms. Connor's crucifix?

A: No. I didn't terminate for that reason alone. Mr./Ms. Connor complained to his/her supervisor, Donna Corleone, that Mr. Price was bothering him/her about his/her religious practices and he/she was not going to work at a place where he/she was grilled about his/her religious beliefs.

Q: So did Mr./Ms. Connor threaten to resign from his/her position of employment?

A: That's what Donna told me. Donna was afraid that we were going to lose Carol as a result of the incident. She did not want to jeopardize losing a new employee.

Q: What did Ms. Corleone say to you about the incident?

A: She said that Carol was uncomfortable about the questions that Jim was asking him/her about whether he/she went to church and how often.

Q: When did you eventually talk to Carol about the incident?

A: May 15, C.Y.-2.

Q: Did anybody ever file a charge of religious discrimination with regard to Mr. Price's conduct at GEM Corp.?

A: Not to my knowledge.

Q: Did anybody ever file a charge of religious harassment with regard to Mr. Price's conduct at GEM Corp.?

A: Not to my knowledge.

Q: Do you know if Mr. Price had an employment contract with GEM Corp.?

A: No, he was an at-will employee.

Q: What was your first impression of Mr. Price when you worked with him?

A: I thought he was distracted at work. He was preoccupied with talking about personal matters.

Q: What do you mean when you say personal matters?

A: Religion. He always wanted to talk about religion.

Q: How did you respond to Mr. Price's insistence about talking about religion?

A: I told him that I did not want to talk about it. I told him that work was not the appropriate place to talk about religion. And I told him that he needed to concentrate on his duties and responsibilities.

Q: Why was Mr. Price ultimately terminated?

A: He was terminated for a cumulative number of reasons.

Q: Could you identify the reasons Mr. Price was terminated?

A: Well, he was harassing employees about their religious beliefs and sexual preferences. He was giving Bibles to people at work who did not want them. He was more focused on preaching his beliefs than he was on supervising the lab. He would leave his shift early and leave the lab unattended. He was involved in a nasty altercation with me on May 10, C.Y.-2, when he wanted to talk about his suspension. He just disrupted the evening shift.

Q: Did Jim Price ever give you a Bible?

A: Yes.

Q: Did you accept it?

A: No.

Q: How did you respond to Mr. Price's offering you a Bible?

A: I tried to give it back to him and he would not take it. He just left it on my desk.

Q: Were you offended?

A: I was offended that he kept trying to talk to me about religion at work.

Q: But were you offended that what he offered you was the Bible?

A: I don't have anything against the Bible, if that is what you are getting at. I already have a Bible. I may not read it, but that is my business, not his.

Q: Did you ever make anti-Semitic remarks to Mr. Price or anybody else at GEM?

A: No. Never.

Q: What did he say to you when you refused his offering?

A: He said that even if I didn't read it, the good Lord would be willing to hold the door for me.

Q: What do you think Mr. Price meant by that?

A: I don't know. That the Bible makes a good doorstop. Your guess is as good as mine.

Q: Was Jim aware that you were agnostic when he tried to give you a Bible?

A: I think he was.

Q: Do you think, in his mind, that he knew he was offending you by giving you a Bible?

A: I think he knew it made me uncomfortable. I always told him that I did not want to talk about religion with him.

Q: Can you give me an example of an incident where Jim offended a co-worker by discussing their sexual preference?

A: One example was with Rusty. She is a lesbian. Jim told her that God was going to send her to Hell if she did not change her ways. I counseled Jim about it.

Q: Why didn't you identify all of the reasons you just articulated to me in your written notice of termination for Jim Price?

A: I didn't think that I had to include every single incident into the termination notice. Many of the things I mentioned were already in his personnel file. The incident with Carol was just the last straw. It didn't seem necessary.

Q: During Mr. Price's employment with GEM and ultimate termination, did he violate any of GEM's Rules of Conduct?

A: Yes.

Q: Do you remember which Rules he violated?

A: He violated Rules 4 and 5.

Q: How so?

A: He refused to stop discussing religious matters with other GEM employees even after I warned him on several occasions. And his conduct altogether was viewed unfavorably by management.

Q: How did you first become aware of Mr. Price's behavior?

A: One of the daytime supervisors, Paula McDonald, informed me.

Q: What did Ms. McDonald tell you?

A: She told me that Jim had been lecturing a gay employee about living in sin and tried to give a Bible to a Muslim coworker. Apparently, Jim was insistent about converting Javed Quershi to Christianity.

Q: What do you mean when you say that Jim was lecturing a gay employee?

A: He would put his hands on her shoulders and tell her that she needed to give up her lifestyle or otherwise she would be going to Hell. He would always tell them that he could cure them of their disease. He told them that he would put them in his prayers so that they would be cured of their disease.

Q: Did you ever inform Human Resources about Mr. Price's actions at work?

A: Yes. I remember emailing Jonny Joyce regarding Mr. Price.

Q: Who is Jonny Joyce?

A: He/She was the head of GEM's Human Resources Department.

Q: I am showing you an email from you to Mr./Ms. Joyce dated March 20, C.Y.-2.
        Do you recognize it?

A: Yes.

Q: What did you say to Mr./Ms. Joyce in the e-mail?

A: There were some behavioral problems with Jim involving religion, and it was
        affecting some other employees at GEM. I informed Mr./Ms. Joyce of the
        situation and asked for some advice on the matter. I wanted to know what steps I
        should take to alleviate the problems we were having.

Q: Did you get a response back from Human Resources?

A: Yes.

Q: I am showing you an e-mail from Barbara Simmons, Mr./Ms. Joyce's assistant, to
        you dated March 21, C.Y.-2. Do you recognize it?

A: Yes.

Q: What did it say?

A: She told me that I should speak with Jim as soon as possible and inform him that
        this behavior cannot continue. They suggested that I document his behavior and
        write him up. She told me that we could get into trouble if we didn't stop his
        behavior.

Q: Do you know what was meant when Human Resources informed you that GEM
        could get into trouble for Mr. Price's behavior?

A: Yes. We could get into trouble for allowing harassment and discrimination in the
        workplace.

Q: Did you ever talk to Mr. Price about your e-mail correspondence with Human
        Resources?

A: Yes. Paula McDonald and I wrote Jim up and had a meeting with him.

Q: What happened at the meeting?

A: We showed Jim the write-up so that he could understand the seriousness of his actions. We showed him my e-mail to Human Resources and the e-mail response stating that they wanted us to take action. We told him that his antics had to stop.

Q: How did Mr. Price respond?

A: The meeting seemed like it took an eternity. Jim was not happy and he did not feel that he should have to stop talking to people about religion. He asked that if it offended someone for him to talk about baseball, should he then not talk about baseball.

Q: How did you respond to that?

A: I told him that if something offends somebody else, then he should not talk about it. Then he asked me if he could speak to people who wanted to talk about religion?

Q: What did you say to that?

A: I told him that it was best not to talk about religion in the workplace, but as long as nobody is offended by it, then it would be okay to discuss.

Q: How did the meeting end?

A: Towards the end of the meeting, things were getting out of control. Jim kept asking these ridiculous questions, and I kept telling him that he could not discuss religion with people at work who did not want to discuss it.

Q: Do you know if the write-up that you presented to Mr. Price ever made it into his personnel file?

A: I don't know, but I would assume so.

Q: Did you put a copy of it in his file?

A: I don't recall.

Q: Are you aware of whether Ms. McDonald put a copy of the write-up in the personnel file?

A: No.

Q: Did you hold any other meetings with Mr. Price regarding his actions at GEM?

A: There was one other meeting, but it didn't have anything to do with religion. Jim had previously been suspended for a day because of his insubordinate behavior towards me on May 10, C.Y.-2.

Q: How did that meeting go?

A: The meeting took place in my office and Paula McDonald was present. We tried to discuss the suspension Jim served for leaving the shift early. He said that it was unfair and it should not have happened.

Q: What did you say to Mr. Price?

A: I told him that because of his attitude, the meeting was over, and that I was not going to discuss it with him any further.

Q: How did Mr. Price react?

A: He was furious. He slammed his hand down on my desk. I stood up from my desk and told him the meeting was over and to get out of my office.

Q: What did Mr. Price do?

A: When I stood up, he stood from the other side of my desk and we were face to face. I told him to get out of my face. I tried to walk around my desk and leave my office, but Jim was between me and the door.

Q: What did you do?

A: I told him to get out of my face and get out of my office. Eventually he left.

Q: Was Paula present for the whole altercation?

A: Yes. And she seemed pretty frightened by it.

Q: Did either you or Ms. McDonald record what happened during the meeting?

A: Yes. I asked Paula to document what she witnessed that day. Paula wrote up an informal report about the incident and gave it to me. Then I used her notes to write up the formal action report.

Q: What did you do with the formal report?

A: I informed Human Resources about the incident and placed the report in Jim's personnel folder.

Q: Did you place Ms. McDonald's report into Mr. Price's personnel file?

A: No. I didn't.

Q: Why not?

A: Her statement was written long hand. It was hard to read. Having both statements in Jim's personnel file would have been confusing.

Q: Did you impose another suspension on Mr. Price?

A: I didn't get a chance. I wrote up the formal warning from Paula's notes, but before I could present it to Jim another incident occurred which led to his termination.

Q: What incident was that?

A: That was the incident with Carol Connor.

Q: Tell me what happened that led to Mr. Price's termination.

A: The Lab was having a party for the receptionist that was leaving. During the party, Jim made some comments to Carol Connor, who was the new receptionist. Carol felt uncomfortable about the comments. On his/her way home from the party, Carol called his/her supervisor, told her about the incident, and asked if he/she could expect these occurrences to happen again. This incident was just a couple of days after the last incident in my office. We had warned Jim about his behavior twice in the past. Now he was already offending the new guy/girl. There was nothing we could do to change his behavior. We had to let him go.

Q: Who told you about the conversation between Mr. Price and Mr./Ms. Connor?

A: Donna Corleone. She is Carol's friend and a supervisor on the day shift.

Q: Did you issue a notice of termination to Mr. Price?

A: Yes.

Q: Why are there no performance-related problems recorded in Mr. Price's notice of termination?

A: We had been over his actions so many times before. His behavior was not going to stop. He refused to correct it. I didn't think that I had to list every single thing present in his personnel folder. It was already there. I just thought we were issuing the last straw type of thing.

Q: Did you fire Mr. Price for his conversation with Carol Connor?

A: No. I did not. It was his overall misconduct and insubordination. His behavior was affecting my work. It was disturbing other staff members. No matter what I did or said to Jim, he was unwilling to correct his behavior.

Q: Have you ever denied an employee's request for leave?

A: I have in the past on a couple of occasions.

Q: What would be the basis of denying an employee's request for leave?

A: Any number of reasons. If we are understaffed or if we have too much work to do. Our business is very unpredictable and sometimes you can't just slip away.

Q: Have you ever denied a request for leave from Mr. Price?

A: I believe so.

Q: Do you remember when that may have been?

A: I don't remember exactly when, but I do remember that once he wanted to take off for almost two weeks. I couldn't have him out of the lab for that long of a period so I had to deny his request.

Q: Did anybody ever come to GEM's management and indicate that they wanted to file a formal charge against Mr. Price because he was harassing them at work?

A: No.

Q: Why didn't anybody come forward?

A: The employees that I spoke to said that they did not come forward for fear of retaliation. For many of them, Jim was their immediate supervisor.

Q: To whom exactly did you speak?

A: Javed and Rusty.

I affirm under penalty of perjury that my answers are full and complete.

_____   *Terri Saks*
                              TERRI SAKS

Deposition of Jonny Joyce

Date: 5/25/C.Y.-1

Q: Mr./Ms. Joyce, who is your employer?

A: I'm not employed, currently.

Q: And did you at any point work for GEM Corporation?

A: Yes.

Q: And when did you work for GEM?

A: C.Y.-12, I believe, I'm not positive on that, until November C.Y.-2.

Q: What was your title when you worked at GEM?

A: I was the Director of Human Resources.

Q: Were you the Director of Human Resources at the time Mr. Price was terminated?

A: Yes.

Q: I'm showing you the GEM Corporation Employee Handbook. Recognize it?

A: Yes.

Q: And is that employee handbook dated August 1, C.Y.-7?

A: Yes.

Q: If you would, look in that handbook, Mr./Ms. Joyce, and flip the page to the "Equal Employment Opportunity" section.

A: Okay.

Q: Can you tell us why this section was put in the handbook and what it deals with?

A: It was put in here in order to cover GEM Corporation with regards to our emphasis on a lack of harassment of employees.

Q: Is it fair to say, Mr./Ms. Joyce, that's GEM's harassment policy?

A: Well, that section and the section entitled "Unlawful Harassment Policy."

Q: And that section deals not only with sexual harassment but all other types of harassment that are prohibited under federal and state law, right?

A: That's correct.

Q: Is there a section that deals with GEM maintaining a harassment free workplace?

A: Yes, both from supervisory people as well as employees.

Q: Is there a section in the handbook that addresses rules of conduct?

A: The rules of conduct are addressed throughout the employee handbook, but I don't think there is a specific section entitled "Rules of Conduct." The closest would be the section entitled "Unacceptable Job Performance/Disciplinary Action."

Q: Could you tell us what the purpose is of having rules of conduct in the employee handbook?

A: It's basically to spell out what rules of conduct were expected of employees and supervisory personnel.

Q: What happened or what could happen if there was a violation of one of those rules of conduct?

A: Employees could be terminated or they could be written up.

Q: Is there a rule that says that employees may not neglect the employee's duty or leave work without prior express permission?

A: Yes.

Q: And is it fair to say that, if there's a violation of one of those rules, that GEM's policy could be discipline up to and including termination?

A: That's correct.

Q: Mr./Ms. Joyce, was it GEM's procedure when employees received their handbooks to sign something called an acknowledgement and receipt of the handbook?

A: Yes.

Q: So if Mr. Price had signed something like this, that would be the normal procedure?

A: Yes.

Q: Okay. Now, prior to March, C.Y.-3, did you have any personal knowledge about Mr. Price's performance problems at the laboratory?

A: No.

Q: How was the lab managed during your tenure in terms of who had control over what decisions were made at the lab and where those decisions were made?

A: They were made with the executives at the lab.

Q: From C.Y.-3, up through June C.Y.-2, who was the Vice-President of Laboratory Operations in the GEM Laboratory?

A: Terri Saks.

Q: What was your function as Human Resources Director during that time?

A: Basically support and benefits.

Q: And when you say "support," what does that mean?

A: The lab was a separate entity. Even though it was a part of GEM Corporation, it was a separate entity, and they were responsible for their own hiring, firing, that kind of thing. What we did in Human Resources was basically payroll kinds of information, benefits kind of information back and forth, and then if there was a problem and – disciplinary problem as far as work performance was concerned, someone in our office might get involved.

Q: Did you have any knowledge or were you involved in the decision to promote Mr. Price from medical technologist to night shift supervisor?

A: No.

Q: Mr./Ms. Joyce, do you recognize this March C.Y.-2 e-mail from Ms. Saks?

A: Yes.

Q: Did you receive that on or about March 20, C.Y.-2?

A: Yes.

Q: What was it about?

A: Basically, an employee was talking with other employees about religion and their religious beliefs, about gay people or gay employees, telling them that he could cure them, and about conversion, basically. The overall tone of it is harassing other employees by another employee who was a supervisor.

Q: Did you respond?

A: Yes, what I said was that we had strict policies regarding harassment of employees and that the supervisor at the lab needed to document all of these behaviors and basically stick to the harassment issue as far as we would not tolerate that.

Q: Did you have an occasion to talk to Saks about issues relating to Price?

A: I believe that we spoke. In each telephone conversation I geared myself toward the harassment issue, documenting the harassment issue, and his work performance issue.

Q: Do you recall an incident on May 10, C.Y.-2, regarding a workplace violence issue with Mr. Price?

A: I remember receiving a phone call from Terri Saks that she felt that she had been threatened by Mr. Price on or about that date.

Q: What advice did you give Ms. Saks?

A: Basically, that it was a harassment issue, it was a misconduct issue, it was an insubordination issue. She needed to document that and terminate him.

Q: Mr./Ms. Joyce, did you have any knowledge about Mr. Price being written up for leaving a shift early in May of C.Y.-2?

A: No.

Q: Mr./Ms. Joyce, did you have an occasion to review the written notice of termination in this case back in May of C.Y.-2?

A: No, I don't think that I had an opportunity to review that.

Q: Did Mr. Price ever complain to you about alleged anti-Semitic remarks made by Ms. Saks in the workplace?

A: No.

Q: During Mr. Price's employment with the company, on how many occasions did you have a chance to speak to him?

A: I'm not sure that I ever did.

Q: Did you tell Terri Saks to terminate Mr. Price's employment?

A: At one point I did say, "Yes, you need to get rid of this guy if he's violent."

Q: Not because of his religious beliefs?

A: Not because of his religious beliefs.

Q: Did you review and approve his termination letter?

A: No.

Q: Is it fair to say, when you were notified on March 20, C.Y.-2, by Ms. Saks via e-mail, that she was notifying you of a harassment problem and not an expression of religious belief?

A: Yes.

Q: Is there a difference?

A: Yes.

Q: Tell us what the difference is between an expression of religious belief and religious harassment, if you know.

A: Well, in my opinion, harassment is when someone else comes and says to you that they are – they feel uncomfortable or intimidated because of the discussion being aimed pointedly at them.

Q: So if Mr. Price was discussing his religious beliefs with another employee who also welcomed that discussion, would that be okay?

A: So long as it didn't interfere with the work product.

Q: So if Mr. Price was on a lunch break and he decided that he would discuss religion with another employee who welcomed that, was that okay?

A: Yes.

Q: So as long as the employee that he was talking with did not feel uncomfortable or intimidated by it, GEM did not say do not discuss religion in the workplace?

A: That's correct.

Q: Did you have a chance to discuss with Carol Connor his/her comments to Donna Corleone?

A: No.

Q: Why not?

A: Terri Saks was the one in charge of the lab at that time.

Q: Did you have a chance to investigate the claim?

A: I wouldn't investigate the claim. I didn't know about it until after the fact.

I affirm under penalty of perjury that my answers are full and complete.

Jonny Joyce
_____
JONNY JOYCE

EXHIBIT #1

GEM Corporation

A Leader in Medical Equipment & Training

Employee Handbook

1. Notice Concerning Personnel Policies and Procedures

All employees of the Company are "employed at-will" which means that when a term of employment is for an indefinite period of time, either party may terminate the employment at any time, for any reason or no reason at all. The employee has the right to quit his/her job and the Company has the right to terminate the employment of the employee for whatever reason. Should there ever be a contract of employment between GEM and its employees, that contract must be in writing and signed by the employee and the President or CEO to be valid.

1.1 Acknowledgment and Receipt

Your signature on the Acknowledgment and Receipt Form on **Appendix H** indicated that you have carefully read this notice in its entirety, that you fully understand all its provisions, and you have had an opportunity to ask any questions that you may have.

. . .

5. Equal Employment Opportunity

GEM maintains a strong policy of equal employment opportunity for all employees and applicants for employment. We hire, train, promote, and compensate employees on the basis of personal competence and potential for advancement without regard for race, color, religion, sex, national origin, age, marital status, or disability, as well as other classifications protected by applicable state or local laws. Our equal employment opportunity philosophy applies to the terms and conditions of employment of GEM's employees.

6. Unlawful Harassment Policy   *Nothing Mr. Price did amounts to unlawful harassment*

GEM is committed to providing a work environment that is free of discrimination and unlawful harassment. Actions, works, jokes, or comments based upon an individual's sex, race, color, national origin, age, religion, disability, marital status or any other legally protected characteristic will not be tolerated. This policy is necessary to stress GEM's strong opposition to all forms of unlawful harassment, and in particular, sexual harassment, and to identify the complaint procedures available to victims and the applicable disciplinary penalties for violations of this policy.   *— No complaint filed by "victims"*

GEM condemns unlawful harassment in any form in the workplace, and we recognize our duty to provide you with an environment free from such conduct. GEM is committed to preventing and promptly correcting any unlawful behavior. All management personnel have been directed to take immediate action to ensure that their subordinate employees, visitors, customers, vendors or clients are not subjected to any form of unlawful harassment or intimidation.

GEM will give complaints of unlawful harassment swift and serious attention and take appropriate action in response to each complaint. Each complaint shall be investigated thoroughly and rapidly, and appropriate discipline up to, and including discharge, shall be imposed upon those found to have violated this policy. All personnel are subject to this policy. There will be no reprisals or retaliation taken against any employee for making allegations or inquiries concerning unlawful harassment.

COMPLAINT PROCEDURE – Any employee who believes that he or she has been subjected to unlawful harassment should report such behavior immediately. Allegations of unlawful harassment should be brought to the attention of your direct supervisor. However, if for some reason you do not wish to bring a complaint to the attention of your direct supervisor, you may bring it to the attention of the CEO, President, Human Resources Manager or any member of the management team. Once a complaint is made or if GEM obtains knowledge of inappropriate behavior in violation of this policy, appropriate members of the management team will investigate this matter promptly and thoroughly by taking statements and interviewing witnesses where appropriate.

Please sign the form attached hereto as Appendix A to acknowledge that you understand this policy. This policy supercedes and replaces any other unlawful harassment or sexual harassment policies at GEM. If you have any questions regarding JAMES's unlawful harassment policy, complaint procedure or investigation procedure, please contact the CEO, President, Human Resource Manager or any member of the management team.

. . . .

7.2 Unacceptable Job Performance/Disciplinary Action

GEM expects the highest standards of behavior from its employees. Employees must comply with all work rules at all times. Failure to comply with any of the following rules may subject the employee to disciplinary action, up to and including termination. These rules ARE NOT INTENDED TO COVER ALL conduct or work performance situations. GEM reserves the right to determine the type of employee conduct that may be grounds for disciplinary action or immediate dismissal. Additionally, the following rules are NOT INTENDED TO CREATE AND SHOULD NOT BE RELIED UPON AS A BASIS FOR ASSUMING a "for cause" requirement for termination or as otherwise altering the express policy of GEM that the employment relationship be EMPLOYMENT AT-WILL.

Accordingly, occurrences of any of the following violations, because of their seriousness, may result in immediate dismissal without prior notice or warning:

1. Willful violation of any Company rule; any deliberate action that is detrimental to GEM's efforts to operate profitably.

2. Engaging in criminal conduct or acts of violence, or making threats of violence toward anyone on Company premises or when representing GEM; fighting, or horseplay or provoking a fight on Company property, or negligent damage of property.

3. Insubordination or refusing to obey instructions properly issued by your manager pertaining to your work; refusal to help out on a special assignment.

4. Engaging in any type of conduct which is insubordinate to GEM executives or supervisors.

5. Threatening, intimidating, or coercing fellow employees on or off the premises at any time, for any purpose.

6. Any act of unlawful harassment, or any other type of harassment against a GEM employee, visitor, customer, vendor, or guest.

7. Leaving work before the end of a workday or not being ready to work at the start of a workday without approval of your manager; stopping work before time specified for such purposes.

8. Leaving your work station during your work hours without the permission of your manager, except to use the restroom.

This list is not all-inclusive. Notwithstanding this list, all employees remain employed at-will.

Progressive Discipline Policy: All unacceptable behavior, as determined solely by GEM, may lead to immediate dismissal from employment. GEM is not required to provide any warnings before terminating your employment. However, to the extent possible and subject to GEM's sole discretion, unacceptable behavior which does not lead to immediate dismissal may be dealt with in the following manner:

- Verbal Warning
- First Written Warning
- Suspension
- Dismissal

Written warnings may include the reasons for the manager's dissatisfaction and any supporting evidence. You will have an opportunity to defend your actions and rebut the opinion of your manager at the time the warning is issued. Disciplinary actions may also include suspensions or other measures deemed appropriate to the circumstances. GEM is not required to provide any employee with a warning or suspension prior to dismissal. Many situations require immediate termination of employment, and it is within GEM's sole discretion to determine when termination is warranted.

All pertinent facts will be carefully reviewed, and, if appropriate, the employee will be given a full opportunity to explain his or her conduct before any decision is reached.

7.3 Termination

We hope to retain good employees. However, employment at GEM is for no specified time, regardless of length of service. Just as you are free to leave for any reason, we reserve the same right to end our relationship with you at any time, with or without notice, for any reason not prohibited by law.

. . . .

11.1 Vacations

GEM encourages employees to take their earned vacation. It is felt that vacation time is important to family considerations and the overall vitality and enthusiasm of the employee.

All full-time employees are eligible for vacation. All full-time employees will accrue vacation beginning on their start date or anniversary date with GEM. Depending upon your length of service, you can earn a minimum of one (1) week per year and a maximum of four (4) weeks per year.

The number of vacation hours an employee can earn is determined by length of service:

Years of Employment	Weeks of Vacation Accrued Annually
After one (1) year	1
After two (2) to five (5) years	2
After five (5), but less than ten (10) years	3
After ten (10) years	4

Every effort will be made to grant your vacation at the time your desire, however, vacations must not interfere with your department's operation and therefore must be approved by your manager at least one (1) month in advance. If any conflicts arise in requests for vacation time, preference will be given to the employee with the most seniority.

EXHIBIT #1

APPENDIX H

Acknowledgment and Receipt of GEM's Employee Handbook

This will acknowledge my receipt of the Company's Employee Handbook. This will also acknowledge that I have read, or will read, the Handbook in its entirety. I also acknowledge that I have been given the opportunity to ask any questions I may have about anything in the Handbook.

I understand that this Handbook does not create any type of employment contract between me and the Company, and that my employment is at-will and not for any definite period of time. I further understand that the policies, procedures, and benefits set forth in this Handbook may be unilaterally amended, modified, or deleted by the Company, at any time, with or without prior notice.

My signature below indicates that I have carefully read this notice in its entirety, that I fully understand all its provisions, and I have had an opportunity to ask any questions that I have.

_5/17/C.Y.-4_   _Jim Price_____
Date   Employee Signature

_5/17/C.Y.-4_   _Max Wilkinson_____
Date   Supervisor

EXHIBIT #2

From: Terri Saks [tsaks@gemcorp.com]
Sent: Monday, March 20, C.Y.-2 3:46 PM
To: Jonny Joyce [jjoyce@gemcorp.com]
Subject: INAPPROPRIATE SUPERVISORY BEHAVIOR?

I need your advice about what to do with my evening supervisor. He
is driving my staff AND me crazy with his religious fervor! At one
point last week I actually told him his comments to ME were
inappropriate, insulting and requested that he STOP! Now I find
out he is approaching other staff. I feel this is a definite
problem overall for a supervisor to talk to staff about their
religious beliefs, however he has gone way past just annoying to
possible harassment. He has told two gay employees he can CURE
them. He is continuously trying to CONVERT a Muslim employee to
whatever religion he belongs to. No employee has come to me to
actually express a grievance BUT I would like to be prepared or do
what I can to stop this if there is an option for me BEFORE I have
a problem!! HELP!!

End of Message

EXHIBIT #3

From: Barbara Haines [bhaines@gemcorp.com]
Sent: Tuesday, March 21, C.Y.-2 11:22 AM
To: Terri Saks [tsaks@gemcorp.com]
Cc: Jonny Joyce [jjoyce@gemcorp.com]
Subject: Re: INAPPROPROATE SUPERVISORY BEHAVIOR?

TERRI: THIS REPLY IS FROM BARBARA AS JOYCE IS OUT OF TOWN AND WILL
HAVE TO RESPOND ON HER RETURN.

GEM CORPORATION HAS STRICT POLICIES REGARDING HARASSMENT OF
EMPLOYEES. I WOULD SUGGEST THAT YOU DOCUMENT THIS SUPERVISOR'S
BEHAVIOR AND WRITE HIM UP. HE HAS TO UNDERSTAND THAT HE CANNOT DO
THIS ON COMPANY TIME BECAUSE OBVIOUSLY HE IS NOT DOING HIS WORK IF
HE IS TRYING TO CONVERT EVERYONE.

STICK TO THE HARASSMENT OF EMPLOYEES AND SPEAK TO HIM IMMEDIATELY
OR WE CAN GET IN TROUBLE FOR NOT STOPPING IT RIGHT AWAY.

End of Message

--- Terri Saks <tsaks@gemcorp.com> wrote:

> I need your advice about what to do with my evening supervisor.
He
> is driving my staff AND me crazy with his religious fervor! At
one
> point last week I actually told him his comments to ME were
> inappropriate, insulting and requested that he STOP! Now I find
out > he is approaching other staff.
> I feel this is a definite problem overall for a supervisor to
talk to > staff about their religious beliefs, however he has gone
way past
> just annoying to possible harassment. He has told two gay
employees > he can CURE them. He is continuously trying to CONVERT
a Muslim
> employee to whatever religion he belongs to. No employee has
come to > me to actually express a grievance BUT I would like to be
prepared or > do what I can to stop this if there is an option for
me BEFORE I have > a problem!! HELP!!
>
>
>
> **End of Message**
>
>

EXHIBIT #4

WRITTEN WARNING: WITH CORRECTIVE ACTION

NAME: James Price   **DATE OF OCCURENCE:** 5/05/C.Y.-2

Supervisor Presenting Warning: Terri Saks

1) Behavior resulting in warning: On May 5, C.Y.-2, Mr. Price left his shift before testing was complete.

2) Desired behavior and steps to achieve: Do not leave shift before testing is complete.

3) Time frame to resolve: Immediately

4) Action taken: One (1) day suspension without pay.

5) Benefit for change: More efficient work flow; improved safety and confidence of night shift.

6) Result on no change: LOSS OF SUPERVISORY POSITION OR TERMINATION

SIGNATURE OF PRESENTER____*Terri Saks*____ DATE _*May 8, C.Y.-2*_

EMPLOYEE SIGNATURE_____*Jim Price*_____DATE ___*May 8, C.Y.-2*_

**NOTE: EMPLOYEE SIGNATURE ONLY DENOTES
ACKNOWLEDGEMENT OF REPORT, NOT AGREEMENT**

EXHIBIT #5

WRITTEN WARNING: WITH CORRECTIVE ACTION

NAME: *James Price*   **DATE OF OCCURENCE:** *5/10/C.Y.-2*

Supervisor Presenting Warning: *Paula McDonald*

1) Behavior resulting in warning: *Jim got into a loud argument with Terri in our office today. He yelled at her and slammed his fist on the table. She stood up from the table and told Jim to leave. Jim stood up and got in her face. He was blocking her exit from the room. Terri pushed Jim's face out of her way and told him to get out of her way or she would fire him. He finally walked out of the office.*

2) Desired behavior and steps to achieve:

3) Time frame to resolve:

4) Action taken:

5) Benefit for change:

6) Result on no change:

SIGNATURE OF PRESENTER_____ DATE_____

EMPLOYEE SIGNATURE_____ DATE_____

NOTE: EMPLOYEE SIGNATURE ONLY DENOTES
ACKNOWLEDGEMENT OF REPORT, NOT AGREEMENT

EXHIBIT #6

WRITTEN WARNING: WITH CORRECTIVE ACTION

NAME: James Price   **DATE OF OCCURENCE:** 5/10/C.Y.-2

Supervisor Presenting Warning: Terri Saks

1) Behavior resulting in warning: While trying to discuss technical staffing, Jim insisted that we discuss his suspension. I told him that we would not discuss it. He slammed his fist on the desk where I was sitting. I stood up and instructed him NOT to speak to me in that manner. He stood up from his chair got in my face, blocking my exit from the office. I demanded that he leave my office several times before he left.

2) Desired behavior and steps to achieve: Jim needs to get control of his temper and fits of anger. He should never express such anger toward another employee or insubordination to his immediate supervisor.

3) Time frame to resolve: IMMEDIATELY

4) Action taken: Indefinite suspension without pay.

5) Benefit for change: Better employee relationships and supervisor communication.

Did not present this corrective action as Jim was terminated for another reason.
- T. Saks

6) Result on no change: TERMINATION

SIGNATURE OF PRESENTER ___*Terri Saks*___ DATE ___*May 11, C.Y.-2*___

EMPLOYEE SIGNATURE_____ DATE_____

**NOTE: EMPLOYEE SIGNATURE ONLY DENOTES
ACKNOWLEDGEMENT OF REPORT, NOT AGREEMENT**

Never filed

EXHIBIT #7

WRITTEN WARNING: WITH CORRECTIVE ACTION

NAME: James Price   **DATE OF OCCURENCE:** 5/15/C.Y.-2

Supervisor Presenting Warning: Terri Saks

1) Behavior resulting in warning: Despite at least 2 separate warnings, Jim continues to discuss RELIGION with GEM employees. Carol Connor discussed his/her discomfort with his/her immediate supervisor, Donna Corleone, regarding Jim Price discussing what church he/she attended. When Mr./Ms. Connor told Jim NONE, he lectured him/her.

2) Action taken: TERMINATION

SIGNATURE OF PRESENTER___*Terri Saks*_____ DATE _*May 15, C.Y.-2*___

EMPLOYEE SIGNATURE_____*Jim Price*_____DATE___*May 15, C.Y.-2*___

**NOTE: EMPLOYEE SIGNATURE ONLY DENOTES
ACKNOWLEDGEMENT OF REPORT, NOT AGREEMENT**

EXHIBIT #8

SUBMIT TO PERSONNEL

REQUEST FOR LEAVE

NAME: Jim Price

TYPE OF LEAVE REQUESTED: Vacation

REASON FOR LEAVE: Spiritual Retreat

AMOUNT OF LEAVE: 2 Days

BEGINNING: 9/15/C.Y.-3

ENDING: 9/16/C.Y.-3

Signed: *Jim Price*

Approved /   By: *Terri Saks*

Confirmed:

EXHIBIT #9

SUBMIT TO PERSONNEL

REQUEST FOR LEAVE

NAME: Jim Price

TYPE OF LEAVE REQUESTED: Vacation

REASON FOR LEAVE: Trip to Holy Land, Israel

AMOUNT OF LEAVE: 6 Days

BEGINNING: 12/21/C.Y.-3

ENDING: 12/28/C.Y.-3

Signed: *Jim Price*

Approved / By: *Terri Saks*

Confirmed: ______

Jury Instructions

Members of the jury, you have now heard all the evidence and the closing argument of the attorneys. It is my duty to instruct you on the law that applies to this case. You will have a copy of my instructions with you when you go to the jury room to deliberate.

I will now tell you the law that you must follow to reach your verdict. You must follow that law exactly as I give it to you, even if you disagree with it. If the attorneys have said anything different about what the law means, you must follow what I say. In reaching your verdict, you must not speculate about what I think your verdict should be from something I may have said or done.

Pay careful attention to all the instructions that I give you. All the instructions are important because together they state the law that you will use in this case. You must consider all of the instructions together. You must decide this case based only on the law and the evidence.

A witness is a person who has knowledge related to this case. You will have to decide whether you believe each witness and how important each witness's testimony is to the case. You may believe all, part, or none of a witness's testimony. In deciding whether to believe a witness's testimony, you may consider, among other factors, the following:

1.   How well did the witness see, hear, or otherwise sense what he or she described in court?

2.   How well did the witness remember and describe what happened?

3.   How did the witness look, act, and speak while testifying?

4.   Did the witness have any reason to say something that was not true? Did the witness show any bias or prejudice? Did the witness have a personal

relationship with any of the parties involved in the case? Does the witness have a personal stake in how this case is decided?

5.   What was the witness's attitude toward this case or about giving testimony?

Sometimes a witness may say something that is not consistent with something else he or she said. Sometimes different witnesses will give different versions of what happened. People often forget things or make mistakes in what they remember. Also, two people may see the same event, but remember it differently. You may consider these differences, but do not decide that testimony is untrue just because it differs from other testimony.

However, if you decide that a witness has deliberately testified untruthfully about something important, you may choose not to believe anything that witness said. On the other hand, if you think the witness testified untruthfully about some things but told the truth about others, you may accept the part you think is true and ignore the rest.

You must not be biased in favor of or against any witness because of his or her race, sex, religion, occupation, sexual orientation or national origin.

Plaintiff has the burden in this case to prove each element of his claim by a preponderance of the evidence. The term "preponderance of the evidence" means the greater weight and degree of credible evidence admitted in this case. Simply put, Plaintiff must prove it is more likely than not that each element of his claim is true.

The issue for your determination in this case is the intent with which GEM acted in terminating Mr. Price's employment. Mr. Price claims that he was discharged from employment by GEM because of his religion. GEM denies that

Mr. Price was discriminated against in any way and asserts that GEM reasonably

and in good faith believed that Mr. Price was harassing other employees by

engaging in unwelcome religious discussions and that Mr. Price was insubordinate

to his supervisor.

You should be mindful that the law applicable to this case requires only that

GEM not discriminate against Mr. Price because of his religion. So far as you are

concerned in this case, GEM may discharge Mr. Price for any other reason, good or

bad, fair or unfair, and you must not second guess that decision or permit any

sympathy for Mr. Price to lead you to substitute your own judgment for that of

GEM even though you personally may not favor the action taken and would have

acted differently under the circumstances. GEM was under no obligation to provide

Mr. Price with each and every reason for his termination in the final notice of

termination. Neither does the law require GEM to extend any special or favorable

treatment to Mr. Price because of his religion.

On the other hand, it is not necessary for Mr. Price to prove that his religion

was the sole or exclusive reason for GEM's decision to terminate his employment.

It is sufficient if Mr. Price proves that his religion was a motivating factor that made

a difference in GEM's decision to terminate his employment.

To prove his religious discrimination claim under Title VII of the Civil

Rights Act of 1964, Mr. Price must prove the following four elements by a

preponderance of the evidence:

1.   That he was a member of and/or practices a particular religion; and

2.   That he was qualified for and satisfactorily performed the job at
       issue; and

3.   That he suffered from some adverse employment action; and

4. That someone outside the protected class of which he is a member

was treated differently.

The parties agree, and I instruct you, that Mr. Price was permitted to

practice his religion in the workplace by engaging in consensual religious

discussions to the extent that he did not harass other employees. The parties further

agree, and I instruct you, that GEM could lawfully discharge Mr. Price if it

reasonably and in good faith believed that he was harassing other employees by

engaging in unwelcome religious discussions, and/or that he was insubordinate to

his supervisor.

It will be up to you, the members of the jury, to determine whether, as Mr.

Price claims, his termination was unlawful, that is, motivated by GEM's unlawful

religious discrimination, or whether, as GEM claims, Mr. Price's termination was

lawful, that is, due to GEM's reasonable and good faith belief that Mr. Price was

harassing other employees by engaging in unwelcome religious discussions and Mr.

Price was insubordinate to his supervisor.

The parties have stipulated that Mr. Price was an at-will employee of GEM

at the time that he was discharged. In an employment at-will situation, both the

employee and the employer have the right to terminate the employment relationship

at any time and for any reason or no reason, so long as it is not for an illegal or

unlawful reason. Because Mr. Price was an at-will employee, GEM had the legal

right to terminate his employment unless the decision to discharge him was based

upon his religion as to constitute illegal discrimination under Title VII.

Your foreperson shall preside over your deliberations. All jurors should

participate in all deliberations and vote on each issue. The votes of ten or more

[Handwritten marginal notes:]
Neither McDonnell, Burdine, suggest this. Title VII protects individuals, not groups & not individuals compared to groups.
- Should be that religion was a motivating factor in adverse employment
- LittleJohn v. NY (2d cir 795 f3d 297 2015)
- Proven by preponderance of evidence that Δ would have discharged π regardless of religion
- Model instructions 8th cir.
- McDonnell douglass is for summary J, not jury instructions, strict adherence not necessary, all that is necessary is proof of discriminatory intent direct or circumstantial, Costa v. Desert Palace 299 f3d 838 (9th 202)
- Instruct "Because of prohibited reason"

jurors are required to reach a verdict. The verdict must be in writing and the verdict

form has been prepared for you. It is as follows:

[READ VERDICT FORM]

In just a few moments, you will be taken to the jury room by the bailiff.

The first thing you should do is elect a foreperson who will preside over your

deliberations like the chairperson of a meeting. It is the foreperson's job to sign and

date the verdict form when all of you have agreed on a verdict in this case and to

bring the verdict back to the courtroom when you return.

In closing, let me remind you that it is important that you follow the law

spelled out in these instructions in deciding your verdicts. There are no other laws

that apply to this case.

UNITED STATES DISTRICT COURT

CENTRAL DISTRICT OF THE STATE OF GOLDEN

JAMES PRICE,	)	
Plaintiff,	)	
	)	CASE NO: 17-cv-4923
v.	)	
	)	
GEM CORPORATION,	)	
Defendant.	)	
	)	

We, the Jury, answer the question submitted to us as follows:

By a preponderance of the evidence, do you find that Plaintiff's termination was unlawful in that it was motivated by religious discrimination?

ANSWER: Yes _____   No _____

_____   _____
Date   Foreperson

Rusty Maxell

v.

Terry Chester

(breach of contract)

**IN THE CIRCUIT COURT OF THE
THIRTEENTH JUDICIAL CIRCUIT
IN AND FOR LEAD COUNTY, STATE OF GOLDEN
CIVIL DIVISION**

RUSTY MAXELL d/b/a   )
MAXELL CONSTRUCTION   )
COMPANY   )   CASE NO: CV 52-845
Plaintiff   )
)
)
v.   )
)
TERRY CHESTER   )
Defendant   )
)

**IN THE CIRCUIT COURT OF THE
THIRTEENTH JUDICIAL CIRCUIT
IN AND FOR LEAD COUNTY, STATE OF GOLDEN
CIVIL DIVISION**

RUSTY MAXELL d/b/a	)	
MAXELL CONSTRUCTION	)	
COMPANY	)	CASE NO: CV 52-845
Plaintiff	)	
	)	COMPLAINT FOR BREACH OF
	)	CONTRACT
v.	)	
	)	Jury Trial Demanded
TERRY CHESTER	)	
Defendant	)	

COMPLAINT

Plaintiff, Rusty Maxell, sues Defendant, Terry Chester, and alleges as follows:

1.   Plaintiff and Defendant are residents of Lead County, therefore, jurisdiction is proper in this court.

2.   On November 17, C.Y.-3, Terry Chester entered into a Contract (attached hereto as Exhibit 1) with Maxell Construction Company (hereinafter referred to as "Maxell") in which Chester agreed to pay Maxell $800,000 dollars to build a custom home on a lot located at 2479 Longmire Road in Silverado.

3.   The Contract specified that Defendant make payments in four installments upon completion by Maxell of certain, designated stages of construction with a final payment of 25% of the contract price due within thirty days after completion by Maxell and occupancy by Defendant.

4.   Construction of the home was completed on March 11, C.Y.-2 and owner occupied house on April 15, C.Y.-2.

5.   Defendant failed to render the final payment within the thirty day period prescribed by the Contract and has disregarded further attempts by Maxell to collect the amount due under the Contract.

6.   Construction of the home was done in a workmanlike manner and perfectly conformed to the Contract excepting that non-specified drywall was installed.

7.   Maxell has performed all other conditions, covenants, and promises required by it on its part to be performed in accordance with the terms and conditions of the Contract.

PRAYER FOR RELIEF

WHEREFORE, Rusty Maxell prays for judgment against Defendant as follows.

1.   Judgment in the amount of $180,000.00 dollars plus prejudgment interest derived from the $200,000 dollars still owed under the Contract minus a $20,000 allowance for use of non-specified drywall;

2.   Reasonable attorney's fees;

3.   Cost of suit; and

4.   For such other and further relief as the Court deems just and proper.

DATED: October 25, C.Y.-2   Respectfully submitted,

                                              Jessica Fielding
                                              Jessica Fielding
                                              Attorney for Plaintiff

Exhibit 1

Maxell Construction Company
879 San Angelo St. • Silverado, GO 76891

(909) 555-2276

For valuable consideration, the receipt and sufficiency of which is hereby acknowledged, the undersigned parties agree as follows:

1. General Description of the Work. The Contractor shall perform all the Work required by the Contract Documents for:

The construction of a custom home at 2479 Longmire road in accordance with the "Royal Chateau" blueprints supplied by Owner.

2. Time of Commencement and Completion. The Work under this Agreement shall commence on 12/1/C.Y.-3 and be completed not later than 4/2/C.Y.-2. *TIME IS OF THE ESSENCE.*

3. Payment. The Owner shall pay the Contractor for the performance of the Work: $800,000.00

4. Fee Schedule. The Contractor shall be paid a fee as set forth below in Article 5 of the General Conditions:

5. Miscellaneous Items. The Contracting parties further agree as follows:

Window-Wrap molding on all windows, install Weathergard extra thick insulation, Granite countertops in kitchen, use Builtrite Mold-No-More drywall, Tuocci decorative tiles in entry-way.

General Terms and Conditions

1. Contractor Responsibilities

1.1. *General Duties*—Contractor shall furnish and pay for everything necessary or proper to fully perform and complete the Work (as hereinafter defined), including all labor, materials, equipment, tools, construction equipment and machinery, supplies, facilities, services, scaffolding, appliances, water, heat, utilities, and transportation. Contractor shall supervise and direct the Work using his best skill and attention. Contractor shall be solely responsible for all construction means and for coordinating all portions of the Work. The term "Work" includes all labor necessary to produce the construction required by the Contract Documents, and all materials and equipment incorporated or to be incorporated in such construction.

1.2. *Warranties*—Contractor warrants to Owner that all materials and equipment incorporated in the Work will be new and of recent manufacture unless otherwise specified, and that all Work will be of good quality, free from faults and defects and in conformance with the Contract Documents and all governing federal, state and local laws, rules and regulations. If, within one year after completion of the Work or within such larger period of time as may be prescribed by law or by the terms of any applicable special guarantee required by the Contract Documents, any of the work is found to be defective or fails to conform with the Contract Documents, Contractor, at its own expense, shall correct the defects promptly upon notification by Owner.

1.3. *Taxes, Permits, and Royalties*—Contractor shall pay all sales, consumer, use, and other similar taxes required by law and shall secure and pay all permits, fees, licenses, royalties, and inspections necessary for the proper execution and completion of the Work. Cost of such items shall be included in Contractor's bid on lump sum Work.

1.4. *Compliance with Law and Safety Standards*—Contractor shall give all notices and comply with all applicable laws, ordinances, rules, regulations, and lawful orders of any public authority bearing on the performance of the Work or the safety of persons or property, or their protection from damage, injury, or loss. Contractor shall erect and maintain, as required by existing conditions and progress of the Work, all reasonable safeguards for safety and protection. Contractor shall comply with all provisions of the Federal Occupational Safety and Health Act and other applicable state and local laws and regulations pertaining to safety in the construction industry.

1.5. *Responsibility for Those Performing the Work*—Contractor shall be responsible for the acts and omissions of its employees and all subcontractors, their agents and

percent will be made within thirty days after completion by Builder and occupancy by Owner.

4.2 *Withholding Payments and Termination*—If Contractor defaults Owner may, after seven days written notice to Contractor and without prejudice to any other remedy he may have, make good such deficiencies and may deduct the cost thereof from the payment then or thereafter due Contractor or, at Owner's option, may terminate the Contract and finish the Work by whatever method Owner deems expedient. If the cost of such deficiencies or of finishing the Work exceeds the unpaid balance in connection with a lump sum or guaranteed price contract, then Contractor shall pay the excess cost to Owner.

5. Costs

5.1 *Reimbursable Costs*—The amount of payments for any unforeseen costs incurred in the performance of this contract will be based on costs, hereinafter set forth in the Reimbursement Schedule [omitted], necessarily incurred in the proper performance of the Work and paid by Contractor. Owner shall not be liable to Contractor or any of its subcontractors for any extra work unless authorized in writing by Owner. Such costs shall be at rates not higher than the standard paid in the locality of the Work, except with prior consent of Owner.

This Agreement was executed the ____*11th*____ day of __*Nov*__ in the year ____*C.Y.-3*____

Owner: *Terry Chester*
Date: *11/17/C.Y.-3*
Contractor: Rusty Maxell
Date: 11/17/C.Y.-3

employees, and all other persons performing any of the Work under the direction of Contractor.

1.6. *Cleaning Up*—Contractor at all times shall keep the premises free from accumulation of waste materials or rubbish caused by his operations. At the completion of the Work, Contractor shall promptly remove all his waste materials and rubbish from and about the site as well as his tools, construction equipment, machinery and surplus materials, and shall clean all glass surfaces and shall leave the site "Broom Clean" or its equivalent.

2. Insurance

2.1 *Owner's Property Insurance*—Unless otherwise provided, Owner shall purchase and maintain property insurance upon the entire Work at the site to the full insurable value thereof. This insurance shall include the interest of the owner, Contractor, Subcontractors in the Work and shall insure against the perils of Fire, Extended Coverage, Vandalism and Malicious Mischief. This insurance does not cover construction tools and equipment and temporary construction facilities owned by Contractor or his Subcontractors.

2.2 *Contractor's Liability Insurance*—Before any work is started, Contractor must satisfactorily furnish to owner evidence of insurance coverage by executing the Certificate of Insurance form which is attached hereto and incorporated herein by this reference [omitted]. Contractor shall maintain insurance in such amounts and for such coverages as shown on the Certificate of Insurance form until final completion of the Work and shall ensure that Owner and all parties indemnified pursuant to Article 3 below are added as additional insureds on the coverage.

3. Indemnity

Before any work is started, Contractor shall execute and return to Owner Contractor's Indemnification Agreement attached hereto [omitted]. Said agreement is incorporated herein by this reference.

4. Payments

4.1 *Method of Payment*— Contractor may make application for periodic progress payments upon the completion of the following stages of construction: (1) 25 percent upon commencement of construction; (2) 25 percent upon completion of the framing; (3) 25 percent upon completion of the roof. Owner shall pay Contractor on or about fifteen (15) days after receipt and approval of an application for payment. Final payment of 25

IN THE CIRCUIT COURT OF THE
THIRTEENTH JUDICIAL CIRCUIT
IN AND FOR LEAD COUNTY, STATE OF GOLDEN
CIVIL DIVISION

RUSTY MAXELL d/b/a)	
MAXELL CONSTRUCTION)	
COMPANY)	CASE NO: CV 52-845
Plaintiff)	
)	DEFENDANT'S ANSWER TO
)	COMPLAINT FOR BREACH OF
v.)	CONTRACT AND
)	COUNTERCLAIM FOR
TERRY CHESTER)	DAMAGES
Defendant)	
)	

ANSWER

Defendant, Terry Chester, answers Plaintiff's Complaint as follows:

1. Defendant admits that jurisdiction is proper in this court.

2. Defendant admits the allegations contained in paragraph 2.

3. Defendant admits the allegations contained in paragraph 3.

4. Defendant admits the allegations contained in paragraph 4.

5. Defendant admits that the final payment on the contract was not tendered

but denies each and every other allegation in paragraph 5.

6. Defendant denies each and every allegation contained in paragraph 6.

7. Defendant denies each and every allegation contained in paragraph 7.

Defendant, Terry Chester, asserts the following affirmative defense:

1.   The Contract specified that Plaintiff would use only Builtrite, Mold-No-More mold resistant drywall in the construction of the home (see Exhibit 1 to Complaint). Plaintiff, however, breached the contract by installing Genericorp standard drywall. Because Plaintiff breached his duties under the contract, Defendant is relieved of his duty to make the final payment under the contract.

DATED: November 20, C.Y.-2   Respectfully submitted,

David Anderson
David Anderson
Attorney for Defendant

Witness List

Witnesses for Plaintiff:

1. Rusty Maxell

2. Pat Beasley

Witnesses for Defendant:

1. Terry Chester

2. Randy Ernst

Each side must call both witnesses listed for their respective side.

All witnesses may be either gender.

Stipulations

1. Federal Rules of Evidence apply.

2. Each witness who gave a deposition did agree under oath at the outset of the deposition to give a full and complete description of what occurred and to correct the deposition for inaccuracies and completeness before signing it.

3. All exhibits in the file are authentic and, unless otherwise noted, are the original of that document.

4. Other than what appears in the depositions, there is nothing exceptional or unusual about the background of any of the witnesses that would bolster or detract from their credibility.

5. All dates are denoted by C.Y. (current year) and C.Y.-1 indicating, for example, that the date is the current year minus one.

6. All pretrial motions shall be oral.

7. No party may "invent" witnesses or evidence not specifically mentioned in this problem.

8. "Beyond the record" is not a proper objection. Rather, attorneys shall use cross-examination as a means of challenging a witness whose testimony strays beyond the facts contained in the depositions.

9. The law is accurately set forth in the jury instructions.

10. The plaintiff and defendant may call only the two witnesses listed on their respective witness list. Each party may call an additional witness by deposition or witness statement. Any such testimony is subject to objections pursuant to the Federal Rules of Evidence. If a witness is called by deposition or witness

statement, the opposing party may cross-examine that witness by deposition or

witness statement.

Deposition of Rusty Maxell

Date: March 21 C.Y.-1

Q: Before we talk about the events in question, I want to start out by asking a few more general questions. How long have you been building homes?

A: Well, as a general contractor for about 18 years, but I was working construction before that. I guess about 25 years in all.

Q: Are you the sole owner of Maxell Construction Company?

A: That's right, it's my business and I've built it from the ground up.

Q: How is your company doing?

A: Well, it's gotten pretty big now, I've got about fifty employees that are usually split into three or four crews depending on the jobs that I have going at any given time. And you know there is always turnover here and there but yeah, I would say approximately fifty people.

Q: And does Maxell Construction Company primarily build houses?

A: Uh, yeah that's probably fair to say. Building homes is probably 60 or 70 percent of my business but you know sometimes I build commercial buildings or other structures, you know it just depends on the work that comes my way.

Q: Okay, thank you Mr./Ms. Maxell. Now let's turn to the matter at hand. How did you first meet Terry Chester?

A: I believe he/she called my company asking for an estimate on a house.

Q: Which you gave?

A: Sure, I looked over the plans that he/she submitted, inspected the site, factored all of his/her requests and came up with the figure that we ultimately went with, $800,000. It was a big house, right at 4,000 square feet. We haggled a little bit, but I'm not the kind of person who plays games, you know. If I say the job is going to cost this much then that is how much it is going to cost. I try to deal straight with people. Anyway, Terry ultimately agreed and we wrote up a contract for the whole shootin' match.

Q: Alright, and then what happened?

A: Well, everything went according to plan. Construction moved along on schedule and everything seemed to be going great. I even finished the house a little early. That's when the trouble started.

Q: I assume that you are referring to the failure to make the last payment?

A: Yeah, during the entire job Terry had always made the payments on time. Well, pretty much, he/she asked for an extension on one occasion for some reason, which I gave him/her. This is what I get for being a nice guy. Anyway, so I finish the job and Terry seemed completely happy with the house. Anyway, a couple of weeks later Terry calls and tells me that I used the wrong drywall and refused to pay unless I come and fix it.

Q: And why didn't you?

A: Why didn't I fix it?

Q: Yes.

A: Because it would have been ridiculous. I would have had to pull out all the drywall in the house, completely gutting the thing. It would have cost a fortune. I have to make a living you know. I mean $800,000 sounds like a lot of money but I barely see ten percent of that, and that's if I'm lucky. When I give an estimate I have to figure in the cost of materials, the cost of labor, how much I'm going to have to pay all my employees, hire subcontractors, rent equipment, and all the other expenses that go into building a house. I generally want to try and clear about ten percent off a job so after I add up all the expenses I add on 12-or 13 percent, whatever makes a nice round number usually. That way I have some wiggle room too. I mean, almost every time something ends up costing more than I think, so a lot of times I only end up making 7 or 8 percent on a job. This job is no different; as it stands I'm only going to be making about 10 percent on this job, that's $80,000. Now, the cost of replacing the drywall would be anywhere from $70,000 to $80,000 which would almost completely destroy my profit margin. It just isn't worth the trouble, and I know Terry knew about the drywall.

Q: Why do you say that?

A: Because Terry went to the construction site a couple of times a week. He/She was obsessive about it. Really anal about the whole thing you know, always asking questions and getting bent out of shape whenever he/she thought something was wrong. Terry just liked to complain. This one time some of my guys were putting in the wrong windows, there was a mix-up from another job I had going on and the orders got switched. Terry caught that real quick and threw a fit until I got them switched out. Anyway, I specifically remember touring the site with Terry while we were putting in the drywall and he/she did like he/she always did, inspected everything top to bottom, and never said a word about the drywall. I bet you Terry hatched the plan to cheat me right then and there.

Q: But you were aware that Terry Chester specifically requested Builtrite Mold-No-More drywall in the contract.

A: Of course I knew, Terry wrote it in on the contract while we were writing it out, along with all of his/her other requests, but it's not like I did it on purpose or anything, and he/she still got his/her house. The drywall won't affect the value of the home one bit.

Q: And why didn't you use that drywall?

A: Look, like I said at any given time, I have several projects going on and I oversee them all. I try and make sure everything is perfect. Look, if you look at the contract Terry made several other special requests in the construction of the home and I honored each and every one of them. I just never noticed that we were using the wrong drywall, with everything that I have to oversee sometimes a few minor things just slip through the cracks.

Q: And the drywall was one of those things?

A: Yeah, like I said I try to make sure things get done right, but in this case the wrong drywall just got ordered by my construction foreperson on the Chester job.

Q: You are referring to Randy Ernst?

A: Yeah, what a piece of work.

Q: How do you mean?

A: Well he/she had been working for me for a couple of years and he/she seemed to be a really on the ball kind of a person. So when an opening came up I bumped him/her up to construction foreperson. I didn't realize he/she had- how should I say it- issues.

Q: What do you mean?

A: He/She would often drink before coming to work, sometimes even drink at work. He/She'd also get my guys all riled up for no reason, you know, just all around trouble. He/She was good when he/she was sober and working, but I ultimately couldn't take anymore so I ended up firing him/her not too long ago.

Q: And it was Randy's responsibility to order supplies, including the drywall.

A: That's right.

Q: Let's turn to Terry Chester, I take it that it is your belief that he/she is simply blowing things out of proportion?

A: Well, yeah I mean come on, it's just drywall. Like I said, the drywall that you use on a house has no real effect on the value of the home so Terry still got pretty much exactly what we contracted for.

Q: So what do you feel this is really about then?

A: I think that Terry just wants to get out of paying me by screwing me over, finding some ridiculous detail and complaining about it, that's what I think. If I don't get this last payment on the job then I will actually be losing a lot of money, which doesn't seem fair at all considering that Terry is currently living in the house that I built for him/her. For crying out loud, I have offered to reduce by $20,000 what Chester owes me. That is more than the difference in the price of the drywall.

    I have reviewed the transcript of my deposition. This is a complete and accurate account.

Rusty Maxell

Rusty Maxell

Deposition of Pat Beasley

Date: March 23 C.Y.-1

Q: Alright, so let's begin by establishing a few things, you work for Builder's Supply

Company, correct?

A: Yes, that's right. I am one of the Customer Sales Representatives.

Q: And what exactly does a Customer Sales Representative do?

A: Well I work with clients to make sure that they get the supplies that they need. We

have all kinds of customers, from laypersons, to small, independent contractors and even

mid to large size general contracting companies. I work with them all to determine what

supplies they need in order to best achieve their construction or remodeling goals.

Q: And how long have you been working at Builder's Supply?

A: It has been about eight years now.

Q: And how well do you know Rusty Maxell?

A: Not that well personally but on a professional level, he/she is one of our biggest

customers and he/she has been ordering from us ever since I first started working at

Builder's Supply. We have a pretty solid working relationship. He/She's a great person.

Tends to use the best materials in his/her projects, which is great for me because I get a

percentage commission. I took over his/her account about five years ago so I have had

quite a bit of interaction with him/her.

Q: What do you mean when you say that you "took over his/her account?"

A: Well, a lot of our regular customers have standing accounts with us to expedite

things. Rusty is always ordering stuff from us and I am his/her contact at Builder's

Supply. All he/she needs to do is call me and I make sure that he/she gets everything he/she needs. Rusty generally knows exactly what he/she wants, but occasionally he/she will ask what I recommend, especially when new products come out. It's part of my job to stay on top of new developments in the industry so that I can help my customers make informed decisions. It's really a good system, the customers get great service and we make a percentage of whatever they buy on commission.

Q: Do you usually deal directly with Mr./Ms. Maxell when he is making orders?

A: Usually, Rusty takes a very hands-on approach to his/her business. He/She works really hard and tends to do a lot of work himself/herself. He/She is always using the old saying "If you want something done right, you have to do it yourself." But you know, sometimes his/her construction forepersons will do the ordering too, it just depends.

Q: Okay, well, let's turn to the day of January 17, C.Y.-2. Do you remember the day in question?

A: If you mean the day that Randy Ernst ordered the drywall, yeah, I remember.

Q: Yes, exactly now what can you tell me about that exchange?

A: Ernst called and we kind of chatted for a minute or two, you know, just kind of about whatever, I didn't know him/her that well but sometimes he/she does the ordering and sometimes comes by the warehouse to pick stuff up. Anyway, so then he/she asks, "What's the cheapest dry wall you have?", and I tell him/her, "Genericorp standard drywall" and then he/she proceeded to order enough of that drywall to use on the house that he/she was working on.

Q: Can you tell me the differences between the Builtrite and the Genericorp drywall?

A: Well, first both companies make a few different kinds of drywall, but if you just mean these particular kinds well, there are a lot of differences. First of all Builtrite tends to make higher quality products in general.

Q: Would you say that Genericorp's products are inferior?

A: No, I didn't say that at all. If Genericorp made bad products we wouldn't carry them. But, on the other hand, you get what you pay for. Builtrite definitely has the edge in terms of quality, but they charge a premium for it. Of course, the Mold-No-More drywall is one of Builtrite's more expensive products and it will run you about 70% more than standard drywall.

Q: Tell me about Mold-No-More drywall.

A: It's made differently than regular drywall. Most drywall is made with a gypsum plaster core and an outer layer of paper. The Mold-No-More drywall uses a glass-like material instead of paper and also uses a special blend of gypsum plaster to make it more mold resistant.

Q: Do a lot of people buy the Mold-No-More drywall?

A: Well, it's still a fairly new product, but we are located in a moderately humid area where mold can be a concern, so I have seen more and more people using it.

Q: You said mold resistant, is it not mold proof?

A: I'm certainly not a scientist, but from my years working with building supplies I have learned and seen a lot. For instance, I know that mold will grow on almost anything given the right conditions and enough time, but in my experience with this drywall versus other drywall it does seem to help. The fact that it doesn't use any paper means that moisture is much less likely to become trapped in the drywall, which is the potential

problem with regular drywall.

Q: You mentioned that there is a price difference between the different kinds of drywall,

about what difference is there?

A: I'm not sure off the top of my head what the exact price difference is, but between our

cheapest drywall, the Genericorp, and the Builtrite Mold-No-More, which is one of the

more expensive, I would say the difference in cost is about 70 percent, more or less. In

building your average home I would say that this comes out to about $10,000 to $12,000

depending on square footage. Of course, in a big house like the one Rusty was building

the difference is probably closer to $18,000.

Q: And in terms of appearance, how similar do the two products look?

A: Honestly, they are very different. The standard drywall of course has the paper on it,

the Genericorp version is blue in color and has "Genericorp" printed all over it. On the

Mold-No-More drywall, there is no paper. The material that they use on the outside

gives it a very distinctive look because it is clear, with a slight yellowish tint. It also has

"Builtrite Mold-No-More mold resistant drywall" printed prominently in each of the

corners.

Q: So just by looking at either drywall it would be clear what kind of drywall it is?

A: That's right.

Q: What would it take to completely replace all of the drywall in a 4,000 square foot

home?

A: It would be a huge job. You would have to go in and tear out everything and then

replace it. It would take at least a couple of weeks and cost a fortune. First, you would have to buy all new drywall, which would cost around $60,000. Then there is $10,000 or so in painting. Then, of course, there is the cost of labor, which would probably be around $25,000, so all in all you are talking about $95,000, maybe more.

I have reviewed the transcript of my deposition. This is a complete and accurate account.

Pat Beasley

Pat Beasley

Deposition of Terry Chester

Date: March 17, C.Y.-1

Q: Alright Terry, how about we start from the beginning. How did you first begin

interacting with Mr./Ms. Maxell?

A: Well, you know, I was looking to build a house because my family needed a new place to

live. I had already bought the lot, and had the plans and everything, I just needed a builder to,

you know, actually build it.

Q: So how did you find Mr./Ms. Maxell?

A: Oh well, I was asking around and looking in the phone book and asked several

contractors for estimates on the job.

Q: And Mr./Ms. Maxell's was the lowest?

A: No actually, his/hers was actually only the second or third lowest, but he/she had good

references and a great reputation so I figured he/she would be the best choice, boy was I

wrong.

Q: And when exactly did this all take place?

A: This was in July of C.Y.-3

Q: Then what happened?

A: We went back and forth for a while and then ultimately we hammered out the details and

wrote up a contract.

Q: And what were the terms of that contract, generally speaking?

A: We agreed on the price of $800,000. The terms that we agreed to set out a timetable for payment. I had to pay 25% down, 25% after the foundation was poured, 25% once the roof went on, and then the final 25% after the house was completed.

Q: Ok, and about something you said earlier, you said that you "needed a new place to live," why was that?

A: Well, me and my family were forced to leave our old house. It had a terrible infestation of black mold. We only discovered the problem after our youngest child, Eric, started to have breathing problems. We went to several doctors to try and figure out what was wrong and no one could figure it out. After a couple of months my wife/husband started having some breathing problems, too. Finally, one doctor suggested we have the house tested for environmental causes. That's when we discovered that we had mold. It was so extensive that we had no option but to leave the house, which was ultimately condemned.

Q: I understand. How many children do you have?

A: I have three, Eric is now 8, Joel is 10, and Samantha is 11.

Q: And when did all this happen?

A: This happened like three years ago in April of C.Y.-4. That was the reason why I specified in the contract that I wanted the mold resistant drywall. I had seen a commercial for it on TV and I thought that it would be a great way to ensure that my family didn't get sick like that again. I even went down to one of those big box construction warehouse places and talked to them about mold resistant drywall. They showed me the special drywall and how it was different from regular drywall.

Q: Where did you go after you left your old house?

A: We were renting an apartment while the new house was being built.

Q: Ok, now what happened after you signed the contract with Mr./Ms. Maxell?

A: Everything went great for a while, construction stayed on time for the most part and I was pretty happy. I made all the payments pursuant to the contract and everything seemed to be going according to plan.

Q: Did you ever visit the construction site?

A: Yes, lots of times. My kids loved watching our house being built and I was very interested in monitoring the progress.

Q: Did you ever complain about anything during construction?

A: Well, not exactly complain, no, but sometimes I had concerns about things that I would ask Rusty about. I mean, I don't know anything about building houses and I just wanted to make sure that everything was going alright. Like, there was this one time when I noticed that they were putting in the wrong windows, Rusty fixed that though. I only noticed because I wanted some special, decorative windows installed. They look very different from regular windows.

Q: But you didn't notice when Rusty used Genericorp instead of Mold-No-More drywall?

A: Well, I wasn't there every day, and it wasn't my job to notice things like that. I mean, I don't know anything about building houses. That's why I hired him/her!

Q: When did you first discover that there was a problem?

A: It was about two weeks after I moved in, I decided to put in a surround sound system in my living room and so I hired this outfit to do the wiring. They had to go through the walls in some places and while they were working I told them that I had had special drywall installed to help prevent mold. But the worker said that the drywall just looked like ordinary drywall. And that's when we discovered it was the wrong stuff.

Q: What did you do then?

A: I called Maxell to tell him/her about the problem but he/she just sort of shrugged it off like it was no big deal. But he/she knew it was important to me, I had told him/her the whole story and specifically asked for that drywall, I even wrote it into the contract! But when I told him/her that I wanted it fixed, he/she said that it would be way too expensive to tear out and replace and refused to do it.

Q: And then what did you do?

A: What do you think I did? I told him/her that either he/she could come and fix his/her mistake or that I wasn't going to make the final payment on the contract.

Q: Did Mr./Ms. Maxell take any action at all?

A: Not other than to have his/her secretary call every other day, demanding that I pay them and send a few threatening letters.

Q: And how did you respond to these?

A: At first I just kept telling him/her that I would pay as soon as he/she fixed his/her mistake, but after a while I just started ignoring them.

I have reviewed the transcript of my deposition. This is a complete and accurate account.

Terry Chester
Terry Chester

Deposition of Randy Ernst
Date: March 20 C.Y.-1

Q: Ok Mr./Ms. Ernst, why don't you start by telling us how you first came to work for Mr./Ms. Maxell.

A: Well, I have been working construction almost all my life, working for different contractors, doing different things. Then one day, several years back one of my buddies who worked for Rusty told me that they needed some experienced people so I went over, talked with Rusty who offered me a job on the spot.

Q: And when were you made a construction foreperson?

A: After I had been working there for a couple of years. Rusty approached me and asked if I wanted a promotion.

Q: And when was this?

A: About three years ago.

Q: And how did you come to be involved in this matter?

A: Alright, well, it's pretty simple really. I was the foreperson on the Chester job, so I obviously knew a lot about what was going on.

Q: What does the foreperson do?

A: Pretty much everything, makes sure the work is going according to plan, supervises the workers, coordinates the subcontractors, you know, all of that stuff.

Q: So it's fair to say that as far as that particular job is concerned, you are pretty much the boss?

A: Yeah, pretty much, I mean of course I had to answer to Rusty, but as far as the day to day operations went, yeah.

Q: Did you know about the specification to use Mold-No-More drywall in construction of the house?

A: Yes.

Q: And did you realize that the drywall that you installed was in fact Genericorp standard drywall?

A: Of course, like I said, I know what goes on at my jobsite.

Q: So why did you install the standard drywall despite knowing that you were supposed to use the Builtrite drywall?

A: It wasn't like that, it wasn't really my fault.

Q: How is that, if you knew that you were installing the wrong drywall?

A: Because Rusty told me to use the other drywall.

Q: Rusty Maxell told you to use the Genericorp drywall?

A: Yeah, well, pretty much.

Q: What do you mean by "pretty much?"

A: Well, you know, a little while after we started construction Rusty visited the site and, you know, we started looking at the numbers and everything and he/she was just complaining about how everything was costing a little more than he/she thought and how he/she wouldn't be making as much money on the job as he/she wanted. And then he/she said, "You know what's really killing us? This drywall. The stuff probably doesn't even work, anyway."

Q: And you took that to mean that you should go ahead and use the cheaper drywall?

A: Well, yeah, it was all in the way he/she said it, sort of like he/she wanted me to do it without having to come right out and say it. He/She just had this tone and sort of gave this look that made it pretty clear to me that that is what he/she wanted to do.

Q: Now, it's my understanding that you no longer work for Mr./Ms. Maxell, is that correct?

A: Yeah, so what?

Q: Can you tell me exactly what precipitated that?

A: Me getting fired?

Q: Yes.

A: It was all crap. Rusty is a total jerk. I worked for him/her for all this time and then, bam!, just like that, he/she throws me out in the cold.

Q: And what reason did he/she give for firing you?

A: Mainly because of my drinking, but it's not like that made a difference, I always did a good job and it really wasn't any of his/her business.

Q: So you only drank in your personal time?

A: Well, you know, pretty much yeah. Sometimes I might have a drink before heading to a job site or you know take a long lunch or something but still, I would only ever have a couple of beers, it's not like they even affected me. And lots of times when Rusty came to visit the job site or whatever, we would go to lunch and we'd both have a beer.

Q: So why do you think he/she fired you?

A: I don't really know, I think he/she just wanted me gone because I was always standing up for my workers and stuff, you know? Rusty was always trying to cut costs and a lot of times that really ended up coming down on the workers who, you know, I had to deal with everyday. I was always telling Rusty that he/she needed to pay them more, but he/she never listened. Lately though there was a lot of grumbling and of course I was sticking up for the workers, and I think Rusty thought that without me to encourage them, they would just stop complaining.

I have reviewed the transcript of my deposition. This is a complete and accurate account.

Randy Ernst

Randy Ernst

Dr. Joann Sloan, M.D.

7634 Thompson St. • Silverado, GO 76894
(909) 555-1652 • JSloan@silveradomedical.com

August 14, C.Y.-4

Terry Chester
5779 Longview drive
Silverado, GO 76891

Dear Mr. and Mrs. Chester,

Now that we have confirmed that your house was infested with black mold, I am now able to make a conclusive diagnosis concerning your son, Eric. Mold exposure accounts for all your son's symptoms, which should dissipate in a few weeks once he has been removed from further exposure. I am confident that Eric will make a full recovery, but I advise you to get Eric out as soon as possible, as further exposure could cause permanent respiratory problems. I am glad that we have finally discovered what has been ailing your son and can now take some effective measures to get him well.

Sincerely,

Joann Sloan

Dr. Joann Sloan, M.D.

Silverado Medical Group

Jury Instructions

Members of the jury, you have now heard all the evidence and the closing argument of the attorneys. It is my duty to instruct you on the law that applies to this case. You will have a copy of my instructions with you when you go to the jury room to deliberate.

I will now tell you the law that you must follow to reach your verdict. You must follow that law exactly as I give it to you, even if you disagree with it. If the attorneys have said anything different about what the law means, you must follow what I say. In reaching your verdict, you must not speculate about what I think your verdict should be from something I may have said or done.

Pay careful attention to all the instructions that I give you. All the instructions are important because together they state the law that you will use in this case. You must consider all of the instructions together. You must decide this case based only on the law and the evidence.

A witness is a person who has knowledge related to this case. You will have to decide whether you believe each witness and how important each witness's testimony is to the case. You may believe all, part, or none of a witness's testimony. In deciding whether to believe a witness's testimony, you may consider, among other factors, the following:

1.   How well did the witness see, hear, or otherwise sense what he or she described in court?

2.   How well did the witness remember and describe what happened?

3.   How did the witness look, act, and speak while testifying?

4.   Did the witness have any reason to say something that was not true? Did the witness show any bias or prejudice? Did the witness have a personal relationship with any of the parties involved in the case? Does the witness have a personal stake in how this case is decided?

5.   What was the witness's attitude toward this case or about giving testimony?

Sometimes a witness may say something that is not consistent with something else he or she said. Sometimes different witnesses will give different versions of what happened. People often forget things or make mistakes in what they remember. Also, two people may see the same event, but remember it differently. You may consider these differences, but do not decide that testimony is untrue just because it differs from other testimony.

However, if you decide that a witness has deliberately testified untruthfully about something important, you may choose not to believe anything that witness said. On the other hand, if you think the witness testified untruthfully about some things but told the truth about others, you may accept the part you think is true and ignore the rest.

You must not be biased in favor of or against any witness because of his or her race, sex, religion, occupation, sexual orientation or national origin.

Plaintiff has the burden in this case to prove each element of his claim by a preponderance of the evidence. The term "preponderance of the evidence" means the greater weight and degree of credible evidence admitted in this case. Simply put, Plaintiff must prove it is more likely than not that each element of his claim is true.

The claim for your consideration is the claim of Plaintiff against Defendant to recover sums claimed by Plaintiff to be due and unpaid under the contract between the parties for the construction of the building and related improvements.

A contract is a promise or set of promises for the breach of which the law gives a remedy or the performance of which the law in some way recognizes a duty. Failure to perform a contract is a breach. The essential elements of this claim are [1] the existence of a contract between the parties; [2] plaintiff's performance [3] defendant's failure to perform [4] damages to plaintiff caused by breach.

Plaintiff contends that he substantially performed his contracted obligations and, therefore, Defendant breached the contract between them by refusing to pay the final installment due under the contract. Defendant maintains that he was relieved of the obligation to pay by Plaintiff's own breach when Plaintiff failed to substantially perform his contracted obligations.

In the case of a construction contract, the building contractor is entitled to payment of the contract price upon proof of "substantial performance" of the work required by the contract. It is not necessary that the building contractor fully and completely perform every item specified in the plans and specifications, which are a part of the contract. The term "substantial performance" means that degree of performance of a contract that, while not equal to full and complete performance, is so nearly equivalent that it would be unreasonable to deny the contractor the payment agreed upon in the contract.

In determining whether the contractor's performance was substantial, the following factors are relevant: (a) the extent to which the owner will be deprived of the benefit which he reasonably expected; (b) the extent to which the owner can be adequately compensated for the part of that benefit of which he will be deprived; (c) the extent to which the contractor will suffer forfeiture; and (d) the extent to which the behavior of the contractor comports with standards of good faith and fair dealing.

The burden is on Plaintiff to prove by a preponderance of the evidence that he substantially performed his obligations under the contract (and change orders) for the construction of the work.

Your foreperson shall preside over your deliberations. All jurors should participate in all deliberations and vote on each issue. The votes of ten or more jurors are required to reach a verdict. The verdict must be in writing and the verdict form has been prepared for you. It is as follows:

[READ VERDICT FORM]

In just a few moments, you will be taken to the jury room by the bailiff. The first thing you should do is elect a foreperson who will preside over your deliberations like the chairperson of a meeting. It is the foreperson's job to sign and date the verdict form when all of you have agreed on a verdict in this case and to bring the verdict back to the courtroom when you return.

In closing, let me remind you that it is important that you follow the law spelled out in these instructions in deciding your verdicts. There are no other laws that apply to this case.

IN THE CIRCUIT COURT OF THE
THIRTEENTH JUDICIAL CIRCUIT
IN AND FOR LEAD COUNTY, STATE OF GOLDEN
CIVIL DIVISION

RUSTY MAXELL d/b/a)
MAXELL CONSTRUCTION)
COMPANY)
Plaintiff)   CASE NO: CV 52-845
)
)   VERDICT FORM
)
v.)
)
TERRY CHESTER)
Defendant)
)

We, the Jury, answer the questions submitted to us as follows:

QUESTION NO. 1: Do you find by a preponderance of the evidence for Plaintiff?

ANSWER: Yes _____   No _____

If you answered the above question "No", you will not answer the remaining questions, but will simply sign the Verdict.

If you have answered Question No. 1 "Yes", then you must answer Question No. 2.

QUESTION NO. 2: By a preponderance of the evidence, how much, if any, do you find Plaintiff is entitled to recover?

ANSWER: $_____

So say we all,

_____   _____
Date   Foreperson

State of Golden

v.

Sunny Grifford

(DUI/hit and run)

IN THE CIRCUIT COURT OF THE SEVENTH JUDICIAL CIRCUIT

IN AND FOR LEAD COUNTY, STATE OF GOLDEN

CRIMINAL DIVISION

STATE OF GOLDEN	)	
	)	
v.	)	CASE NO: CR 94-663
	)	
SUNNY GRIFFORD,	)	
Defendant	)	
	)	

IN THE CIRCUIT COURT OF THE SEVENTH JUDICIAL CIRCUIT

IN AND FOR LEAD COUNTY, STATE OF GOLDEN

CRIMINAL DIVISION

THE 4th DAY OF NOVEMBER, C.Y.-1

STATE OF GOLDEN	)))	**MISDEMEANOR COMPLAINT**
v.	))	CASE NO: CR 94-663
SUNNY GRIFFORD, Defendant	)))	

COMES NOW the undersigned and states that he is informed and believes, and upon such information and belief declares:

COUNT I

On or about October 5, C.Y.-1, at and in the County of Lead, the crime of operating a motor vehicle while under the influence of alcohol, in violation of section 502 of the Golden Vehicle Code, a misdemeanor, was committed by Sunny Grifford.

COUNT II

On or about October 5, C.Y.-1, at and in the County of Lead, the crime of leaving the scene of an accident, in violation of section 392 of the Golden Vehicle Code, a misdemeanor, was committed by Sunny Grifford.

Jennifer Warner
Declarant and Complainant

Witness List

Witnesses for the State:

1. Sam Jackson * * *
2. Donna Kevins * *

Witnesses for Defendant:

1. Sunny Grifford *
2. Sonia Grifford * *

Each side must call both witnesses listed for their respective party.

* This witness must be a male.

* * This witness must be a female.

* * * This witness may be either gender.

Stipulations

1. Federal Rules of Criminal Procedure and Federal Rules of Evidence apply.

2. Each witness, except Defendant, who gave an interview or statement (collectively "witness statement") reviewed the officer's report of his or her witness statement and verified it was accurate.

3. All exhibits in the file are authentic and, unless otherwise noted, are the original of that document.

4. Other than what appears in the officer's report of the witness statements, there is nothing exceptional or unusual about the background of any of the witnesses that would bolster or detract from their credibility.

5. All dates are denoted by C.Y. (current year) and C.Y.-1 indicating, for example, that the date is the current year minus one.

6. All pretrial motions shall be oral.

7. No party may "invent" witnesses or evidence not specifically mentioned in this problem.

8. "Beyond the record" is not a proper objection. Rather, attorneys shall use cross-examination as a means of challenging a witness whose testimony strays beyond the facts contained in the witness's statement.

9. It is stipulated that the State of Golden State driver's license is Defendant's driver's license and that all information on the license is correct. It is further stipulated that the photograph and information is that of Defendant. Except for the weight and age, the description of Defendant should comport with the physical description of the witness playing Defendant.

10. It is stipulated that October 5, C.Y.-1 was a Saturday.

11. The "Reliable Wireless" record of the cell phone calls made to 392-5039 from 556-1632 is authenticated under Federal Rule of Evidence 902(11) and is admissible as a certified business record under Federal Rule of Evidence 803(6).

12. Golden Vehicle Code section 502 reads as follows: "It is unlawful for any person who is under the influence of any alcoholic beverage or drug, or under the combined influence of any alcoholic beverage and drug, to drive a vehicle."

13. Golden Vehicle Code section 392 reads as follows: "The driver of any vehicle involved in an accident shall immediately stop the vehicle at the scene of the accident and shall provide his or her name, address and insurance information to all injured parties and to police, and shall also render reasonable assistance to any injured party, including transportation or arrangement of transportation to a hospital."

14. The prosecution and defense may call only the two witnesses listed on their respective witness list. Each party may call an additional witness by deposition or witness statement. Any such testimony is subject to objections pursuant to the Federal Rules of Evidence. If a witness is called by deposition or witness statement, the opposing party may cross-examine that witness by deposition or witness statement. The parties have agreed to waive Confrontational Clause objections for only this witness.

SILVERADO POLICE DEPARTMENT

DRIVING-UNDER-THE-INFLUENCE ARREST REPORT

Case No. 73519-391	Arrestee's Name (Last) (First) (M.I.) GRIFFORD SUNNY X.		Social Security No. 493-30-3920		Telephone 493-2009

Address 997 N. 52nd ST.	City SILVERADO	Sex M	Occupation TEACHER, SILVERADO HIGH SCHOOL		

Descent XXX	Hair XXX	Eyes XXX	Height XXX	Weight 175	Birthdate 9/30/C.Y.-31	Age 31

Charge(s) 1. VC 502 – DRIVING UNDER INFLUENCE 2. VC 392 – HIT AND RUN	Location of Occurrence INTERSECTION OF BORCHARD AND LAS BRISAS

Location of Arrest 997 N. 52ND ST., SILVERADO	Date and Time Arrested 10/5/C.Y. -1 2300 HOURS	Special Medical Problems NONE

Clothing	Shirt/Blouse BATHROBE	Dress/Suit	Tie	Coat	Belt	Socks	Shoes SLIPPERS

Property NONE

Currency NONE	Jewelry NONE

Vehicle License and State 9EKD4930, GO	Vehicle Description	Make MERCEDES	Model S600	Year C.Y. -1	Color BLK

Vehicle Disposition IMPOUNDED

Reason for Release BAIL POSTED	Released To SONIA GRIFFORD, WIFE

Arresting Officer (Name and Number) JACKSON, 34076	Date 10/5/C.Y.-1	Signature *Sam Jackson*

SILVERADO POLICE DEPARTMENT

DRIVING-UNDER-THE-INFLUENCE ARREST REPORT

REPORT TYPE: **INVESTIGATION NARRATIVE**
OFFICER REPORTING: **SAM JACKSON** (initialed: *S.J.*)
DATE: **10/5/C.Y.-1**

On this date, at approximately 21:30 hours, I received a dispatched call concerning a hit and run in the area of North Silverado. The suspect was last seen traveling northbound on Borchard Avenue in a black Mercedes with front end damage. I responded to the area in search of said Mercedes.

I failed to locate the Mercedes. At approximately 21:50 hours, dispatch received a call from a woman who identified herself as Donna Kevins, who related she was involved in the previously reported hit and run accident and knew where the driver lived. She reported the address of the driver as 997 N. 52nd Street, Silverado.

I arrived at said address at 22:00 hours and observed a black Mercedes parked slightly askew, blocking the driveway of the residence. The car was parked approximately 20 feet from the streetlight illuminating the general area. Upon closer inspection, I determined that the car had what looked like recent body damage on the right front fender. I placed my hand on the hood of the car and could not discern any warmth.

While I was inspecting the car, a man, later identified as Sunny Grifford, came out of the 997 N. 52nd Street residence wearing a bathrobe and holding a partially filled martini glass. He walked down the driveway toward me and said, "Hello, can I help you?" I informed him that I was investigating a vehicle accident that occurred earlier in the evening. I asked him about the damage to his fender. Mr. Grifford replied, "Yeah, I ran a stop sign yesterday and had a little fender-bender." During this exchange I smelled a strong odor of an alcoholic beverage emitting from his person. I asked him if he was driving the vehicle at the time of the accident and he said he was. I asked him when the accident had occurred, and he related it had happened the previous day.

I told Mr. Grifford I was investigating a hit and run that had occurred at approximately 21:30 hours this evening. At that point, Mr. Grifford turned, somewhat unsteadily, and began walking back toward the front door of his residence. I ordered him to remain and he complied. At that time, a woman, later identified as Sonia Grifford, came out of the residence. She identified herself as Sunny Grifford's wife and demanded to know what was going on. I told her that I was questioning her husband about a hit and run accident that had occurred that evening. Mrs. Grifford immediately became angry and related to me that she and her husband had been home together since the late afternoon.

As I was questioning Mrs. Grifford, a dark blue Taurus pulled up to the curb in front of the Grifford residence and a woman later identified as Donna Kevins exited the vehicle and began running toward Mr. Grifford, yelling obscenities. Before I could restrain her, she reached Mr. Grifford and pushed him in the chest and began kicking him. She was yelling that he was a "terrible person," and that she "couldn't believe he could be capable of doing something like that." I separated the two and threatened to arrest Ms. Kevins for assaulting Mr. Grifford, as well as interfering with a police investigation. I then asked her why she was there. She related that Mr. Grifford had rammed his car into her car and driven away. She confirmed that Grifford was the driver who had left the accident which she had reported. At this point, Mr. Grifford became agitated and attempted to shove Ms. Kevins. I put Mr. Grifford in the back of my patrol car to separate the two and called for backup.

When backup arrived, I instructed Officer Jake Hayes to stand by and cautioned him that Ms. Kevins may attempt to interrupt the ongoing investigation.

Believing that Mr. Grifford had as recently as a half hour ago operated his car, I subjected him to a series of field sobriety tests to determine his level of impairment. Mr. Grifford was able to successfully perform the Romberg and alphabet field sobriety tests, but failed the heel to toe and leg raise. See attached FST report.

Based on my observations, I formed the opinion that Mr. Grifford had been impaired at the time he was operating a motor vehicle. He was placed under arrest without incident and was told he would have his blood alcohol level measured by a breath test.

Mr. Grifford refused to take the breath test, even though I advised him three times, reading directly from the DUI face sheet. Grifford stated he had a lawyer friend who told him never to take a breathalyzer test if he had been drinking at all because "the tests lie and the cops will get you even if you didn't do anything." After Grifford refused to provide a chemical sample, I placed him in my police cruiser to transport him to the Silverado Police Department.

At this time, a tow truck from Rick's Towing arrived. I spoke with the tow truck driver, Mike, who stated that his dispatch received a call from Mama Red's Auto Body requesting that they tow Mr. Grifford's Mercedes to Rick's Towing's storage lot and then deliver the car to Mama Red's. Mike did not know when the request was made.

Mike related that he was told the call was an emergency, and that he was to get to the address as soon as possible. He related that they had been swamped the past couple of days and wasn't able to get there immediately.

At this point Mr. Grifford stated, "Of course, now they show up to tow my car. I called those jerks yesterday."

As I was getting into my cruiser, I noticed some dark colored paint in the scrape on Grifford's right front fender. Holding the paint up to the light, I wasn't able to determine the color of the chips, just that they were dark. I sent the paint chips to the lab for analysis, but they were subsequently misplaced and have not been located.

Sam Jackson
Officer Sam Jackson

SILVERADO POLICE DEPARTMENT

DRIVING-UNDER-THE-INFLUENCE ARREST REPORT (CONTINUATION)

Arrestee's Name (Last, First, M.I.) GRIFFORD, SUNNY X.	MPD Case No. 73519-391	Traffic Collision ☑ Yes ☐ No	Driving established by: ☐ Officer ☑ Witness(es) ☐ DUI Checkpoint

ORIGIN

SOURCE OF ACTIVITY:

SEE NARRATIVE

ELEMENTS OF OFFENSE

☐ A/O ☑ Other: (DONNA KEVINS) saw the vehicle driven by the defendant do the following:

☐ Almost strike object or vehicle	☑ Involved in collision	☑ Driver appeared intoxicated
☐ Braking erratically	☐ Unsafe lane change	☑ Rapidly accelerating/decelerating
☐ Fail to stop for a stop sign	☐ Improper turn or position	☑ Swerving
☐ Slow response to signs/signals	☑ Unsafe movement right/left	☐ No lights during darkness
☐ Fail to stop for red signal	☐ Violation of signs	☐ High beams on illegally
☐ Following too closely	☐ Violation of markings	☐ Violated right-of-way
☑ Weaving in between lanes	☐ Slow speed (___ in a ___ zone)	☐ Wrong side of roadway
☐ Weaving within lane	☐ Speeding (___ in a ___ zone)	☐ Entered established DUI checkpoint

☐ Other/Details: _____

☑ A/O ☐ Other: (_____) ☐ stopped ☑ contacted the defendant at ___997 N. 52nd STREET, SILVERADO___

BREATH	COMPLEXION	EYES	SPEECH	COORDINATION	BEHAVIOR
☑ Alcohol	☐ Normal	☑ Bloodshot	☑ Slurred	☑ Unsteady	☑ Cooperative
☑ Strong	☑ Flushed	☐ Watery	☐ Slow	☐ Staggered	☐ Uncooperative
☐ Moderate	☐ Red	☐ Red	☐ Mumbled	☐ Needs Support	☐ Belligerent
☐ Slight	☐ Pale	☑ Droopy	☐ Rapid	☐ by officer	☐ Laughing/Carefree
☐ Marijuana	☐ Blotchy	☐ Glassy	☑ Thick	☐ object(s)	☐ Crying
☐ PCP	☐ Other	☐ Clear	☐ Talkative	☐ Fell	☐ Indifferent
☐ Other		☐ Fixed	☐ Hesitant	☑ Swaying	☐ Combative
		☐ Other	☐ Other	☐ Other	☐ Argumentative
					☐ Fluctuating

CHEMICAL TEST ADMONITION (30291 GVC)

1. You are required by state law to submit to a chemical test to determine the alcohol and/or drug content of your blood.
2. ☑ a. Because I believe you are under the influence of **alcohol**, you have the choice of taking a breath, or urine test.
   ☐ b. Because I believe you are under the influence of **alcohol and drugs**, you have a choice of taking a breath, blood or urine test.
3. If you refuse to submit to, or fail to complete a test, your driving privilege will be suspended for 1 year or revoked for 2 or 3 years. A second offense within ten years of a separate violation of driving under the influence, including such a charge reduced to reckless driving, or vehicular manslaughter will result in a 2-year revocation.
4. Refusal or failure to complete a test may be used against you in court. Refusal or failure to complete a test will also result in a fine and imprisonment if this arrest results in a conviction of driving under the influence.
5. You do not have the right to talk to an attorney or have an attorney present before stating whether you will submit to a test, before deciding which test to take, or during the test.

☑ Refusal.	Admonition Given By JACKSON	Serial # 34076

ADDITIONAL CHEMICAL TEST ADMONITION (30293 GVC)

1. If you take a breath test, a sample will **NOT** be saved and you or your attorney will **NOT** have a breath sample to test for alcohol content.
2. If you want any remaining sample saved for your use, you must choose to take a blood or urine test which will be retained at no cost to you and may be tested by any party in any criminal prosecution.
   Advised ☐ Before test was chosen.
       ☐ After the breath test. Do you wish to take a blood or urine test?

Response: REFUSED	Admonition Given By JACKSON	Serial # 34076

DISPOSITION OF DEFENDANT:

☑ MPD JAIL   ☐ COUNTY JAIL   ☐ JUVENILE HALL   ☐ NOTIFY WARRANT

REPORTING OFFICER JACKSON	SERIAL NUMBER 34076	DATE 10/5/C.Y.-1	SIGNATURE Sam Jackson

SILVERADO POLICE DEPARTMENT

DRIVING-UNDER-THE-INFLUENCE ARREST REPORT (CONTINUATION)

Arrestee's Name (Last, First, M.I.)	MPD Case No.
GRIFFORD, SUNNY X.	73519-391

Are you sick or injured? ☐ Yes ☑ No	Are you diabetic or epileptic? ☐ Yes ☑ No	Do you take Insulin or Dilantin? ☐ Yes ☑ No
Do you have any physical defects? ☐ Yes ☑ No	Are you under the care of a doctor/dentist? ☐ Yes ☑ No	Are you taking any medication? ☐ Yes ☑ No

Corrective lenses: ☐ Glasses ☐ Contacts ☑ None	When did you last sleep? LAST NIGHT	How long? 7.5 HOURS	What have you eaten today? BREAKFAST, LUNCH, DINNER

What have you been drinking? WINE, MARTINIS	How much? 5 GLASSES WINE, 2 MARTINIS	Where? RESIDENCE	Time of first drink? 17:00 HOURS	Time of last drink? 21:00 HOURS

FIELD SOBRIETY TEST ADMONITION (To be given only in case of a refusal to submit to test.)
The Field Sobriety Test is given to determine the extent to which alcohol and/or drugs have impaired your mental or physical processes. Your refusal to submit to all or part of the test WILL be commented on in court and a jury will be instructed that your refusal may show a consciousness of guilt on your part.

Will you take the Field Sobriety Test now?

Response: __I HAVEN'T BEEN DRIVING, BUT FINE.__	Admonition Given By: JACKSON	Serial # 34076

Officer: __JACKSON__ Time: __22:15 HOURS__	Location: Surface/Lighting/Weather FLAT / OVERHEAD LIGHTING / CLEAR

ROMBERG / FINGER TO NOSE	HEEL TO TOE	LEG RAISE
R F ☐ ☐ 1. SWAYS WHILE BALANCING (Side-to-side or front-to-back while feet do not move.) ☑ ☐ 2. MOVES FEET TO BALANCE (Moves feet from original position.) ☐ ☐ 3. USES ARMS TO BALANCE (Raises arms 6 inches or more from side.) ☐ ☐ 4. FALLS (Falls away from standing position. Moves one or both feet.) ☐ ☐ 5. OPENS EYES (Cannot maintain balance and keep eyes closed.) ☐ ☐ 6. CANNOT TILT HEAD (Cannot maintain balance with head tiled back.) ☐ 7. UNABLE TO TOUCH TIP OF NOSE WITH EACH ATTEMPT ☐ ☐ 8. UNABLE TO DO THE TEST	☑ 1. LOSES BALANCE DURING INSTRUCTIONS (Does not maintain heel-to-toe position throughout instructions.) ☐ 2. STARTS BEFORE INSTRUCTIONS ARE FINISHED (Does not wait until told to begin as per the instructions.) ☑ 3. STOPS WHILE WALKING (Pauses several seconds after a step.) ☑ 4. DOES NOT TOUCH HEEL-TO-TOE (Leaves 1/2 inch or more between heel & toe on any step and/or fails to walk even with line.) ☑ 5. STEPS OFF THE LINE (Steps so that one foot is entirely off of line.) ☑ 6. USES ARMS TO BALANCE (Raises one or both arms 6 inches or more from sides to assist with balance.) ☑ 7. LOSES BALANCE WHILE TURNING (Removes pivot foot from the line while turning.) ☑ 8. INCORRECT NUMBER OF STEPS ☐ 9. UNABLE TO DO THE TEST	Lft. Rgt. ☑ ☑ 1. SWAYS WHILE BALANCING (Side-to-side or back-and-forth motion while maintaining one leg stand position.) ☑ ☑ 2. USES ARMS TO BALANCE (Moves arms 6 or more inches from side to maintain balance.) ☐ ☑ 3. HOPPING (Able to keep one leg raised but resorts to hopping to maintain balance.) ☑ ☑ 4. PUTS FOOT DOWN (Not able to maintain position putting raised foot down one or more times during 30 second count.) ☐ ☐ 5. UNABLE TO DO THE TEST **ALPHABET** ☐ 1. INCORRECT ALPHABET (Letters misplaced or omitted.)

REPORTING OFFICER JACKSON	SERIAL # 34076	DATE 10/5/C.Y.-1	SIGNATURE Sam Jackson

SILVERADO POLICE DEPARTMENT

DRIVING-UNDER-THE-INFLUENCE ARREST REPORT (CONTINUATION) (initialed: *S.J.*)

FIELD SOBRIETY TEST INFO SHEET

GENERAL INSTRUCTIONS

I explained and demonstrated each FST prior to asking Mr. Grifford to complete the test. I further explained that I would tell him when to begin each test and if he had any questions on how to perform the tests to ask, so I may further explain the test.

ROMBERG

Mr. Grifford was instructed to assume a modified stance of attention with his heels together and his head held slightly back for 30 seconds.

FINGER TO NOSE

Mr. Grifford was instructed to tilt his head back, close his eyes, extend his arms and then, on my command, touch his finger to his nose.

HEEL TO TOE

Mr. Grifford was instructed to walk an imaginary straight line placing the heel of one shoe at the toe of the other. He was instructed to take seven steps forward and then seven steps back.

LEG RAISE

Mr. Grifford was instructed to stand with one leg raised about six inches from the ground. He was then instructed to count aloud to 30 while keeping the leg off the ground. He was then instructed to repeat the test with the other leg.

ALPHABET

Mr. Grifford was instructed to recite the alphabet.

SILVERADO POLICE DEPARTMENT

DRIVING-UNDER-THE-INFLUENCE ARREST REPORT (CONTINUATION)

REPORT TYPE: **SUSPECT INTERVIEW**
OFFICER REPORTING: SAM JACKSON (initialed: *S.J.*)
DATE: 10/6/C.Y.-1

At the station at 1:00 hours, I read Sunny Grifford his Miranda rights from my Silverado Police Department issued Miranda card. He agreed to speak with me.

He reported he had been involved in a minor traffic collision at approximately 5:35 p.m. on October 4th as he was exiting the Silverado High School parking lot. Grifford reported he ran a stop sign and hit a large, black car, causing a dent in the side of the other car, and some scratches in the paint on Grifford's own car. Grifford related that he didn't want to submit the accident to his insurance, so instead offered the other driver $500 cash from his wallet to "make things right." Grifford related that the other driver agreed, and after the money was paid, Grifford continued on home.

I asked Grifford if he had any information about the other driver. He stated that he didn't. The two did not exchange information. I asked Grifford for a description of the driver. He related it was a young woman with blonde hair. I then asked him for a more detailed description of the other vehicle. He stated he didn't remember anything about the other car except that it was a black SUV.

I then asked Grifford about the evening of October 5th. He related he had a "date" with his wife that evening. He stated he went to the grocery store and ran a few errands that afternoon and arrived home at approximately 4:00. He and his wife made dinner and spent the evening watching movies on the couch. He related he was in the kitchen getting another "Manhattan" martini when he noticed this officer standing in front of his residence and came out to investigate.

Mr. Grifford related that he and his wife had been drinking wine and martinis that evening, but that he had not been out of the house since approximately 4:00 p.m.

I asked Mr. Grifford for his driver's license to complete my paperwork. A copy of that license is attached as Attachment "A" to this report. I noticed his license had expired prior to this date. I asked Grifford about this and he stated he had been "really busy with work and hadn't gotten around to renewing it." He reported that until he got his license renewed, he was only doing essential driving.

I asked Grifford if he knew Ms. Kevins. He dropped his head into his hands and did not speak. After several minutes he told me that he did know her, and that they are both math teachers at Silverado High School.

I inquired as to the nature of their relationship. Again, Grifford dropped his head into his hands and did not speak. Finally, he looked up and said that up until six weeks ago he and Ms. Kevins had been "dating," but that he had broken it off because he wanted to make his marriage work.

I asked him how Ms. Kevins had reacted to his breaking off the relationship and he said that she was irate and threatened to tell his wife. Grifford then volunteered that, to his knowledge, she had not told his wife. He also said that the only time he had seen Ms. Kevins during the past six weeks was at school. Grifford volunteered that on three occasions since the breakup he has received anonymous, threatening notes in his box at work. He said that he kept one of those notes. At that point Grifford instructed his wife to retrieve his jacket from their house. When she returned, Grifford took a note from a jacket pocket and handed it to me. A copy of which is Attachment "B" to this report.

I asked Grifford if Ms. Kevins was fabricating the hit and run story. He replied, "Obviously she is, I haven't been out of my house since the afternoon. This is her getting back at me."

Grifford was continued in custody for approximately three more hours until his wife arranged his bail.

Attachment "A"

GOLDEN

DRIVERS LICENSE

F6063257

SUNNY X. GRIFFORD
997 N. 52ND ST.
SILVERADO, GOLDEN 90392

CLASS: C

SEX: M   EYES: xxx
HEIGHT: x' x"   HAIR: xxx
WEIGHT: xxx   DOB: 9/30/C.Y. -31

Sunny X. Grifford

EXPIRES: 9/30/C.Y. -2

Attachment "B"

YOU'RE A TERRIBLE PERSON! I'LL MAKE YOU SORRY!

SILVERADO POLICE DEPARTMENT

DRIVING-UNDER-THE-INFLUENCE ARREST REPORT (CONTINUATION)

REPORT TYPE: **WITNESS INTERVIEW, SONIA GRIFFORD**
OFFICER REPORTING: **SAM JACKSON** (initialed: *S.J.*)
DATE: **10/6/C.Y.-1**

Mrs. Grifford related that she and her husband had scheduled a "date" for the evening in question. She stated the two had been married for six years and they had been fighting a lot and had recently made a commitment to work on their marriage. One of the things they decided to do was make a standing "date" on Saturday nights.

She stated that Mr. Grifford went to the grocery store to buy food and alcohol for dinner and arrived back around 4:00 p.m. At that time, the two began preparing dinner and remained in the house for the remainder of the evening.

I asked Mrs. Grifford if she had noticed any damage on her husband's car. She reported that the previous day her husband had been in an accident on his way home from work, but had dealt with the matter in cash so it wouldn't go on their insurance.

I asked Mrs. Grifford why Donna Kevins would accuse her husband of hit and run. Mrs. Grifford related that she (Mrs. Gifford) works as an administrative assistant at Silverado High School, and stated that Kevins is crazy and is always causing trouble with the other teachers at Silverado High. I asked if there was any history of trouble between Kevins and her husband and she told me that Kevins had made some romantic overtures in the past toward her husband but that he had not reciprocated.

She then volunteered that Kevins has a reputation at the school as a "nut job" and is always flirting "with anyone in pants." She also told me that last spring, Kevins had a breakdown in her classroom and subsequently took a two month leave for psychiatric reasons. Mrs. Gifford gave me a copy of a letter that she claims she retrieved from Kevins's personnel file. The letter, dated 6/7/C.Y.-1, appears to be from Dr. Garret Strong and is Kevins's "Psychological Evaluation Report." I have attached this letter to the report.

Reviewed and verified by: <u>Sonia Grifford</u>
                                        Sonia Grifford

Attachment "A"

Silverado Medical Group, LLC

Dr. Garret Strong, MD
1376 Oaks Drive
Suite #7
Silverado, GO 99876

6/7/C.Y.-1

Superintendent:

As requested, here is a Psychological Evaluation Report to be placed in Donna Kevins's personnel file at Silverado High School.

The purpose of this Report is to assess Ms. Kevins following a minor work-related breakdown. I observed Ms. Kevins after a mandatory two month leave from her employment at Silverado High School which was imposed because of her breakdown. Based upon my interview and initial observations of Ms. Kevins, I am of the opinion that she is mentally fit to return to work, though I do have a few concerns. During the interview, Ms. Kevins exhibited some of the classic signs of Histrionic Personality Disorder. Histrionic Personality Disorder is a personality disorder characterized by excessive emotionality and attention-seeking behaviors.

My interview with Ms. Kevins uncovered that she may have difficulty gauging the appropriate level of intimacy in her relationships, and may sometimes project her own fantasies onto the behaviors and motivations of others. However, my interview with Ms. Kevins was far too short to make any conclusive diagnosis.

I reiterate that Ms. Kevins is fully capable of returning to work and will in no way be a risk in the workplace. In fact, based on my interview I expect that she will be a highly effective employee. I do recommend, nonetheless, that she be encouraged to seek further counseling for her own personal benefit.

Garret Strong
Dr. Garrett Strong

SILVERADO POLICE DEPARTMENT

DRIVING-UNDER-THE-INFLUENCE ARREST REPORT (CONTINUATION)

REPORT TYPE:	**WITNESS INTERVIEW, DONNA KEVINS**
OFFICER REPORTING:	**SAM JACKSON** (initialed: *S.J.*)
DATE:	**10/6/C.Y.-1**

Ms. Kevins was extremely agitated after arriving at the Grifford residence. I delayed my interview until she regained her composure. I asked Ms. Kevins about what had happened that evening. She told me that she was driving home alone from the Alamo Bar and Grill at about 9:30 that evening when Grifford pulled up alongside her vehicle at the stop light at Borchard and Las Brisas. She related that when she looked over at Grifford he appeared to try to roll down his window, but did not seem to remember how to do so. Instead, he winked at her and blew her a kiss. Kevins related that when the light turned green, Grifford "stepped on it" and swerved into her car, striking her left side fender. She said she almost lost control of her car, but managed to come to a stop. She stated that Grifford gave her the finger and sped away. Kevins immediately called the Silverado Police Department on her cell phone and reported the hit and run accident. Kevins said she was pretty shook up and drove immediately home. But after thinking about it, she got madder and madder. She then called the police dispatch and identified Grifford as the driver, and then drove to Grifford's residence to confront him.

Kevins explained that she and Grifford had had an affair that lasted about six months, but that she broke it off about a month ago. She said that Grifford has been stalking her ever since. I asked her what she meant by this and she stated that Mr.

Grifford has been calling her cell phone at all hours. She also stated that Mr. Grifford has been following her home and showing up at places where he knows she will be. She stated that is what must have happened tonight, "he must have watched me leave the Alamo and then followed me."

In response to what I heard from Ms. Kevins, I subpoenaed Mr. Grifford's cellular phone records for all calls placed to Ms. Kevins's cellular phone, which record is Attachment "A" to this report.

I noticed there was a medium-sized scrape on the left side of Kevins's car.

Reviewed and verified by: *Donna Kevins*
Donna Kevins

Attachment "A"

Record of Cell Phone Calls Made to 392-5039 from 556-1632

Date: 9/5/C.Y.-1 – 10/5/C.Y.-1

Date	Time	Minutes
9/5	9:00 a.m.	1
9/12	4:03 a.m.	1
9/26	1:03 a.m.	2
9/30	4:40 p.m.	1
10/2	2:32 a.m.	39
10/3	5:23 p.m.	3
10/4	1:43 a.m.	9

Sunny Grifford's cell phone number is 556-1632.
Donna Kevin's cell phone number is 392-5039

Jury Instructions

Members of the jury, I thank you for your attention during this trial. Please pay attention to the instructions I am about to give you.

In this case, Sunny Grifford is accused of driving under the influence of alcohol and leaving the scene of an accident. Every person who, while under the influence of any alcoholic beverage, drives a vehicle, is guilty of driving under the influence, a violation of the Golden Vehicle Code section 502, a misdemeanor.

A person is under the influence of any alcoholic beverage when, as a result of drinking an alcoholic beverage, his physical or mental abilities are impaired so that he no longer has the ability to drive a vehicle with the caution characteristic of a sober person of ordinary prudence under the same or similar circumstances.

Every person who as the driver of any vehicle is knowingly involved in an accident must:

1. Immediately stop the vehicle at the scene of the accident;

2. Give his name, current residence address, and the registration number of the vehicle he is driving to the person struck or the driver or occupants of any vehicle collided with, and to any traffic or police officer at the scene of the accident, and the driver shall upon request, if available, exhibit his driver's license to such persons and officer; and

3. If there is no traffic or police officer at the scene of the accident to whom to give the information required, without delay, report the accident to the nearest office of the Department of Golden Highway Patrol or office of a duly authorized police authority and submit with the report the information required in item 2.

A willful failure of a driver of any vehicle to comply with any one of these duties when involved in an accident is a violation of the Golden Vehicle Code section 392, a misdemeanor. The word "knowingly" means that the driver of the vehicle involved knew that an accident had occurred, and knew that he was involved in the accident.

In order to prove a violation of Golden Vehicle Code section 392, each of the following elements must be proved:

1. A person, while driving a motor vehicle, was involved in an accident;

2. That person knew that an accident had occurred and knew that he was involved in the accident;

3   That person willfully failed to perform one or more of the following duties:

a.   To immediately stop at the scene of the accident; or

b.   To give his name, current residence address, the registration number of the vehicle to the person injured or to the driver or occupants of the other vehicle, if any, or to any traffic or police officer at the scene of the accident and though requested, or failed to show his available driver's license.

Sunny Grifford has entered a plea of not guilty. This means you must presume or believe that Sunny Grifford is innocent. This presumption stays with Sunny Grifford as to each material allegation in the indictment through each stage of the trial until it has been overcome by the evidence to the exclusion of and beyond a reasonable doubt.

To overcome Defendant's presumption of innocence, the State has the burden of proving that:

1.   The crime with which Defendant is charged was committed; and

2.   Defendant is the person who committed the crime.

Defendant is not required to prove anything.

Whenever the words "reasonable doubt" are used, you must consider the following: A reasonable doubt is not a mere possible doubt, because everything relating to human affairs is open to some possible or imaginary doubt. It is that state of the case which, after the entire comparison and consideration of all the evidence, leaves the minds of the jurors in that condition that they cannot say they feel an abiding conviction of the truth of the charge. It is to the evidence introduced during this trial, and to it alone, that you are to look for that proof. A reasonable doubt as to the guilt of Defendant may arise from the evidence, a conflict in the evidence, or a lack of evidence. If you have a reasonable doubt, you should find Defendant not guilty. If you have no reasonable doubt, you should find Defendant guilty.

You must decide this case based only on the law and the evidence. It is up to you to decide what evidence is reliable. You should use your common sense in deciding which evidence is reliable and which evidence should not be relied upon in considering your verdict. You may find some of the evidence not reliable or less reliable than other evidence.

A witness is a person who has knowledge related to this case. You will have to decide whether you believe each witness and how important each witness's testimony is to the case. You may believe all, part, or none of a witness's testimony. In deciding whether to believe a witness's testimony, you may consider, among other factors, the following:

1.   Did the witness seem to have an opportunity to see and know the things about which the witness testified?

2.   Did the witness seem to have an accurate memory?

3.   Was the witness honest and straightforward in answering the attorneys' questions?

4.   Did the witness have some interest in how the case should be decided?

5.   Does the witness's testimony agree with the other testimony and other evidence in this case?

6.   Has the witness been offered or received any money, preferred treatment, or other benefit in order to get the witness to testify?

7.   Had any pressure or threat been used against the witness that affected the truth of the witness's testimony?

8.   Did the witness at some other time make a statement that is inconsistent with the testimony he or she gave in court?

9.   Was it proved that the witness had been convicted of a crime?

You may rely upon your own conclusions about the witnesses. A juror may believe or disbelieve all or any part of the evidence or the testimony of any witness.

Defendant in this case has become a witness. You should apply the same rules to consideration of his testimony that you apply to the testimony of the other witnesses.

There are some general rules that apply to your deliberations. You must follow these rules in order to return a lawful verdict:

1.   You must follow the law as it is set out in these instructions. If you fail to follow the law, your verdict will be a miscarriage of justice.

2.   This case must be decided only upon the evidence that you have heard from the answers of the witnesses and have seen in the form of exhibits and these instructions.

3.   This case must not be decided for or against anyone because you feel sorry for anyone or are angry at anyone.

4.   Remember the lawyers are not on trial. Your feelings about them should not influence your decision in this case.

5.   Your duty is to determine if Defendant has been proven guilty or not. It is the judge's job to determine the proper sentence if Defendant is found guilty.

6.   Whatever verdict you render must be unanimous; that is, each juror must agree to the same verdict. The verdict must be the verdict of each juror, as well as of the jury as a whole.

7.   It is entirely proper for a lawyer to talk to a witness about what testimony the witness would give if called to the courtroom. The witness should not be discredited for talking to a lawyer about his or her testimony.

8.   Your verdict should not be influenced by feelings of prejudice, bias, or sympathy. Your verdict must be based on the evidence and the law contained in these instructions.

Deciding a proper verdict is exclusively your job. I cannot participate in that decision in any way. Please disregard anything I may have said or done that made you think I preferred one verdict over another.

Only one verdict may be returned as to the crime charged. The verdict must be in writing and the verdict form has been prepared for you. It is as follows:

[READ VERDICT FORM]

In just a few moments, you will be taken to the jury room by the bailiff. The first thing you should do is elect a foreperson who will preside over your deliberations like the chairperson of a meeting. It is the foreperson's job to sign and date the verdict form when all of you have agreed on a verdict in this case and to bring the verdict back to the courtroom when you return.

In closing, let me remind you that it is important that you follow the law spelled out in these instructions in deciding your verdicts. Even if you do not like the laws, you must apply them. There are no other laws that apply to this case.

IN THE CIRCUIT COURT OF THE SEVENTH JUDICIAL CIRCUIT

IN AND FOR LEAD COUNTY, STATE OF GOLDEN

CRIMINAL DIVISION

STATE OF GOLDEN	)	
	)	
	)	
v.	)	CASE NO: CR 94-663
	)	
SUNNY GRIFFORD,	)	
Defendant	)	
	)	

VERDICT

We, the jury, find as to Defendant, Sunny Grifford, as follows:

As to Count I – Driving Under the Influence in violation of section 502 of the Golden

Vehicle Code:

_____   Guilty

_____   Not Guilty

As to Count II – Leaving the Scene of an Accident in violation of section 392 of the

Golden Vehicle Code:

_____   Guilty

_____   Not Guilty

So say we all.

_____

Foreperson of the Jury

_____

Date

Chapter 7

SAM SPENCER v. TERESA MORE

Sam Spencer

v.

Teresa More

(negligent entrustment accident)

**IN THE CIRCUIT COURT OF THE
THIRTEENTH JUDICIAL CIRCUIT
IN AND FOR LEAD COUNTY, STATE OF GOLDEN
CIVIL DIVISION**

SAM SPENCER	)	CASE NO: CV 63-956
Plaintiff	)	
	)	
	)	
	)	
v.	)	
	)	
TERESA MORE	)	
Defendant	)	
	)	

**IN THE CIRCUIT COURT OF THE
THIRTEENTH JUDICIAL CIRCUIT
IN AND FOR LEAD COUNTY, STATE OF GOLDEN
CIVIL DIVISION**

SAM SPENCER	)	CASE NO: CV 63-956
Plaintiff	)	
	)	COMPLAINT FOR NEGLIGENT
	)	ENTRUSTMENT
v.	)	
	)	
TERESA MORE	)	JURY TRIAL DEMANDED
Defendant	)	
	)	

COMPLAINT

Plaintiff, Sam Spencer, sues Defendant, Teresa More, and alleges:

1. Plaintiff and Defendant are residents of Lead County, therefore, jurisdiction is proper in this Court.

2. On April 3, C.Y. -1, Plaintiff, Sam Spencer, while riding his bicycle, was struck by a motor vehicle negligently operated by Karrie Braves, owned by Defendant Teresa More. Braves failed to exercise due care while operating said motor vehicle. Braves' failure to exercise due care caused her SUV to hit Plaintiff. Plaintiff was operating his bicycle in a reasonable and prudent manner at the time of the accident.

3. Said accident was the proximate cause of Plaintiff's injuries and property damage.

4. Defendant, Teresa More, is liable for the actions of Karrie Braves under the doctrine of negligent entrustment. Defendant, Teresa More, negligently entrusted her

vehicle to Karrie Braves, whom she knew or should have known to be an unlicensed, incompetent, or reckless driver.

WHEREFORE, Plaintiff prays for judgment against Defendant in an amount to be proven at trial, together with interest, costs, attorney's fees, and such other relief as the Court deems just.

Julian Rivera
_____

JULIAN RIVERA
816 Congress Ave., Suite 1700
Sacramento, State of Golden 90263
Golden State Bar 0001118886
Attorney for Plaintiff

IN THE CIRCUIT COURT OF THE
THIRTEENTH JUDICIAL CIRCUIT
IN AND FOR LEAD COUNTY, STATE OF GOLDEN
CIVIL DIVISION

SAM SPENCER
Plaintiff

v.

TERESA MORE
Defendant

)
)
)
)
)
)
)
)
)
)

CASE NO: CV 63-956

ANSWER TO COMPLAINT FOR
NEGLIGENT ENTRUSTMENT

ANSWER

Defendant, Teresa More, answers Plaintiff's Complaint as follows:

1. Defendant admits all allegations in paragraph 1.

2. Defendant denies all allegations in paragraph 2.

3. Defendant denies all allegations in paragraph 3.

4. Defendant denies all allegations in paragraph 4.

Defendant, Teresa More, asserts the following affirmative defenses:

5. At the time of the accident on April 3, C.Y. -1, Plaintiff was negligent in that it was nighttime and Plaintiff was not wearing any reflective clothing. Plaintiff's failure to wear such reflective clothing was the proximate cause of the accident and Plaintiff's injuries.

6. At the time of the accident on April 3, C.Y. -1, Plaintiff was negligent in that he was riding his bicycle against traffic. Moreover, Plaintiff was negligent in that

he was riding his bicycle in the lane designated for motor vehicle traffic. These actions were the proximate cause of the accident and Plaintiff's injuries.

7. On April 3, C.Y. -1, Plaintiff's faculties were impaired due to ingesting alcoholic beverages. Plaintiff's impairment was the proximate cause of the accident and his injuries.

WHEREFORE, having answered Plaintiff's complaint, Defendant prays that the same be dismissed, that judgment be entered in favor of Defendant, that Plaintiff take nothing thereby, and that Defendant be awarded costs, attorney's fees and such other relief as to the Court deems just. Defendant demands a jury trial.

Mike Denton
_____
MIKE DENTON
982 Congress Ave., Suite 2500
Sacramento, State of Golden 90263
Golden State Bar 0001119997
Attorney for Defendant

Witness List

Witnesses for Plaintiff:

1. Sam Spencer *

2. Deputy Chris Cutler * *

Witnesses for Defendant:

1. Teresa More * * *

2. Gale Ruby * *

Each side must call both witnesses listed for their respective side in any order.

*   This witness must be a male.

* *   This witness may be either gender.

* * *   This witness must be a female.

This is a bifurcated trial on the issue of liability only.

Stipulations

1. Federal Rules of Evidence apply.

2. Each witness who gave a deposition did agree under oath at the outset of his/her deposition to give a full and complete description of what occurred and to correct the deposition for inaccuracies and completeness before signing the deposition.

3. All exhibits in the file are authentic and, unless otherwise noted, are the original of that document.

4. It is stipulated that the DMV records of Karrie Braves and Sam Spencer are certified copies and are admissible for all purposes.

5. Other than what appears in the officer's report or witness depositions, there is nothing exceptional or unusual about the background of any of the witnesses that would bolster or detract from their credibility.

6. All dates are denoted by C.Y. (current year) and C.Y.-1 indicating, for example, that the date is the current year minus one.

7. All pretrial motions shall be oral.

8. No party may "invent" witnesses or evidence not specifically mentioned in this problem.

9. "Beyond the record" is not a proper objection. Rather, attorneys shall use cross-examination as a means of challenging a witness whose testimony strays beyond the facts contained in the officer's report or deposition.

10. The plaintiff and defendant may call the two witnesses listed on their respective witness list. Each party may call a third witness by deposition or witness statement. Any such testimony is subject to objections pursuant to the Federal Rules of Evidence. If a witness is called by deposition or witness statement, the opposing party may cross-examine that witness by deposition or witness statement.

11. The Judge ruled on Defendant's pre-trial motion in limine that Exhibit 1, Karrie

Eugenia Braves's Golden Department of Motor Vehicles record, and Exhibit 2,

Karrie Eugenia Braves's Nevada Department of Motor Vehicles record, are

admissible.

12. The law is accurately set forth in the jury instructions.

Lead County Sheriff's   Department

Report: Incident Report

Report by: Deputy Chris Cutler, Badge Number 13208 (initialed: *CC*)

Date: April 12, C.Y. -1

Position/Department: Lead County Sheriff's Department, Investigator, Traffic Division

---

NOTIFICATION: I responded to a call about a fatal collision on April 3, C.Y. - 1 at 19:50 hours. All times, speeds and measurements are approximate, taken with LTI Laser using TDS Recon data collector and a Rol-A-Tape; critical speed scuff measurements were taken with fiber cloth and steel tape.

SCENE: As I arrived at the accident scene it was just turning to night. There were no streetlights. I activated several flares to direct traffic around the involved area. The collision occurred on Thousand Oaks Blvd., approximately a quarter mile west of Rancho Road in Pine City. Thousand Oaks Blvd. is an east/west commercial street that is approximately 64 feet wide, with two 11-foot traffic lanes eastbound and two 11-foot traffic lanes westbound. There is no median divider. There are 10-foot shoulders both east and west bound. There is no designated bike lane. The posted speed limit is 35 mph. The roadway surface is asphaltic concrete. The roadway is delineated by painted lines; there are dotted white lines that separate the east and westbound number one and two lanes and a double yellow line that separates east and westbound traffic.

A white Ford Explorer was facing southbound in the #2 westbound lane of Thousand Oaks Blvd. A bicycle was located on the northside sidewalk. Steve Goodman (DOB: September 4, C.Y. – 50) was standing beside the passenger's door of the Explorer. Goodman was assisting in providing first aid to the two occupants of the Explorer. I spoke with Goodman after the fire department relieved him. Goodman told me he works for the Federal Bureau of Prisons. Goodman said he did not see the collision take place. He drove up on the scene after the fact and felt he should provide first aid. Goodman said he checked on the driver, Karrie Braves, and felt that she was deceased. Goodman said he tried to check for a pulse on her neck, but did not feel any. Goodman then concentrated on passenger Teresa More. Goodman said he held her still and waited for paramedics to arrive.

On the sidewalk abutting the westbound lanes of Thousand Oaks Blvd. an individual later identified as Sam Spencer was being tended to by two unknown individuals. Spencer was lying on his back and was conscious. The bicycle was lying 10 feet east of Spencer.

Lead County Fire Department Truck #30 arrived on scene and began working on extricating the occupants of the Explorer and treating Spencer. Diagram 1 is a sketch of the area after the collision (see next page for diagram):

Diagram 1: Layout of area after collision

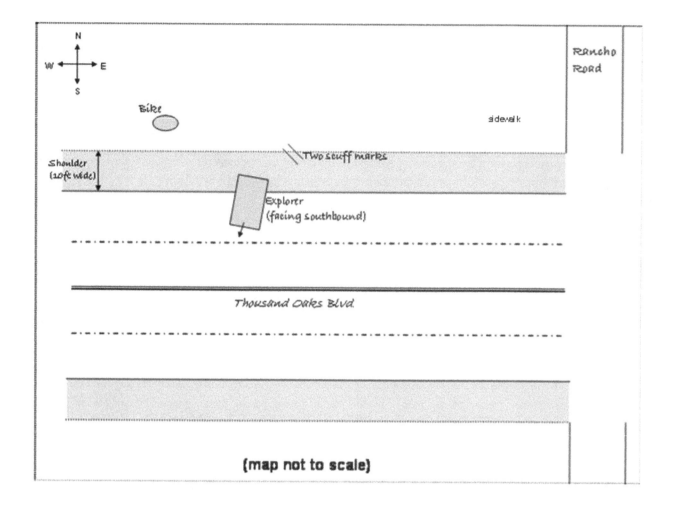

(map not to scale)

DAMAGE: The Explorer had contact damage along the right front side and extensive rollover damage. All three left side windows were shattered as well as the left side of the vehicle's windshield. The steering wheel was broken and free-turning.

The passenger side seatbelt was cut by emergency personnel, suggesting it was in use at the time of collision. Braves was still wearing her seatbelt when I arrived. I cut the seatbelt to allow the Coroner's office to remove Braves' body from the vehicle.

The bicycle was bent nearly in two, the handlebars bent back to within two inches of the frame. The front tire was found 44 feet from the bicycle's location.

PARTIES AND STATEMENTS: Karrie Braves was identified as the driver of the Explorer. American Medical Response paramedics pronounced Braves dead at the scene at 20:10 hours. The Lead County Medical Examiner was notified and responded to the scene. Braves' cause of death was determined to be multiple blunt force injuries.

I attempted to interview the passenger in the Explorer, Teresa More, at Mercy Hospital, where she was being examined after the accident. She was crying and, as best as I could make out, she said, "It's my fault, it's all my fault – I should have been more careful."

I was unable to interview the bicycle rider, Sam Spencer, at Mercy Hospital in that he was undergoing surgery.

FOLLOW-UP INVESTIGATION: Witnesses and parties described a third vehicle, a BMW, possibly involved in a "road rage" encounter with the Explorer prior to and at the time of the collision. In a media release my department asked for persons involved or witnesses to the collision to come forward. To this day no one has come forward. Witnesses also mentioned seeing a Lead County bus in the immediate vicinity of the accident.

After making several phone calls to the Lead County and the Golden State Department of Transportation, I located the driver of the bus that several witnesses spoke about. I spoke with the driver, Gale Ruby (DOB: December 31, C.Y.-48, lives at 25607 Calle Segundo in Rolling Hills, Golden State), on the telephone and he/she told me the following:

> He/She was westbound on Thousand Oaks Blvd., just east of Rancho Road, when he/she received a phone call from his/her supervisor asking if the headlights on his/her bus were on. Ruby told her supervisor that his/her lights were on but that she would pull over and check. As Ruby began to pull over just east of Rancho Road two cars were coming up alongside the left side of his/her bus and he/she could see them in his/her left side rear-facing mirror.

Ruby saw a vehicle that he/she described as a white
SUV, which he/she later confirmed was the aforementioned
Explorer and a little BMW car approaching "fairly fast." Ruby
said it looked like the two vehicles might have been
"involved." From his/her mirror she noticed that the SUV was
cutting off the BMW.

Ruby stated that as the two vehicles passed his/her
location, the Explorer was in the number two westbound lane
and that the BMW was in the number one westbound lane.
Just as the two vehicles passed his/her location the BMW
appeared to veer into the number two lane and the SUV looked
like it swerved to the right and then struck that guy on the bike.
The bike and rider went flying. After hitting the bike the
Explorer then jerked left, just missed the BMW and rolled.
Ruby stated he/she thought the two vehicles (the Explorer and
the BMW) were going no less than 45 miles per hour, probably
50 when they passed his/her location. The posted limit in this
portion of the road is 35 miles per hour.

I gave Ruby my phone number and asked him/her to have anyone
who may have been on the bus that day call me if they saw the collision. As
of 5/23/C.Y.-1, I have not received any phone calls.

One witness, who gave his name as Humberto Galves, told me he worked at
Enrique's Mexican Restaurant and that Spencer had just left the restaurant before the
accident. Galves told me that Spencer was "more or less a regular in the lounge at
Enrique's." Galves told me that Spencer had been drinking beer but that he "looked
kinda okay" when he left. Galves explained that he ran out to the street when he heard
the accident.

When I later attempted to contact Galves for my follow-up, he could not be
reached at the phone number he had left me. I also attempted to contact him at Enrique's
but was informed that he no longer worked there.

SKID AND SCUFF MARKS: I found two scuffmarks on the shoulder beginning seven
feet from the north curb, which were eight feet in length, traveling in a northwest
direction.

SPEED CALCULATIONS: Placing a 50-foot cord across the arc of the left front tire
scuffmark, I measured the middle ordinate of the critical speed scuff; I found the middle
ordinate to be 5 1/8 inches. Using the middle ordinate and the published track width of
the Explorer of 5.446 feet, I determined the radius of the critical speed scuff to be 609.28
feet. Using this radius and range of assigned drag factors of between .7 to .8, I calculated
the Explorer's speed to be between 54.98 miles per hour and 60.51 miles per hour.

SUMMARY: The Explorer was westbound on Thousand Oaks Blvd. in the number two lane. The Explorer struck the eastbound cyclist approximately six to seven feet from the north curb. The Explorer then took evasive action turning left and rolled the vehicle onto the passenger side continuing over onto an upright position.

CAUSE: Based on the information available at the time of this report, it appears that the Explorer was engaged in some manner of "road rage" incident with the non-involved driver of a BMW and while driving erratically and without devoting her full attention to the conditions ahead of her drove onto the westbound shoulder and struck the bicyclist. It is my determination as a traffic investigator for the past five years investigating approximately thirty traffic fatalities that the driver of the Explorer was the primary cause of the accident.

Deposition of Sam Spencer

Date: April 25, C.Y. - 1

Q: Before we talk about the accident I want to back up and fill in some of the personal

     information about you. You're married?

A: Yes, Karen and I have been married for 12 years.

Q: Any children?

A: Adam, he's ten.

Q: Okay, let's turn to the accident. Where were you going?

A: Home.

Q: Where were you coming from?

A: Enrique's – the Mexican restaurant there on Thousand Oaks Blvd.

Q: You were riding a bike that day?

A: We only lived a mile or so from the restaurant – it was good exercise.

Q: I understand – but I just want to be clear, you didn't possess a valid driver's license at the

     time.

A: That's right.

Q: Why was that?

A: I've got two DUI's – they pulled my license.

Q: When were those DUI's?

A: I don't see what this has to do with what happened to me.

Q: Please answer the question.

A: One was about three years ago and the second was about four months before the accident.

     I really screwed up by drinking and driving and I thank God that I didn't hurt anyone! I

     would never have forgiven myself if someone had gotten hurt because I was being stupid.

Q: I am handing you what has been marked as Exhibit A, which is report from the Golden

Department of Motor Vehicles. It has your name on it. Is the information on this report

correct?

A: Yes.

Q: Are you employed, Mr. Spencer?

A: No, I'm between jobs right now.

Q: Were you employed at the time of the accident?

A: No, I'd just been laid off from my job as a janitor at Amgen.

Q: Okay, let's turn to the events just prior to the accident. Had you had anything to drink at

Enrique's?

A: Probably two beers – since that second DUI I limit myself.

Q: You say probably two beers. Can you be any more specific than that?

A: I can tell you for certain I was only drinking beer – nothing else.

Q: But you can't pinpoint exactly how many beers?

A: I'm giving you my best guess.

Q: Were you drinking or visiting with anyone inside the bar?

A: No one in particular. I was just hanging out.

Q: What time did you arrive at the restaurant?

A: I don't know – maybe 3.

Q: The accident happened about a quarter 'til 8. Were you inside the restaurant that whole

time?

A: That's right – just hanging out.

Q: Let's turn to your bike. What kind of bike is it?

A: It's no kind of bike now. It was completely destroyed when she smashed into me.

Q: What kind of bike was it?

A: I don't know, one of those beach cruiser bikes with the fat wheels.

Q: Were there any lights on the bike?

A: No.

Q: Were you wearing any kind of reflective clothing that night?

A: It wasn't fully dark, it wasn't necessary. The sun had just gone down about a half hour before.

Q: If I understand things correctly, you were riding on the street just before the accident?

A: That's right. I was riding on the shoulder.

Q: So you were riding eastbound on the westbound side of the street?

A: Yeah, but I was hugging the curb. I was out of the traffic lanes in the shoulder and I wanted to see the on-coming traffic.

Q: How close would you say you were to the curb?

A: Couldn't have been more than a foot or two.

Q: As you were riding tell me what happened just before the accident.

A: Like I said, I was hugging the curb and then out of nowhere this big old white SUV is right in front of me.

Q: What happened then?

A: I'm not sure – I think I tried to jerk the bike to the left, but there wasn't enough time.

Q: What do you recall next?

A: Flying through the air. It was a weird feeling – it felt like I was going to die.

Q: Tell me about your injuries.

A: I had to have surgery because I went flying off my bike and broke my wrist, my

collarbone and I really screwed up my sciatic nerve.

Q: Tell us your condition now.

A: Well, as you can see I'm stuck in this wheelchair because I have a partial tear in my

sciatic nerve. Doc says he's not sure if I'll ever walk again.

Q: Tell us how these injuries have changed your life.

A: Where to even begin…I can't walk. I can't run with my son. I don't even think that I can

ever work as a janitor again. I have nightmares at night. My life will never be the same.

I have reviewed the transcript of my deposition. This is a complete and accurate account.

Sam Spencer
_____
Sam Spencer

GOLDEN DEPARTMENT OF MOTOR VEHICLES

Samuel Spencer

DOB: May 20, C.Y. – 35

Address: 4809 Hill Dr., Pine City, Golden 91358

Driver's License Number: 45B30498

Registered Vehicle: Honda Accord, License #4JEP493

April 15, C.Y. – 3	Golden Vehicular Code § 6641 (driving under the influence of alcohol)
	Pled guilty
	30 day suspended sentence effective this date
January 4, C.Y.-1	Golden Vehicular Code § 6641 (driving under the influence of alcohol)
	Pled guilty
	1 year suspended license effective this date

(EXHIBIT A)

Deposition of Teresa More

Date: April 24, C.Y. - 1

Q: Mrs. More, I know this is difficult for you, but we are here, of course, to examine the events of April 3rd. I first want to ask some questions about Ms. Braves, your daughter. Was she living with you at the time of the accident?

A: No, she had moved to Las Vegas in C.Y. – 3 and has lived there ever since.

Q: What kind of work was she in?

A: She was a showgirl at the Folies Bergere show at the Tropicana. She was always beautiful and it was nice she could make a living from her looks.

Q: Where in Las Vegas did she live?

A: Karrie lived at 2762 Pointer Ave. She was 27. Such a sweet girl. What a terrible waste this has all been.

Q: Why did she happen to be in Pine City at the time of the accident?

A: Every four weeks she got off for a few days and she would usually come home and stay with me and her dad.

Q: So she was visiting you on April 3rd?

A: Yes.

Q: As I understand it, during the accident Ms. Braves was driving your car and you were a front seat passenger, is that right?

A: That's right. She loved driving. Anywhere we went, she drove.

Q: You are aware that Karrie was convicted of vehicular manslaughter, aren't you?

A: I remember we went to court and they took her license.

Q: How old was she when she was convicted of manslaughter?

A: She was only 18 or 19.

Q: You knew the court took Karrie's license because of the manslaughter, right?

A: Yes, they suspended her license for five years.

Q: Did your daughter serve any time?

A: Yes, she went to jail for 60 days.

Q: After your daughter got out of jail, she moved to Nevada, right?

A: That's right. Because her license was suspended, I had to drive her everywhere and I got tired of it. I bought her a plane ticket and helped her get set up in Las Vegas. There, she wouldn't need a car because she could get a job close to her house and walk.

Q: Are you aware that your daughter's license was also suspended by Nevada?

A: I knew once she got her license back she got a couple of tickets.

Q: Mrs. More, weren't you aware that her license had been suspended?

A: She had been squabbling with the Nevada DMV.

Q: Was it your belief that her license had not been suspended?

A: I didn't know for certain either way. Karrie said she had gotten some speeding tickets and they were pestering her. It didn't seem fair to me.

Q: Was she a good driver?

A: Yes. Sometimes she drove a little fast for my taste, but I'd say she was a good driver.

Q: When you say fast, what do you mean?

A: Sometimes she could be a little impatient with drivers who weren't going as fast as she would have liked. But she was always in control and never reckless.

Q: Was she impatient on April 3rd, the day of the accident?

A: Karrie didn't do anything to cause the accident.

Q: Where were you and Karrie going that day?

A: To pick up my prescription and run a few other errands.

Q: Let's talk about the accident. As I understand, things got started at the four way stop at Erbes Street and Coleena Avenue here in Pine City. Is that right?

A: Yes, there is a four way stop sign there and we got there just a little bit before that other woman in that little BMW. Karrie slowed down and came to a stop. It wasn't a complete stop, but it was better than what that other woman did.

Q: What do you mean?

A: The little BMW raced up to the intersection and clearly got there after Karrie, but jetted out in front of us. Karrie was rolling into the intersection and had to hit the brakes so we didn't hit her. After that happened, Karrie pulled behind the BMW and started tailing her. Karrie was upset about being cut off, she had been anxious to get home and when the woman in the BMW flipped her off, she just had it.

Q: When did the woman in the BMW flip Karrie off?

A: Just after she made her right turn at the four-way stop at Erbes and Coleena. That's when she cut us off.

Q: Did the woman do anything else?

A: She was probably yelling at us, but all of our windows were up, so I didn't hear anything.

Q: What did Karrie do?

A: Karrie didn't swear in front of me, but she said under her breath, "That bitch." Then, she just backed off.

Q: What happened next?

A: We came up to the light at Thousand Oaks Blvd. and both of us turned right. Karrie followed the BMW for a bit, and then pulled beside that woman in the BMW.

Q: So both cars were traveling west on Thousand Oaks?

A: Yes.

Q: Which lane was each car in?

A: That woman in the other car was in the fast lane and we were in the slow lane.

Q: What happened next?

A: Just when we went past a bus, the woman swerved right at us and Karrie turned away to keep from getting hit. Then, we hit that poor man on his bike. Next thing I remember, we were screeching and rolling over.

Q: Did you say anything when you saw the man on the bike?

A: I didn't have time.

Q: What do you remember next?

A: When we stopped rolling, I looked over at Karrie and just knew that something horrible had happened. A mother knows these things. I couldn't move much. I started to breathe heavily and then someone came over and tried to keep me calm. The paramedics arrived. I kept asking about Karrie. They were only working on getting me out of the car. I told them, "Stop, work on Karrie, she's so young, she has her whole life in front of her." They ignored me. I knew she was dead. If not, they would have been trying to save her too.

Q: How fast was Karrie driving at the time of the accident?

A: I don't know.

Q: What happened to the BMW?

A: I have no idea. And to think she was the one who started it all.

Q: Do you recall telling the paramedics "it's all my fault"?

A: Not really. I was probably thinking that if I had been driving this would not have happened. I mean, if it had been me behind the wheel, I would be dead and Karrie would still be alive. She had so much of her life ahead of her.

Q: Mrs. More, wouldn't you agree that if your daughter had not been so concerned with the driver of the BMW that she would have been able to avoid the accident?

A: My daughter is dead and I can't walk because that woman tried to hit us. We were where we were supposed to be, that other car wasn't.

I have reviewed the transcript of my deposition. This is a complete and accurate account.

Teresa More

Teresa More

Deposition of Gale Ruby

Date: April 28, C.Y. – 1

Q: Mr./Ms. Ruby, I understand you drive a bus. Is that correct?

A: I've been a bus driver for Golden State for eighteen years.

Q: I suspect you have seen a lot of strange and peculiar things as a bus driver.

A: More than I like to think about.

Q: Mr./Ms. Ruby, I want to turn to the accident you witnessed on April 3·rd. What time did you come on duty that day?

A: I started at 4:00 in the afternoon.

Q: What route were you driving?

A: I was on my standard route that day. I run from Pine City into the west end of the San Fernando Valley. It is a 33-mile loop.

Q: So that route takes you along Thousand Oaks Blvd. in Pine City?

A: I am generally in the vicinity of where the accident happened a little after 7:45 p.m. Give or take.

Q: So just to be clear, you were westbound on Thousand Oaks Blvd. about 7:45 on April 3rd?

A: That's right.

Q: What was the first thing that drew your attention?

A: Well, I had just finished pulling over to make sure my headlights were on when I noticed in my side mirror two cars coming up from behind me. So they would have been traveling westbound.

Q: What drew your attention to these cars?

A: They appeared – how can I say this – they appeared to be involved.

Q: Tell me what you mean.

A: The sports car kept cutting in front of the SUV and then rapidly accelerating.

Q: Describe the two cars.

A: Like I said, one was a sporty little BMW and the other was a white SUV.

Q: Over what period of time were you able to observe their interaction?

A: I can't tell. I guess it couldn't have been too long. Maybe 10 seconds.

Q: All the time they were coming in your direction as you were traveling westbound?

A: That's right.

Q: What happened next?

A: After confirming that my headlights were on, I begin to pull away from the curb. As I was pulling away from the curb the SUV nearly sideswiped me. It looked like the SUV driver was trying to avoid being hit by the sports car. I had to pull to my right to avoid a collision.

Q: What happened next?

A: Oh, it was awful. Just a little bit after they passed me the SUV collided with someone on a bicycle who was coming from the other direction. I didn't even see the guy on the bike until the last minute. Looked like he was right out in the traffic lane.

Q: What happened next?

A: Then, the SUV jerked left and rolled over. I knew right away that these were going to be serious injuries. It was just sickening.

Q: At the time the SUV struck the man on the bike, can you estimate the SUV's speed?

A: I can't say for certain, but I guess 45, 50 miles per hour.

I have reviewed the transcript of my deposition. This is a complete and accurate account.

Gale Ruby

Gale Ruby

GOLDEN DEPARTMENT OF MOTOR VEHICLES

Karrie Eugenia Braves

DOB: January 19, C.Y. – 28

Address: 582 Sparks Avenue, Pine City, Golden 91362

Registered Vehicle: No vehicle currently registered.

April 15, C.Y. – 8   Golden State Vehicular Code section 191 (misdemeanor vehicular

manslaughter)[*]

Pled guilty

Served 60 days in county jail beginning this date

License suspended for five years beginning 60 days from this date

36 months probation

(EXHIBIT 1)

---

[*] Golden State Vehicular Code section 191 provides: "Misdemeanor vehicular manslaughter is the killing of a human being without malice aforethought, in the reckless driving of a vehicle, where the killing was either the proximate result of the commission of an unlawful act, not amounting to a felony, but without gross negligence, or the proximate result of the commission of a lawful act that might produce death, in an unlawful manner, but without gross negligence."

NEVADA DEPARTMENT OF MOTOR VEHICLES

Karrie Eugenia Braves

DOB: January 19, C.Y. - 28

Address: 2762 Pointer Avenue, Las Vegas, NV 89102

Registered Vehicle: Ford Contour, Nevada License #HT2TRT

April 25, C.Y. – 3   Nevada Vehicle Code section 14020 (speeding)

                        Pled guilty

                        Forfeited bail $540.00

March 17, C.Y. -2   Nevada Vehicle Code section 14020 (speeding)

                        Pled guilty

                        License suspended for 18 months effective this date.

(EXHIBIT 2)

Jury Instructions

Members of the jury, you have now heard all the evidence and the closing argument of the attorneys. It is my duty to instruct you on the law that applies to this case. You will have a copy of my instructions with you when you go to the jury room to deliberate.

I will now tell you the law that you must follow to reach your verdict. You must follow that law exactly as I give it to you, even if you disagree with it. If the attorneys have said anything different about what the law means, you must follow what I say. In reaching your verdict, you must not speculate about what I think your verdict should be from something I may have said or done.

Pay careful attention to all the instructions that I give you. All the instructions are important because together they state the law that you will use in this case. You must consider all of the instructions together. You must decide this case based only on the law and the evidence.

A witness is a person who has knowledge related to this case. You will have to decide whether you believe each witness and how important each witness's testimony is to the case. You may believe all, part, or none of a witness's testimony. In deciding whether to believe a witness's testimony, you may consider, among other factors, the following:

1.   How well did the witness see, hear, or otherwise sense what he or she described in court?

2.   How well did the witness remember and describe what happened?

3.   How did the witness look, act, and speak while testifying?

4.   Did the witness have any reason to say something that was not true? Did the witness show any bias or prejudice? Did the witness have a personal relationship with any of the parties involved in the case? Does the witness have a personal stake in how this case is decided?

5.   What was the witness's attitude toward this case or about giving testimony?

Sometimes a witness may say something that is not consistent with something else he or she said. Sometimes different witnesses will give different versions of what happened. People often forget things or make mistakes in what they remember. Also, two people may see the same event, but remember it differently. You may consider these differences, but do not decide that testimony is untrue just because it differs from other testimony.

However, if you decide that a witness has deliberately testified untruthfully about something important, you may choose not to believe anything that witness said. On the other hand, if you think the witness testified untruthfully about some things but told the truth about others, you may accept the part you think is true and ignore the rest.

You must not be biased in favor of or against any witness because of his or her race, sex, religion, occupation, sexual orientation or national origin.

Plaintiff has the burden in this case to prove each element of his claim by a preponderance of the evidence. The term "preponderance of the evidence" means the greater weight and degree of credible evidence admitted in this case. Simply put, Plaintiff must prove it is more likely than not that each element of his claim is true.

Plaintiff claims that he was harmed because defendant negligently permitted Karrie

Braves to use defendant's vehicle. To establish this claim, Plaintiff must prove all of the

following:

1. That Karrie Braves was negligent in operating the vehicle;

2. That Teresa More was an owner of the vehicle operated by Karrie Braves;

3. That Teresa More knew, or should have known, that Karrie Braves was

    incompetent or unfit to drive the vehicle;

4. That Teresa More permitted Karrie Braves to use the vehicle; and

5. That Karrie Braves' incompetence or unfitness to drive was a substantial factor in

    causing harm to Sam Spencer.

Negligence is the doing of something which a reasonably prudent person would

not do, or the failure to do something which a reasonably prudent person would do, under

circumstances similar to those shown by the evidence. It is the failure to use ordinary or

reasonable care. Ordinary or reasonable care is that care which persons of ordinary

prudence would use.

Liability is to be apportioned among persons whose fault caused or contributed to

a loss or injury, in proportion to their percentage of fault; as a result you are first required

to decide whether an actor's negligence was a proximate cause of Plaintiff's loss or

injury. Proximate cause is defined as a reasonably close causal connection between the

conduct and the resulting loss or injury. The law defines cause in its own particular way.

A cause of injury or harm is something that is a substantial factor in bringing about an injury

or harm.

There may be more than one cause of an injury. When negligent conduct of two or more persons contributes concurrently as a cause of an injury, the conduct of each is a cause of the injury regardless of the extent to which each contributes to the injury. A cause is concurrent if it was operative at the moment of injury and acted with another cause to produce the injury. It is no defense that the negligent conduct of a person who is not a party was also a cause of the injury.

In this case Defendant has filed a special defense alleging that Plaintiff's injuries were caused by Plaintiff's own negligence. Defendant must prove the elements of this special defense by a preponderance of the evidence. Specifically, Defendant must prove that Plaintiff was negligent and that such negligence was the cause of any of Plaintiff's injuries.

I have previously instructed you that Defendant is under the obligation to exercise the care which a reasonably prudent person would use under the circumstances. The plaintiff is also under the same obligation. A plaintiff is negligent if the plaintiff does something which a reasonably prudent person would not have done under similar circumstances; or fails to do that which a reasonably prudent person would have done under similar circumstances.

As I have explained, Plaintiff has claimed that the accident was caused by Defendant's negligence and Defendant has claimed that it was caused by Plaintiff's own negligence. If you find that negligence on the part of BOTH parties was a substantial factor in causing the accident, then the law is that Plaintiff can recover damages from Defendant only to the extent of Defendant's fault and may not recover damages to the extent that he himself was at fault.

If Plaintiff was more at fault than Defendant, then Plaintiff cannot recover any damages. Here is an example to make this rule clear: If Plaintiff was 20% at fault and Defendant was 80% at fault, Plaintiff recovers 80% of his damages. If Plaintiff was 50% at fault and Defendant was 50% at fault, Plaintiff recovers 50% of his damages. However, if Plaintiff was more than 50% at fault, he was more at fault than the party he has sued, and he recovers no damages.

Your foreperson shall preside over your deliberations. All jurors should participate in all deliberations and vote on each issue. The votes of ten or more jurors are required to reach a verdict. The verdict must be in writing and the verdict form has been prepared for you. It is as follows:

[READ VERDICT FORM]

In just a few moments, you will be taken to the jury room by the bailiff. The first thing you should do is elect a foreperson who will preside over your deliberations like the chairperson of a meeting. It is the foreperson's job to sign and date the verdict form when all of you have agreed on a verdict in this case and to bring the verdict back to the courtroom when you return.

In closing, let me remind you that it is important that you follow the law spelled out in these instructions in deciding your verdicts. There are no other laws that apply to this case.

**IN THE CIRCUIT COURT OF THE
THIRTEENTH JUDICIAL CIRCUIT
IN AND FOR LEAD COUNTY, STATE OF GOLDEN
CIVIL DIVISION**

Sam Spencer   )
      Plaintiff   )   **VERDICT FORM**
)
      vs   )   Case No. CV 63-956
)
Teresa More   )
      Defendant.   )

We, the Jury, answer the questions submitted to us as follows:

QUESTION NO. 1: Do you find by a preponderance of the evidence that Defendant was negligent in entrusting her vehicle to Karrie Braves?

        ANSWER: Yes _____   No _____

If you answered the above question "No", you will not answer the remaining questions, but will simply sign the Verdict. If you have answered Question No. 1 "Yes", then you must answer the remaining questions.

QUESTION NO. 2: Do you find by a preponderance of the evidence that Defendant's negligent entrustment was the cause of Plaintiff's injuries?

        ANSWER: Yes _____   No _____

QUESTION NO. 3:   Do you find by a preponderance of the evidence that Plaintiff's actions were the cause of his injuries?

        ANSWER: Yes _____   No _____

QUESTION NO. 4: To what percentage to you attribute the fault of each party?

        PLAINTIFF: _____ %
        DEFENDANT: _____ %

Dated this _____ day of _____, 20___.

_____
  Foreperson

Chapter 8

Nicole Gail

v.

Peter Novak

(excessive force)

IN THE CIRCUIT COURT OF THE SEVENTH JUDICIAL CIRCUIT

IN AND FOR LEAD COUNTY, STATE OF GOLDEN

CIVIL DIVISION

NICOLE GAIL Plaintiff, v. PETER NOVAK Defendant.	CASE NO: CV 78-534

IN THE CIRCUIT COURT OF THE SEVENTH JUDICIAL CIRCUIT

IN AND FOR LEAD COUNTY, STATE OF GOLDEN

CIVIL DIVISION

NICOLE GAIL Plaintiff,	))))	CASE NO: CV 78-534
	))	COMPLAINT FOR BATTERY BY PEACE OFFICER
v.	))	JURY TRIAL DEMANDED
PETER NOVAK Defendant.	)))	

Plaintiff, Nicole Gail, sues Defendant, Peter Novak, and alleges as follows:

1.   Plaintiff and Defendant are residents of Lead County, therefore, jurisdiction is proper in this Court.

2.   On August 11, C.Y. -1, Peter Novak, an officer in the Silverado Police Department, responded to a call at the commercial establishment called Without A Paddle, located at 27038 Rayford Road in Silverado, GO.

3.   Peter Novak utilized excessive force in arresting Nicole Gail, unnecessarily using his TASER® gun, or electrical control device, multiple times, administering prolonged and painful electrical shocks,

4.   As a result of Peter Novak's excessive use of force, Plaintiff suffered numerous injuries including burns to her skin and clothes, damage to her vision, and extreme pain and emotional anguish.

PRAYER FOR RELIEF

WHEREFORE, Nicole Gail prays for relief against Defendant as follows:

1.   Judgment in the amount of $10,000 for hospital bills and medical expenses; $200,000 for damage to Plaintiff's vision, and extreme pain; $100,000 for pain and mental anguish and punitive damages in the amount of $1,000,000.

2.   Reasonable attorney's fees;

3.   Cost of suit; and

4.   For such other and further relief as the Court deems just and proper.

DATED: October 24, C.Y.-1   Respectfully submitted,

Jessica Fielding

Jessica Fielding

IN THE CIRCUIT COURT OF THE SEVENTH JUDICIAL CIRCUIT

IN AND FOR LEAD COUNTY, STATE OF GOLDEN

CIVIL DIVISION

NICOLE GAIL Plaintiff,	))))	CASE NO: CV 78-534
	))	ANSWER TO PLAINTIFF'S COMPLAINT
v.	))	
PETER NOVAK Defendant.	)))	

Defendant, Peter Novak, hereby answers the Complaint of Plaintiff, Nicole Gail, by admitting, denying and affirmatively alleging as follows:

1.   Defendant admits that jurisdiction is proper in this Court.

2.   Defendant admits the allegations in paragraph 2.

3.   Defendant admits that he did use his TASER® gun to subdue and arrest Nicole Gail, but denies the remaining allegations.

4.   Defendant denies the allegations in paragraph 4.

Affirmative Defense

1.   Defendant is a member of the Silverado Police Department and as such is entitled to use all necessary force in order to uphold the laws and make arrests. All force used during the arrest of Nicole Gail was necessary and proper for the safety of Peter

Novak, others, and to prevent the destruction of public property. Therefore, Plaintiff's

complaint fails to state a claim and Plaintiff should take nothing thereby.

DATED: November 20, C.Y.-1   MAHER & KLINE

                                               *Jenna Wilson*_____
                                               BY: JENNA WILSON
                                               Attorneys for Defendant Peter Novak

Witness List

Witnesses for Plaintiff:

1. Nicole Gail *

2. Albert Redfield * *

Witnesses for Defendant:

1. Peter Novak * *

2. Drew McCann * * *

Each side must call both primary witnesses listed for their respective side.

*   This witness must be a female.

**   This witness must be male.

* * *   This witness may be either gender.

This is a bifurcated trial on the issue of liability only

Stipulations

1. Federal Rules of Evidence apply.

2. Plaintiff and the Silverado Police Department have reached an out of court settlement. The terms are confidential.

3. Each witness who gave a deposition did agree under oath at the outset of his/her deposition to give a full and complete description of what occurred and to correct the deposition for inaccuracies and completeness before signing the deposition.

4. All exhibits in the file are authentic and, unless otherwise noted, are the original of that document.

5. All depositions were signed under oath.

6. Other than what appears in the witness statements or depositions, there is nothing exceptional or unusual about the background of any of the witnesses that would bolster or detract from their credibility.

7. All dates are denoted by C.Y. (current year) and C.Y.-1 indicating, for example, that the date is the current year minus one.

8. All pretrial motions shall be oral.

9. No party may "invent" witnesses or evidence not specifically mentioned in this problem.

10. "Beyond the record" is not a proper objection. Rather, attorneys shall use cross-examination as a means of challenging a witness whose testimony strays beyond the facts contained in the witness's statement or deposition.

11. Neither party shall request Plaintiff, Nicole Gail, to exhibit her injuries.

12. Plaintiff and Defendant may call only two witnesses listed on their respective witness list. Each party may call a third witness by deposition only. Any deposition testimony is subject to objections pursuant to the Federal Rules of Evidence. If a witness is called by deposition, the opposing party may cross-examine that witness by deposition.

13. The law is accurately set forth in the jury instructions.

14. It is stipulated that the within this jurisdiction the blood alcohol content level of .08% is presumed to be under the influence of alcohol.

15. The physical description of a witness should be tailored to that of the student playing the witness, except for the height, weight, and age.

SILVERADO POLICE DEPARTMENT

ARREST AND BOOKING FORM

Crime/Incident	Case Number
PC 401 – Drunk and Disorderly Conduct PC 387 – Resisting Arrest PC 701 – Assaulting a Peace Officer VC 1022 – Unauthorized Use of Motor Vehicle	66514-891
Date & Time Reported 08/11/C.Y.-1 23:15	Location of Occurrence 27038 Rayford Rd., Silverado

SUSPECT							
Name (Last, First, Middle) Gail, Nicole L.			Residence Address 1301 Wilkins St., Silverado				
SEX F	DESCENT XX	HAIR XX	EYES XX	HEIGHT 5'9"	WEIGHT 160	BIRTHDATE 1/15/C.Y.-38	AGE 38
Location of Arrest 27308 Rayford Rd., Silverado			Blood Alcohol Content (BAC) .10				
Occupation Bank Teller			Employer First Bank of Silverado				

Arresting Officer: Novak *(initialed PN)*

SILVERADO POLICE DEPARTMENT

Report Type: Arrest Narrative

Report by: Officer Peter Novak *(initialed PN)*

Date: 8/12/C.Y.-1

On 8/11/C.Y.-1, at approximately 11:30 p.m., I was dispatched to *Without A Paddle*, a local sports bar and restaurant located at 27038 Rayford Road. Dispatch informed me that there had been a 911 call that a woman was being disruptive inside the bar. Officer Marquez was also dispatched to the scene.

I arrived just prior to Officer Marquez. There were a large number of cars in the parking lot. It was dark and the lot was not well lit. I waited for Officer Marquez to arrive. After he arrived, we made our way to the entrance. As we entered, we were intercepted by a bar patron, later identified as Drew McCann. McCann appeared agitated and nervous. He/She informed us that the suspect had been kicked out of the bar because she was disruptive and that when she left the bar she climbed into his/her vehicle. McCann indicated to us the location of his/her vehicle, a gray Honda CRV, which was on the far west side of the parking lot.

Officer Marquez and I then approached the vehicle and noted a figure in the front passenger seat. I approached the passenger side door and opened it. I saw a female (later identified as suspect Nicole Gail) sitting inside the car and ordered her to exit. She refused to comply and yelled at me to leave her alone. I again ordered the suspect from the vehicle. My request was met with a string of obscenities. Ms. Gail shouted, "Don't touch me, I have a gun!" I then drew my standard issue electronic taser device and informed the suspect that if she did not exit the vehicle that I would be forced to subdue her. After the suspect again ignored my command to exit the vehicle I proceeded to use the taser to apply a 15-20 second burst. The suspect began yelling and flailing her arms and exited the vehicle.

As I attempted to handcuff her, she continued to resist. I ordered her to stop struggling and put her arms behind her back. She continued to yell and flail around. I used the taser once again applying a 10-15 second burst. At this point the suspect collapsed to the ground but continued to yell and struggle so I pressed the taser directly to her person in order to drive stun her with another 5 second burst. Immediately thereafter, Officer Marquez was able to handcuff her and place her in the back of my patrol car.

Inside the patrol vehicle, the suspect once again began yelling and kicking. She was kicking the front seats so hard that they began to bend forward. I ordered her to stop. When she refused I applied another 10 second burst with the taser. After this Marquez and I were able to remove her from my vehicle and were in the process of transferring her to Marquez's cruiser which was equipped with a suspect divider in the back seat. During the transfer the suspect continued struggling and was tasered again. At this point the suspect collapsed to the ground, and appeared to briefly lose consciousness. However, she quickly came to and complied with my command to enter the rear seat of Marquez's vehicle.

Officer Marquez stayed with the suspect while I entered the bar and took witness statements before having the suspect transported to the station for booking at approximately 00:30 hours on 8/12/C.Y.-1. During booking the suspect was

administered a breathalyzer test which indicated that her blood alcohol level was .10.

Deposition of Nicole Gail

Date: November 25, C.Y. - 1

Q: Good afternoon Ms. Gail, how are you today?

A: Fine, I guess.

Q: Before we go any further can you tell me how old you are?

A: I'm 38 years old.

Q: And are you married Ms. Gail?

A: Not anymore, I got divorced a couple of years ago.

Q: On August 11th of C.Y.-1, you were at a bar?

A: Yes.

Q: What was the name of the bar?

A: I don't really remember the name, something silly.

Q: Was it called *Without A Paddle*?

A: Yeah, that sounds right.

Q: What were you doing there?

A: One of my good friends had gotten married earlier that day; I was one of the bridesmaids. After the reception a lot of us decided to go out to a bar. That was around 9:30 p.m.

Q: How did you get there?

A: I got a ride from one of my girlfriends at the wedding.

Q: Why didn't you ride home with her?

A: She had already left the bar. I wasn't ready to go yet so I decided to stay.

Q: How were you planning to get home?

A: I don't know, there were a bunch of us there, I figured I could catch a ride with

       one of them, or maybe that I would meet someone at the bar.

Q: What did you do when you got to the bar?

A: We were just hanging out. You know, dancing and drinking, just celebrating and

       having a good time.

Q: How much were you drinking?

A: I don't know. We were just having a good time.

Q: But you don't remember how much you were drinking?

A: Not exactly, I guess.

Q: Well, what do you remember?

A: Like I said, we were just dancing and having a good time when an argument got

       started with this girl that worked at the bar. She was being really difficult about

       something, then we sort of got into it and some words were exchanged.

Q: Into it?

A: You know, just a minor scuffle. I don't really remember it that well. No one got

       hurt or anything. It was just a misunderstanding.

Q: What happened after that?

A: Then they asked me to leave the bar, more like told me, but whatever, I was fine

       with that. One of my friends at the bar offered to give me a ride home. He told

       me to go outside and wait in his car while he took care of his bar tab. So I left and

       went outside to find his car.

Q: And is that what you did?

A: Yeah, at least I thought I did. He said that it was a Honda in the back of the lot next to the fence, I just sort of assumed and I got in the first Honda that I came to that was by the fence. I was waiting in the car for several minutes and then all of a sudden someone pulled open the door and yelled, "Get out of the car!"

Q: What did you do?

A: I was so shocked that I just said "no."

Q: Did you realize that it was a police officer?

A: Not at first. It was dark and I couldn't see who was yelling at me in the parking lot. I was alone and afraid that whoever it was wanted to hurt me. They kept yelling at me so I told them I had a gun so they would leave me alone.

Q: When did you realize they were police officers?

A: It wasn't until I was getting out of the car that I could tell who they were. But by that time the officer was yelling at me very loudly. The cop started shocking me as I was getting out of the car. It was awful. It just hurt so bad. I just remember the pain so intensely.

Q: So you got out of the car?

A: Fell out of the car is more like it. I just sort of melted out the door; I could barely control my body. I just remember the pain, going on and on, like it was never going to end and I just started screaming and trying to get away. But I just kept falling to the ground when I tried to get up.

Q: How many times did the officer taser you?

A: I don't know, to me it just felt like one long continuous shock.

Q: What do you remember after that?

A: The officer stopped tasering me at that point and he and his partner picked me up,

       handcuffed me, and put me in the back of his police cruiser. I was, like, in shock

       or something from being blasted by that thing but as I started to recover, I thought

       that I just had to get away. I mean, at this point I was afraid for my life, so once

       they put me in the car, I started struggling and kicking at the door and window,

       just trying to get away.

Q: Why were you trying to get away from the police?

A: At that point I didn't see him as a police officer anymore, just as a man who

       wanted to hurt me. He started yelling at me again and then he shocked me again.

       I was just screaming for him to please stop, but he didn't. He just kept on going.

Q: Do you remember what happened next?

A: They started to move me to a different patrol car but I don't remember anything

       else because I think I must have passed out.

Q: What kind of injuries did you suffer as a result of being tasered?

A: I hit my head when I fell and scratched myself up pretty good, also there were

       burn marks all over my clothes. Mainly now I still have problems with my vision,

       seeing double or blurred vision. It is better than it was right after it happened but

       it still interferes with my ability to drive and take care of my son.

Q: You have a son?

A: Yes, his name is Christopher.

Q: How old is he?

A: Four years old.

I have reviewed the transcript of my deposition. This is a complete and accurate account.

Nicole Gail
Nicole Gail

Deposition of Al Redfield

Date: November 25, C.Y.-1

Q: Hello, Mr. Redfield, are you ready to begin the deposition?

A: Sure, fire away.

Q: We asked you to bring a copy of your resume. Did you bring one?

A: Yes, here is a copy. [hands document to counsel]

Q: Thank you. I will attach your resume to this deposition and mark it as Exhibit 1.

Is everything in your resume accurate?

A: Yep.

Q: Alright, well looking at your resume here it says that you have your own private

security company, is that right?

A: Yes, Trident Security Services.

Q: And what does Trident do?

A: We are a private security firm. We provide highly trained security personnel to

individuals or entities in a number of different contexts.

Q: Such as?

A: Personal protection, armed security response for private residences and

commercial properties. We can also provide security for private events.

Q: How long has your company been in business?

A: I started Trident three years ago. I decided that I wanted to be the one giving the

orders for a change.

Q: Mr. Redfield, tell us about your experience in law enforcement or security work before you started Trident.

A: I was a deputy sheriff here in Golden for three years.

Q: To what rank did you obtain?

A: Patrol Officer.

Q: I understand that you didn't leave the sheriff's department of your own accord, is that right?

A: I was asked to leave.

Q: In fact, you were fired, weren't you?

A: Yes.

Q: You were fired for using unlawful force against a citizen.

A: That's what Internal Affairs decided. It was a bogus finding.

Q: Well, you never challenged your termination, did you?

A: The deck was stacked, I couldn't see any point.

Q: It is our understanding that you are going to be testifying on behalf of Ms. Gail in this case, is that right?

A: That's right, I am going to be testifying about the proper use of tasers by police officers.

Q: Now, do you know Ms. Gail personally?

A: I've met her.

Q: But did you have any sort of relationship with her before this litigation was commenced?

A: No.

Q: So you were approached by the plaintiff to testify in this case?

A: Yes.

Q: Have you ever served as a witness before in a case like this?

A: It depends on what you mean by a case like this.

Q: Have you ever testified as an expert witness for a plaintiff in a case involving the use of a taser?

A: Yes, I have.

Q: On how many occasions?

A: Four or five, I think.

Q: Which is it, four or five?

A: Five, well, actually now that I think about it I have done it six times before.

Q: Six times, are you sure?

A: Yeah, I'm sure.

Q: So you are not basing your testimony on any personal knowledge of the event in question?

A: No, but I have heard Ms. Gail's account of the incident and I have read the police reports.

Q: And what did that information tell you?

A: That Office Novak went way too far.

Q: "Way too far?"

A: Yes, he did not follow proper procedures in the use of a taser.

Q: Why do you say that?

A: I have conducted training sessions for the manufacturer of tasers at police stations for a while now and I train my security guys how to use them and I can tell you that the way that Novak used his taser was a far cry from any proper protocol.

Q: Have you seen the Silverado Police Department guidelines on the use of tasers?

A: Yes, I have. They are very similar to the sort of guidelines that I use.

Q: And you don't feel that Officer Novak complied with those guidelines?

A: No, he didn't. These things aren't toys. They are dangerous. They are meant to help police officers defuse potentially deadly situations without resorting to lethal force. They aren't some sort of magic bullet that a lazy officer can use whenever he doesn't feel like getting his hands dirty.

Q: But Ms. Gail was getting violent, wouldn't you agree?

A: Sure, but just because a suspect is getting violent is not a call to get trigger-happy with the tasers. You have to take the context of the whole situation into account. When I run the training sessions I discuss different scenarios where a taser would be appropriate, for instance when the officer is outnumbered or when a small framed officer is confronted by a much larger assailant. It is designed to let an officer deal with unpredictable situations. Furthermore, look at the number of times Novak used the taser. He was way out of bounds.

Q: Mr. Redfield, let's turn to the specifics of Ms. Gail's situation. When in your estimation was Officer Novak's use of his taser incorrect?

A: We need to start with the fact that this is a civilian woman being confronted by a male police officer. This officer was not confronted with a particularly dangerous or threatening situation.

Q: But it was night and Ms. Gail was inside a car. Couldn't Officer Novak have

     reasonably been concerned that she was armed?

A: I don't think so. There was no indication Ms. Gail had a weapon. If they had just

     shined a light in the car, they would have seen she was unarmed. The officer

     knew that in all likelihood this was a woman who had just been kicked out of a

     bar and her only problem was too much alcohol.

Q: You indicated that you believe Officer Novak was not justified in using his taser

     several times on Ms. Gail, is that correct.

A: Oh, yeah.

Q: But didn't she continue to struggle and resist throughout the entirety of the

     incident.

A: Listen counsel, once she was outside that car it was clear she was a woman, she

     had no weapons and she presented no threat to the male officers.

Q: Have you ever used a taser before?

A: Of course, many times.

Q: In a real world situation?

A: Well, no, not exactly. Just in training situations and things. I was off the force

     before they ever started adopting tasers so I never had the opportunity. We had to

     handle things the old-fashioned way.

Q: Are you familiar with an article by Matthew W. Saint, entitled "The TASER® as

     a Less Lethal Alternative: Risks and Benefits"?

A: Yep. I read that article in the Police Science Journal.

Q: I am handing you a document which has been marked as Exhibit 2. Is this the

article?

A: Yes, it is.

Q: Thanks, Mr. Redfield.

I have reviewed the transcript of my deposition. This is a complete and accurate account.

Al Redfield
Al Redfield

Exhibit 1

```
Albert Redfield
Trident Security Services
Silverado, Golden 90000
```

Qualifications

- Certified instructor in the use of TASER® guns.

- Trained in multiple forms of hand-to-hand combat including jiu jitsu, kickboxing, and tae kwon-do.

- Extensive training and experience with firearms and tactical operations.

Experience

Trident Security Services, Silverado, GO (Three Years)
Owner
- Coordinate private security force of approximately thirty employees.

- Providing discreet and effective security services in wide variety of circumstances to private and corporate clients.

- Conducting training programs in firearms, hand-to-hand combat, and tactical operations with staff on regular basis.

Golden Sheriff's Department, Conroe, GO (Three Years)
Patrol Officer

United States Marine Corps, Camp Pendleton (Seven Years)
Drill Sergeant
- Conducted basic training for over seven years, training hundreds of troops in combat tactics, the use of firearms, and hand-to-hand combat.

Exhibit 2

"The TASER® as a Less Lethal Alternative: Risks and Benefits"

Police Science Journal
Vol. 73, pages 13-14

AUTHOR: *Matthew W. Saint, MD, PhD*
               Department of Emergency Medicine
               Orange Clinic, Silverado, GO

The TASER® has recently found itself being adopted by an increasing number of law

enforcement agencies around the country. These devices are seen as a boon by many in

the law enforcement community for filling a perceived niche on the scale of degrees of

force available to law enforcement. With physical restraint on the one end and the lethal

use of firearms at the other, the TASER® affords officers an alternative that allows a

suspect to be subdued without posing an undue risk to the officer's safety and without the

risk of death or permanent injury to the suspect. But is the TASER® really as safe as

these agencies claim?

How TASER®s Work

TASER®s work by firing two small barbs using compressed nitrogen. These barbs lodge

themselves in the target's skin and allow the device to deliver a potent electrical shock.

The typical voltage is around 50,000 volts. However, the amperage is relatively low at

around 2.1 mAmps on average. The electrical current can then overcome the target's

muscle control allowing law enforcement officials to subdue them and take them into

custody. Many of the newer TASER®s also allow the user to "drive stun" by driving the device directly to the target's skin. Although this does not have the same effect of incapacitating the target's motor system, it still affects the sensory systems. Pain compliance is the primary goal of the "drive stun."

Injuries caused by TASER®s are generally relatively minor including, minor cuts at the point of penetration, minor burns, and other miscellaneous effects. The effect of prolonged exposure to electrical current is less certain. There have been reports of moderate to severe burns and a number of physiological side effects, some of which seem to be relatively long lasting.

Other Risks

Although no deaths have been directly attributed to the TASER®, there are an increasing number of cases where electric shock has been listed as a contributing factor in the cause of death, or at least that it could not be ruled out. In many of these cases, the target was apparently suffering from excited delirium, a hypermetabolic state often triggered by amphetamines or other narcotics. It is possible that excited delirium alone could account for many of these deaths, however, more research is necessary to determine what kind of effects the TASER® can have on people who are under intense physical or emotional stress.

Deposition of Jonny Speck

Date: November 23, C.Y. - 1

Q: Let's get right to it then, what do you remember of the night in question?

A: Nicole and I and a bunch of our friends had all been to a wedding earlier that evening and after the reception was over we all decided to go out and have a good time.

Q: Was there drinking at the wedding?

A: A little, mainly just champagne, maybe a few beers, there wasn't an open bar or anything. But anyway, after it was over a bunch of us decided we wanted to keep partying so we all decided to go out.

Q: What happened after you got to the bar?

A: We were all just drinking, dancing, laughing. Just having a good time, you know. We weren't looking to cause any trouble or anything. Nicole is a nice girl. I've known her for years. We even hooked up a few times. She wouldn't hurt a fly but she does get a little wild when she's had a few.

Q: What do you mean "wild"?

A: Nothing serious, she just gets loud and doesn't always think before she speaks. Usually, it's actually pretty funny. But I guess it might have gotten a little bit out of hand that night.

Q: What do you mean by "out of hand"?

A: Well, Nicole sort of got herself into some trouble with one of the waitresses at the

      bar. You see, I was over on the other side of the bar talking to this girl I met

      when I noticed a sort of commotion across the room.

Q: What did you see?

A: I just looked over in time to see one of the waitresses pushing Nicole away from

      her. At that point one of the bouncers came over and started talking to Nicole. I

      went over there to find out what was going on. From what I could piece together,

      the waitress had apparently refused to give Nicole any more alcohol and Nicole

      had gotten upset. Typical Nicole now that I think about it.

Q: You weren't surprised by all of this?

A: Not particularly. Like I said, Nicole can get pretty wild when she has been

      drinking.

Q: Has she ever been violent?

A: No nothing like that, she can just act up and yell. She has a short temper when

      she's drunk. This isn't the first time that she has been thrown out of a bar, that's

      all.

Q: What did you do about all of this?

A: Nicole is my friend and she was in no condition to be driving home, so I told her

      that I would give her a ride and that she ought to go wait in my car.

Q: But you didn't go with her?

A: Not immediately no, I mean I had to say goodbye to a few people and close my

      tab and all of that. I figured that she would make it to my car fine.

Q: What kind of car do you drive?

A: A light green Honda SUV.

Q: What happened then?

A: After I finished up at the bar, which took about 5 or 10 minutes, I went outside to

        the parking lot. That's when I saw the police cruisers over near where my car

        was. I heard screaming coming from that direction so I ran over there to see what

        was going on. When I got over there I saw two cops and Nicole on the ground

        screaming. One of them was tasering Nicole while the other one just stood there.

        I didn't know what to do. I mean the police officers looked like they meant

        business and I didn't really know what was going on. Then the cops handcuffed

        Nicole and put her in the patrol car. I couldn't really see what was going on in the

        car, but it was apparent that Nicole was struggling. I heard the officer telling

        Nicole to stop kicking, that she was going to damage the car. Then she started

        screaming again and I could hear that terrible buzzing again and again.

Q: Did you do anything at that point?

A: No, I still wasn't really sure what she had done or what was going on. Then the

        officer started to move her to a different patrol car. Nicki started yelling again

        and then the officer tasered her and she collapsed to the ground. After that the

        officers picked her up, loaded her into the back of the second squad car, and drove

        away.

I have reviewed the transcript of my deposition. This is a complete and accurate account.

                                        _____Jon Speck_____
                                        Jonny Speck

Deposition of Officer Peter Novak

Date: November 26, C.Y. - 1

Q: Officer Novak, how many years have you been a police officer?

A: I joined the Silverado Police Department about seven years ago.

Q: Are you married?

A: I am. I have two kids, a three-year-old girl and an 11-month-old baby.

Q: How did you come to be at *Without A Paddle* on the night of August 11?

A: It was a relatively slow night, I was on the dusk to dawn shift from 7:00 p.m. to

      7:00 a.m. and a call went out on dispatch for a drunk and disorderly out at the bar.

      Me and another officer responded. We got out and an individual approached us in

      the parking lot and reported that some drunk woman had gotten into the

      individual's car and that she wouldn't get out.

Q: Did that person point out the car?

A: Yeah, it was a gray Honda.

Q: What happened next?

A: I approached the car and saw the subject sitting in the front seat. I opened the

      door and ordered her out. She responded in a belligerent fashion and refused to

      comply.

Q: What did you do then?

A: I kept telling her to get out of the car. She refused and yelled that she had a gun.

      It was dark so I couldn't see whether or not she had a gun so I wasn't about to reach in there unprotected to pull her out myself. So, I drew my taser and told her

that if she didn't exit the vehicle I would be forced to use it on her.

Q: Did she comply?

A: No. She still refused to exit the vehicle, so I then did what I said I would and

activated the taser.

Q: Then what?

A: The taser overcame her ability to struggle and we were able to remove her from

the vehicle.

Q: What did you do then?

A: After the initial shock wore off, Ms. Gail began to struggle again. I told her

repeatedly to remain on the ground but she persisted in trying to stand up and

walk away. She continued to scream hysterically until I administered another

shock. At that point we were able to subdue her, place her in handcuffs and get

her into my patrol car. At that point I thought the whole thing was over, but then

she started up again.

Q: What do you mean?

A: Ms. Gail began struggling and screaming once again. She was kicking at the

doors and windows of the patrol car and trying to climb into the front seat. She

was completely hysterical, I was afraid to get near her without getting kicked in

the head or something.

Q: What did you do?

A: I told her to stop, that she was damaging police property and that she had to calm

down. Then I stunned her again in order to subdue her further. After she stopped struggling I proceeded to get her out of my patrol car so that I could transfer her

to the other car on the scene that was equipped with a suspect cage. We didn't

want to take any more chances.

Q: What's a suspect cage?

A: You know, it's one of those steel cage dividers that separates the back and front

seats in police cruisers. They are designed to take a lot of punishment so we

figured that that was our best bet considering how violent she was.

Q: Were you successful?

A: Eventually, but not until Ms. Gail fell and lost consciousness.

Q: Did you find a gun on Ms. Gail or in the car?

A: No, but when a suspect tells you they have a gun, you take them seriously—I

mean, we didn't want to get hurt.

Q: Do you have any formal training in the use of tasers?

A: Of course I do. We all have to take a half-day training course on the tasers before

we are issued one.

Q: What does that training entail?

A: We learn about how they operate and how to use them safely and everything. We

even all have to take a turn being tasered, just so we know what it feels like and

have an idea of its effectiveness.

Q: What is a "drive stun", Officer Novak?

A: A drive stun is where the taser is applied directly to the suspect's person in order

to administer a shock directly, without using the taser's range capabilities. It causes pain but doesn't have much effect on the victim's central nervous system. It's more for pacification than incapacitation.

Q: Did it appear that Ms. Gail was intoxicated during this encounter?

A: Yes, in fact once we got her back to the station I administered a Blood Alcohol Test and determined her BAC level to be around 0.10%.

Q: Are you familiar with the Silverado Police Department Operations Manual?

A: Of course. I am familiar with everything in that manual.

Q: I am handing you what has been marked as Exhibit 3, which are pages 20 through 21 of the manual. Do you know what are on these pages?

A: Those pages set forth the protocol on how to properly use a taser.

Q: Have you ever received any officer disciplinary reports?

A: On a couple of occasions.

Q: How many?

A: Two, but they were written about three years ago.

Q.   I am handing you documents that have been marked as Exhibits 4 and 5. Are these the two officer disciplinary reports?

A: Yes, but I don't see what that has to do with this case.

Q: Was an incident report written up about this case?

A: Yes.

Q: I am handing you a document which has been marked as Exhibit 6. Is this the officer incident report related to this case?

A: Yes, it is.

Q: I am also handing you a document that has been marked as Exhibit 7. Is this a

        photograph of the type of taser gun that you used on the night of on August 11th?

A: Yes.

I have reviewed the transcript of my deposition. This is a complete and accurate account.

Peter Novak

Peter Novak

Exhibit 3

SILVERADO POLICE DEPARTMENT

OPERATIONS MANUAL

6/115 Appropriate Degrees of Force - Taser

The taser is an Electro-Muscular disruption device which uses probes with connective wires propelled by a compressed nitroglycerin cylinder or direct contact points.

When attempts to subdue a suspect by physical control techniques have been or will likely be ineffective, or there is a reasonable expectation that it will be unsafe for officers to approach within contact range of the suspect, officers may utilize their standard issue taser consistent with Department approved training and policy.

The varying degrees of force are not meant to preclude an officer from passing lower degrees of force and utilizing higher degrees of force as may be appropriate.

. . . . .

6/120 Authorized Use of the Taser Gun

The taser gun is a Department approved non-lethal control device and may be discharged in situations discussed in 6/115.

1. Supervisors and officers who have been trained in its proper use are authorized to use the taser gun.

2. The taser gun shall never be used indiscriminately nor shall it be used in anticipation against mere threat of violence, but may be used when there is a credible threat of violence coupled with the present ability to cause injury to a citizen or an officer.

3. The taser gun shall not be used on a suspect once his violent behavior is no longer likely to cause injury, property damage or escape.

4. When the taser gun has been used, a supervisor shall be notified immediately.

5. Whenever a taser gun is discharged, other than at a training session, the discharge will be documented.

Exhibit 4

Silverado Police Department

Officer Disciplinary Report

Current Date: 2/4/C.Y.-3
Date of Offense:1/27/C.Y.-3
Name: Peter Novak   Badge Number: 23-8976
Complaint: Unnecessary Force

This is officer's 1st_x_ 2nd___ 3rd___ 4th___ 5th___ offense of this nature during the
past 12 consecutive months

This is officer's 1st_x_ 2nd___ 3rd___ 4th___ 5th___ offense or combination of offenses
during the past 12 consecutive months

Date of Last Offense: N/A

Previous disciplinary action within the last 12 months: None

Summary of events resulting in disciplinary action:

During routine arrest for a DUI, Officer exercised unnecessary force in handling

the suspect. Officer slammed him on the hood of the car and hit suspect across

the face when he disobeyed officer's orders to remain still. Considering this was

the Officer's first offense of this nature, he will receive an official reprimand but

no suspension.

Exhibit 5

Silverado Police Department

Officer Disciplinary Report

Current Date: 10/22/C.Y.-3
Date of Offense:10/15/C.Y.-3
Badge Number: 23-8976

Name: Peter Novak
Complaint: Unnecessary Force

This is officer's 1st___ 2nd_x_ 3rd___ 4th___ 5th___ offense of this nature during the past 12 consecutive months

This is officer's 1st___ 2nd_x_ 3rd___ 4th___ 5th___ offense or combination of offenses during the past 12 consecutive months

Date of Last Offense: 1/27/C.Y.-3

Previous disciplinary action within the last 12 months: Official reprimand

Summary of events resulting in disciplinary action:

Officer responded to a domestic disturbance call at 02:30 hours on 10/15/C.Y.-3.

Officer Novak arrived and got into a verbal confrontation with the male resident

of the home. Officer then grabbed the suspect and threw him into a wall. After

the suspect was down on the ground, Novak kicked him on the ground before

placing him in handcuffs and taking him into custody. Because this was the

Officer's second offense of this nature in the past year, an official reprimand was

issued as well as a 5 day, unpaid suspension.

Exhibit 6

Silverado Police Department

Officer Incident Report

Current Date: 8/18/C.Y.-1
Date of Incident:8/11/C.Y.-1
Badge Number: 23-8976

Name: Peter Novak
Complaint: Unnecessary Force

Date of last offense: 10/15/C.Y.-3

Previous disciplinary action within the last 12 months: None

Summary of events and conclusions of the investigation:

Officer responded to a drunk and disorderly call at a local bar and restaurant. He

was informed that the suspect was currently involved in the unauthorized use of a

motor vehicle. When officer approached the suspect, she became immediately

belligerent and uncooperative. After officer gave the suspect warning of his

intention to use his department issued taser gun he used it to subdue and arrest the

suspect. Based on the surrounding situations, the Officer's knowledge, and the

suspect's behavior, this committee finds that Officer Novak responded

appropriately. No disciplinary action is recommended.

Exhibit 7

X-26 TASER® issued to all Silverado Police Officers

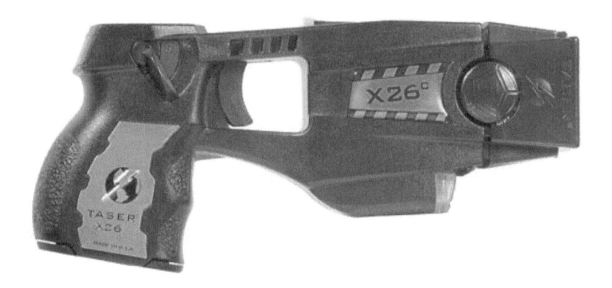

Deposition of Drew McCann

Date: November 27, C.Y.-1

Q: Mr./Ms. McCann, could you please tell us what you observed during the night of August 11th, C.Y.-1?

A: Yes, I had gone to the bar *Without A Paddle* that night after I got off work around 7:30 p.m. I was there with a few friends from work having a couple of drinks and talking.

Q: When did you first observe Ms. Gail?

A: I first noticed her when she began arguing with a waitress near our table.

Q: What was she arguing about?

A: She was trying to order a drink, but the waitress was refusing to serve her. Ms. Gail appeared drunk and was getting very loud. She demanded that the woman get her another drink, but the waitress refused to do so, saying that she had had enough. That seemed to make Ms. Gail angry. She reached over and tried to grab one of the drinks off of the waitress's tray but stumbled, making the waitress drop the entire tray of drinks. I got soaked. Man, I was ticked off. Just because this drunk woman couldn't hold herself together. She totally ruined my suede jacket.

Q: What happened then?

A: Then, the waitress pushed Ms. Gail away and started yelling for the bouncer. She was yelling and swearing at the waitress and then when the bouncer came she started yelling at him. They ultimately told her that she had to leave and that they were calling the cops. That seemed to get her attention because she finally left.

Q: What did you do then?

A: Like I said, I was upset because some of the drinks had spilled on me, so I decided to go ahead and call it a night. I walked out to go home a minute or so later. But when I got to my car I noticed that she was sitting there in my car! I didn't know what the hell she was doing in my car, but I wasn't about to go out there and drag her out myself. So, I started to head back to the bar when two cops showed up. I walked over and told them that this woman who had caused all the commotion inside was sitting in my car.

Q: And what did they do?

A: They went over to go and check things out so I just sort of hung back.

Q: How far were you from the officers?

A: I don't know, probably about 70 or 80 feet.

Q: What did you observe from where you were watching?

A: I saw the officer open my car door and begin talking to her, after a couple of minutes he pulled out his taser and pointed it at her. After that I heard yelling and then she kind of stumbled out of the car. Then, she started yelling and screaming again and flailing around on the ground. The officer kept telling her to calm down, but she just kept screaming hysterically. After that I guess he must have stunned her again because she quieted down for a few seconds while they got handcuffs on her and put her in the back of the patrol car. She was seriously throwing a fit, though.

Q: What do you mean she was throwing a fit?

A: Yelling, screaming, flailing her arms around. It looked like she was trying to hit the officers to me. Didn't surprise me much, though. She was so drunk in the bar and had already gotten into a fight with that waitress inside. I didn't really feel bad for her. She brought it on herself.

Q: What happened next?

A: I couldn't see very well, but there was definitely some activity going on in the police car. After a few minutes the officer pulled Ms. Gail out of the first car and tried to move her over to the second. Then, it looked like she passed out and the other officer came and helped put her into the other squad car.

Q: Is there anything else?

A: Not that I can think of.

I have reviewed the transcript of my deposition. This is a complete and accurate account.

Drew McCann
Drew McCann

Jury Instructions

Members of the jury, you have now heard all the evidence and the closing argument of the attorneys. It is my duty to instruct you on the law that applies to this case. You will have a copy of my instructions with you when you go to the jury room to deliberate.

I will now tell you the law that you must follow to reach your verdict. You must follow that law exactly as I give it to you, even if you disagree with it. If the attorneys have said anything different about what the law means, you must follow what I say. In reaching your verdict, you must not speculate about what I think your verdict should be from something I may have said or done.

Pay careful attention to all the instructions that I give you. All the instructions are important because together they state the law that you will use in this case. You must consider all of the instructions together. You must decide this case based only on the law and the evidence.

A witness is a person who has knowledge related to this case. You will have to decide whether you believe each witness and how important each witness's testimony is to the case. You may believe all, part, or none of a witness's testimony. In deciding whether to believe a witness's testimony, you may consider, among other factors, the following:

1.   How well did the witness see, hear, or otherwise sense what he or she described in court?

2.   How well did the witness remember and describe what happened?

3.   How did the witness look, act, and speak while testifying?

4.   Did the witness have any reason to say something that was not true? Did the witness show any bias or prejudice? Did the witness have a personal relationship with any of the parties involved in the case? Does the witness have a personal stake in how this case is decided?

5.   What was the witness's attitude toward this case or about giving testimony?

Sometimes a witness may say something that is not consistent with something else he or she said. Sometimes different witnesses will give different versions of what happened. People often forget things or make mistakes in what they remember. Also, two people may see the same event, but remember it differently. You may consider these differences, but do not decide that testimony is untrue just because it differs from other testimony.

However, if you decide that a witness has deliberately testified untruthfully about something important, you may choose not to believe anything that witness said. On the other hand, if you think the witness testified untruthfully about some things, but told the truth about others, you may accept the part you think is true and ignore the rest.

You must not be biased in favor of or against any witness because of his or her race, sex, religion, occupation, sexual orientation or national origin.

Plaintiff has the burden in this case to prove each element of his claim by a preponderance of the evidence. The term "preponderance of the evidence" means the greater weight and degree of credible evidence admitted in this case. Simply put, Plaintiff must prove it is more likely than not that each element of his claim is true.

Nicole Gail claims that Officer Peter Novak harmed her by using unreasonable force to arrest her. To establish this claim, Plaintiff must prove all of the following:

1. That Peter Novak intentionally touched her;

2. That Peter Novak used unreasonable force to arrest her;

3. That Nicole Gail did not consent to the use of that force;

4. That Nicole Gail was harmed; and

5. That Peter Novak's use of unreasonable force was a substantial factor in causing Plaintiff's harm.

A police officer may use reasonable force to arrest or detain a person when he or she has reasonable cause to believe that that person has committed a crime. Even if the police officer is mistaken, a person being arrested or detained has a duty not to use force to resist a police officer unless he is using unreasonable force.

In deciding whether Peter Novak used unreasonable force, you must determine the amount of force that would have appeared reasonable to a police officer in Peter Novak's position under the same or similar circumstances. You should consider, among other factors, the following:

(a) The seriousness of the crime at issue;

(b) Whether Nicole Gail reasonably appeared to pose an immediate threat to the safety of Peter Novak or others; and

(c) Whether Nicole Gail was actively resisting arrest or attempting to evade arrest.

Your foreperson shall preside over your deliberations. All jurors should participate in all deliberations and vote on each issue. The votes of ten or more jurors are required to reach a verdict. The verdict must be in writing and the verdict form has been prepared for you. It is as follows:

[READ VERDICT FORM]

In just a few moments, you will be taken to the jury room by the bailiff. The first thing you should do is elect a foreperson who will preside over your deliberations like the chairperson of a meeting. It is the foreperson's job to sign and date the verdict form when all of you have agreed on a verdict in this case and to bring the verdict back to the courtroom when you return.

In closing, let me remind you that it is important that you follow the law spelled out in these instructions in deciding your verdicts. There are no other laws that apply to this case.

IN THE CIRCUIT COURT OF THE SEVENTH JUDICIAL CIRCUIT

IN AND FOR LEAD COUNTY, STATE OF GOLDEN

CIVIL DIVISION

NICOLE GAIL   )   CASE NO: CV 78-534
Plaintiff,   )
)   VERDICT FORM
)
v.   )
)
PETER NOVAK   )
Defendant.   )
)

We, the Jury, answer the question submitted to us as follows:

Do you find from a preponderance of the evidence that Defendant harmed Plaintiff by using unreasonable force to arrest her?

ANSWER: Yes _____   No _____

So say we all,

_____   _____
Date   Foreperson

Chapter 9

CAMERON HILLMAN v. MUTUAL LIFE INSURANCE COMPANY

Cameron Hillman

v.

Mutual Life Insurance Company

(denial of insurance coverage)

**IN THE CIRCUIT COURT OF THE THIRTEENTH JUDICIAL DISTRICT
IN AND FOR LEAD COUNTY, STATE OF GOLDEN
CIVIL DIVISION**

CAMERON HILLMAN	)	
	)	
	)	
v.	)	Case No. CV 49-3023
	)	
MUTUAL LIFE	)	
INSURANCE CO.	)	
	)	

**IN THE CIRCUIT COURT OF THE THIRTEENTH JUDICIAL DISTRICT
IN AND FOR LEAD COUNTY, STATE OF GOLDEN
CIVIL DIVISION**

CAMERON HILLMAN	)	Case No. CV 49-3023
	)	
v.	)	**COMPLAINT**
	)	
MUTUAL LIFE	)	JURY TRIAL DEMANDED
INSURANCE CO.	)	
	)	

Plaintiff, Cameron Hillman, sues Defendant, Mutual Life Insurance Co., and alleges as follows.

1.   Plaintiff is a surviving heir of Perry Hillman, and is the sole named beneficiary of life insurance policy number 17-14785 issued by Defendant in which Perry Hillman is the named insured.

2.   On August 8, C.Y.-2, Perry Hillman died as a result of accidental asphyxiation.

3.   On August 19, C.Y.-2, Plaintiff presented to Defendant a certified copy of a death certificate for Perry Hillman and sought payment of benefits under the life insurance policy issued by Defendant.

4.   On September 25, C.Y.-2, Defendant breached its duties under its life insurance policy when it notified Plaintiff that it would not pay full benefits on the life insurance policy in which Perry Hillman is the named insured.

5.   As a result of Defendant's breach, Plaintiff has sustained economic damages.

WHEREFORE, Plaintiff prays for judgment against Defendant in an amount to be proven at trial, together with interest, costs, attorney's fees, and such other relief as the court deems just.

Plaintiff demands a jury trial.

David White

DAVID WHITE
12114 West Coast Highway
Silverado, Golden
(213) 576-0849
Attorney for Plaintiff

**IN THE CIRCUIT COURT OF THE THIRTEENTH JUDICIAL DISTRICT
IN AND FOR LEAD COUNTY, STATE OF GOLDEN
CIVIL DIVISION**

CAMERON HILLMAN	)	
	)	
v.	)	Case No. CV 49-3023
	)	
MUTUAL LIFE	)	**ANSWER**
INSURANCE CO.	)	
	)	

Defendant, Mutual Life Insurance Co., answers Plaintiff's Complaint as follows:

1.   Defendant generally denies each and every allegation in Plaintiff's Complaint, except that Defendant admits that it issued life insurance policy number 17-14785 with Perry Hillman as the named insured and in which Cameron Hillman is a named beneficiary.

Defendant asserts the following affirmative defenses:

2.   Plaintiff's complaint fails to state a claim upon which relief can be granted.

3.   The death of the named insured resulted from an excluded act, TO WIT, suicide.

WHEREFORE, having answered Plaintiff's complaint, Defendant prays that the same be dismissed, that judgment be entered in favor of Defendant, that Plaintiff take nothing thereby, and that Defendant be awarded costs, attorney's fees and such other relief as the court deems just.

Defendant demands a jury trial.

RD Franklin
   Ruth D. Franklin
48932 Bayshore Ave.
Silverado, Golden
(213) 234-9876
Attorney for Defendant

Witness List

Witnesses for Plaintiff:

1. Cameron Hillman **

2. Casey Kaelin **

Witnesses for Defendant:

1. Det. Alex Fine **

2. Jessica Timberwolf *

Each side must call both witnesses listed for their respective side in any order.

*   This witness must be a female.

**   This witness may be either gender.

This is a bifurcated trial on the issue of liability only.

Stipulations

1. Federal Rules of Evidence apply.

2. Each witness who gave a statement did agree under oath at the outset of his or her statement to give a full and complete description of what occurred and to correct the statement for inaccuracies and completeness before signing it.

3. All exhibits in the file are authentic and, unless otherwise noted, are the original of that document.

4. The reports from the Department of Justice Laboratory, Office of Forensic Services and Coroner's Office are deemed admissible for all purposes. The parties do not contest the accuracy of the statements therein. Cameron Hill and Detective Alex Fine are familiar with these reports and can testify as to the contents of the reports.

5. Other than what appears in the witness statements, there is nothing exceptional or unusual about the background of any of the witnesses that would bolster or detract from their credibility.

6. All dates are denoted by C.Y. (current year) and C.Y.-1 indicating, for example, that the date is the current year minus one.

7. All pretrial motions shall be oral.

8. No party may "invent" witnesses or evidence not specifically mentioned in this problem.

9. "Beyond the record" is not a proper objection. Rather, attorneys shall use cross-examination as a means of challenging a witness whose testimony strays beyond the facts contained in the witness's statement.

10. The insurance policy clause excluding payment of benefits where death is the result of suicide has been ruled valid.

11. The law is accurately set forth in the jury instructions.

12. It is stipulated that in the State of Golden, 0.08% blood alcohol content is the point at which a person is considered intoxicated.

13. The plaintiff and defendant may call only the two witnesses listed on their respective witness list. Each party may call an additional witness by deposition or witness statement. Any such testimony is subject to objections pursuant to the Federal Rules of Evidence. If a witness is called by deposition or witness statement, the opposing party may cross-examine that witness by deposition or witness statement.

Witness Statement of Cameron Hillman

Date: January 10, C.Y.-1

I am Cameron Hillman, the only child of the deceased, Perry Hillman. Although I did not reside with my father, we were fairly close, and we met for dinner at least once a week in the two years preceding his death.

On August 8, C.Y.-2, I went to my father's home to check on him. He had broken his jaw in some sort of "accident" the week before. When I had asked him about how it had happened, he was pretty vague. He said he had fallen, but the doctor who treated him said it looked like a blunt force trauma injury. His housekeeper said that he and his wife, Jessica Timberwolf, had been "drinking and carrying on" the day that he broke his jaw. I am guessing she had something to do with it.

Anyway, after trying to phone my father on August 8, C.Y.-2, and not getting any response, I decided to go to his home to check on him. I arrived at about 7:30 p.m. and found him unconscious on the floor in his study. I checked him and he did not have a pulse, nor was he breathing. I called 911. When the paramedics arrived, they pronounced him dead. I later learned that he had asphyxiated on his own vomit. I believe that Jessica had poisoned him and that is what made him vomit.

About two weeks before he died, Dad told me that he thought that Jessica might be thinking of leaving him. He said that she was becoming increasingly violent, especially after a few drinks, but said that he loved her. It was about a week later that he had the "accident" in which he broke his jaw.

Dad needed surgery to set his jaw, and the surgeons had to fix his mouth in a closed position, using heavy rubber bands to keep him from moving his teeth or jaw. After the surgery, the surgeon, Dr. Brown, told Jessica and me that Dad would need to be on a liquid diet. Dr. Brown also warned us that Dad would need to keep a pair of scissors handy in case his pain medications made him nauseous. This was because, with his jaw banded closed, if he were to vomit he could asphyxiate.

After the coroner took Dad's body, a police officer arrived. He asked for permission to search the home, which I granted. He took a few things, including a glass with a straw in it from a table in Dad's study. I later learned that the glass had the residue of a liquid meal and that traces of seconal and codeine were also present. After the officer left, I entered Jessica's room. Her clothes and other belongings had been cleared out. One thing seemed out of place, though. The scissors that Dad was given and told to keep with him were by the sink in Jessica's bathroom. For me that was the tip-off that she was involved in Dad's death. It began to make sense that she must have put something that would make him sick in his liquid meal and had taken the scissors he would need if he vomited.

When I saw that Jessica had apparently left, but before I put two and two together, I called her cell phone to tell her that Dad had died. There was no answer, and after several attempts, I finally left word for her on her voicemail. I was reluctant to leave that message on her voicemail, but I was having great difficulty reaching her.

Days later, while I was cleaning out Dad's house, I came across a marriage certificate. The certificate showed that he and Jessica had gotten married in Las Vegas. I can't believe my Dad never told me they had gotten married.

Finding the marriage certificate made me remember a conversation I had with Jessica one night at my Dad's house. I had stopped by to check on him and found Jessica in a half-drunken stupor on the couch in the living room. When I asked her where Dad was, she responded by telling me how much she admired women like Anna Nicole Smith. She said she "admired anyone willing to marry a wealthy old guy." But she wondered how Anna Nicole "had the patience to wait around for so long." At the time, I thought that Jessica was just trying to make me upset, so I ignored it. But now, knowing that the two of them had gotten married, I believe Jessica was planning to kill my father and make it look like an accident so she would inherit his money.

About ten years ago, Dad had a rough patch. He lost his job and his then-girlfriend left him all in the same week. It really drove him to the edge. In fact, he tried to end his life by sitting in his car inside the garage with the motor running. He was saved when Casey Kaelin, the housekeeper, found him slumped over the wheel of his car. We talked over the years about his suicide attempt, and he told me repeatedly that he felt foolish to have done such a thing. I am positive that Dad never again considered ending his own life. In fact, just two days prior to his death, we discussed taking a trip together. He said he had wanted to visit the northern island of New Zealand and asked me if I would like to accompany him on that trip in December of C.Y.-2.

I have reviewed my witness statement. This is a complete and accurate account.

Cameron Hillman
Cameron Hillman

Witness Statement of Casey Kaelin

Date: January 20, C.Y. -1

I am Casey Kaelin and I was employed as Perry Hillman's housekeeper from April C.Y.-14 until August 8, C.Y.-2, when Mr. Hillman died.

I first started working for Mr. Hillman a few months after his divorce. He had one child, Cameron Hillman, then a teenager, who lived with his ex-wife. Cameron stayed with Mr. Hillman two weekends each month until Cameron became an adult.

A few years after I started working for Mr. Hillman, there was a most unfortunate incident. Mr. Hillman had been dating a young woman who seemed to be after him only for what he could do for her. And then in one week, Mr. Hillman lost his job and his girlfriend dumped him. He was already down about being out of work, but when that girl walked out on him he really went over the edge. Lucky for him, I arrived at work early and, when I opened the garage, I found him in his car, unconscious, with the motor running. I think if I had been fifteen minutes later, he would have been beyond help.

I never liked Jessica Timberwolf. When she moved into Mr. Hillman's home in C.Y.-4, I almost quit. In fact, I told Mr. Hillman I was leaving, but he talked me into staying and said that I wouldn't have to deal much with Ms. Timberwolf. I had my own room in the house and it was away from the family. I didn't go out of my way to see Ms. Timberwolf, but it was hard to avoid hearing her. She was loud, especially when she was drinking. It worried me that Mr. Hillman started to drink heavily with her. He hadn't been much of a drinker before, but the two of them drank quite a bit. And when they were drinking they sometimes had loud fights.

About a week before Mr. Hillman died, he and Ms. Timberwolf had another really bad fight late one night. I couldn't make out the words through the kitchen door, but there was a lot of yelling. I heard a thump and then a shout from Mr. Hillman. A few minutes later Ms. Timberwolf came through the door and said, "Casey, you remember that famous guitarist, Jimi Hendrix? You know he died from choking on his own vomit?" Then, she laughed and walked into the living room.

The next morning Ms. Timberwolf told me she was taking Mr. Hillman to the Emergency Room, because he had fallen and hurt himself. It turned out he had a broken jaw, and he stayed overnight in the hospital. When he came home, his jaw was set in a clenched position, and he had to have liquid meals. I prepared his meals for him the first three days and then Ms. Timberwolf told me she would do it. That surprised me, because she isn't exactly the domestic type. Still, I saw her using the blender to make Mr. Hillman's liquid meals for him.

The day before Mr. Hillman died, he and Ms. Timberwolf had another loud fight. I couldn't make out much, but heard her say she was finished with him. I could not make out what he said--he couldn't speak very well with his jaw shut. I thought she would leave right there and then, but she went to her room. I was supposed to be off the next day, but didn't want to leave Mr. Hillman alone. So I knocked on Ms. Timberwolf's door to see if it was still okay for me to leave. When she opened the door, she told me to go ahead and take the day off. Then she smiled and said, "You can rest assured that I will take care of Perry." There was something about the way she said it that made me uneasy, but I had plans for my day off. I checked with Mr. Hillman, too, and he said "Jessica will be here, so go ahead and take the day off." As I turned to leave, Mr. Hillman said, "Casey, Jessica really is a good woman. I would be lost without her."

That was the last time I saw Mr. Hillman. The next day, August 8, C.Y.-2, I got a phone call from Cameron telling me Mr. Hillman had died. When I returned to the house, I also learned that Ms. Timberwolf had left.

Cameron told me that Mr. Hillman and Ms. Timberwolf had a secret wedding. Neither Mr. Hillman nor Ms. Timberwolf ever mentioned this to me, but I do remember the two of them taking a week-long vacation to Las Vegas in December, C.Y.-3.

I have reviewed my witness statement. This is a complete and accurate account.

Casey Kaelin
Casey Kaelin

Lead County Sheriff's Department

Report: Investigation Narrative

Report by: Detective Alex Fine *(initialed AF)*

Date: August 9, C.Y.-2

Position/Department: Homicide Division (Three Years)

On August 8, C.Y.-2, at approximately 20:00 hours, I received a call from paramedics reporting that they had responded to a 911 call and had found a deceased male, identified as Perry Hillman, in his home at 1492 Columbus Circle, Silverado. The deceased had apparently died of asphyxiation after vomiting.

I arrived at the residence of the deceased at approximately 20:19 hours and was granted permission to search the home by Cameron Hillman. A walk through did not reveal any sign of disturbance. In the study, where the deceased was found, I located and bagged for later testing a 12 oz. glass with a liquid residue which appeared to have been recently used, as some of the residue was still liquid. I also located and bagged two bottles of prescription medications – seconal and Tylenol with codeine. Both medications were in the name of the deceased. On a portion of the table where the prescription medications were located was a thin, powdery film. Samples of the powder were collected for analysis. There was also a shot glass, with a small amount of golden liquid at its bottom, near a half-empty bottle of Wild Turkey bourbon. I collected both the glass and the bourbon for further testing.

The following day I interviewed Mr./Ms. Casey Kaelin, the deceased's housekeeper. He/She told me that he/she had last seen the deceased on August 7, C.Y.-2, and that he/she had not been present on August 8, as it was his/her day off. He/She reported that the deceased and his wife, Jessica Timberwolf, had argued frequently and, in fact, had been arguing on August 7. He/She had also observed that the couple used alcohol regularly. I asked Mr./Ms Kaelin if he/she noticed anything amiss when he/she returned to the decedent's home and he/she said that the only thing he/she noticed was that Ms. Timberwolf, who had resided at the home of the deceased, appeared to have left the residence and to have taken all her belongings. Mr./Ms. Kaelin had no knowledge as to Ms. Timberwolf's whereabouts and could not state whether she may have left before or after the deceased died. He/She did speculate that Ms. Timberwolf's departure would have dealt a terrible blow to the deceased and recounted that ten years earlier the deceased had attempted suicide after a romantic break up.

Lead County Sheriff's Department

Report: Supplemental Report

Report by: Detective Alex Fine *(initialed AF)*

Date: August 14, C.Y.-2

Position/Department: Homicide Division (Three Years)

On August 12, C.Y.-2, I received the results of the chemical analysis of the contents of the two glasses seized from the deceased's premises, a fingerprint analysis of the glasses and the prescription medication bottles, and a copy of the coroner's report. Attached to this statement are copies of the chemical analyses and a copy of the fingerprint report. Based upon the results of those reports, my investigation and my interview with Casey Kaelin, I concluded that the death was a probable suicide. The adult child of the deceased, Cameron Hillman, has contacted our office on several occasions expressing the view that the deceased was poisoned by Jessica Timberwolf.

I interviewed Ms. Timberwolf, who stated she and Mr. Hillman had separated at the time of his death. Based on my interview with Ms. Timberwolf, I am of the opinion that she played no role in the death of Mr. Hillman. I have assured Cameron Hillman that if any evidence of foul play is brought to our attention, the case will be re-opened.

LEAD COUNTY
DEPARTMENT OF JUSTICE LABORATORY

Report by: T. Dudley Sturt, Chemist

Re: Chemical analysis of evidence seized from residence of Perry Hillman

Date: August 9, C.Y.-2

I have examined the residual contents of two glasses, one bottle of Wild Turkey

brand bourbon, and a tape on which a powder residue was collected. The results are as

follows:

A.   Bottle of Wild Turkey brand bourbon: The content of this bottle, 278.6ml of

liquid, is an alcoholic distillate from a fermented mash of corn, rye and barley malt. The

liquid is 50.5% alcohol. The contents of the bottle were not found to include any

contaminants or adulterants.

B.   Small "shot" glass: On inspection, the shot glass was found to have residue

consistent with the contents of the Wild Turkey brand bourbon bottle described above. No

adulterants or contaminants were detected.

C.   Large (12 oz capacity) glass with "milky" residue: Analysis of residue found

it to be a liquid meal replacement drink (likely Ensure Plus) in which traces of seconal (secobarbital) were noted. The medication appeared to have been infused into the drink by crushing the tablets.

  D. Tape with powder residue: The powder noted in the collection tape was residue from a crushed seconal tablet.

          T. Dudley Sturt
          T. Dudley Sturt, Chemist
          Lead County Office of Forensic Services to
          Department of Justice Laboratory

LEAD COUNTY
OFFICE OF FORENSIC SERVICES

Report by: Amy Rebbin, Latent Fingerprint Examiner

Re: Hillman case

Date: August 9, C.Y.-2

The liquor bottle (Wild Turkey), two medication bottles and two glasses seized from the residence of Perry Hillman were dusted for fingerprint comparison.

The Wild Turkey bottle yielded nine readable latent prints, four of which matched Perry Hillman. The remaining latent prints are of an unknown origin.

The small "shot" glass yielded one latent print consistent with Perry Hillman and no additional prints of a quality suitable for analysis.

The large "12 oz" glass yielded several latent prints that did not match Perry Hillman, but the origin of those prints is unknown. It also yielded a partial palm print consistent with Perry Hillman.

The medication bottle labeled "seconal" yielded one partial print consistent with Perry Hillman and several latent prints that do not match Perry Hillman, but the origins of those prints is unknown.

The medication bottle labeled "Tylenol with codeine" yielded only smudged prints which were not suitable for analysis.

Amy Rebbin
_____
Amy Rebbin

 LEAD COUNTY CORONER'S OFFICE

Autopsy Report

Deceased: Perry Hillman

Doctor: Sam Home, Pathologist

Autopsy Date: August 9, C.Y.-2

My initial impression was that the deceased was a well-nourished 63-year-old Caucasian male, approximately 5'9", weighing 165 pounds. Upon examination, it was noted that a metal apparatus had been affixed to his teeth to hold his jaw immobile, although the rubber closures had been removed. According to the paramedic report, the closures had been removed by the paramedics upon arrival at decedent's residence.

Most of the major organ systems (heart, brain, renal, endocrine) were unremarkable. I noted that the decedent had regurgitated his stomach contents and discovered a significant quantity of the regurgitated contents of his stomach in his brachia and in both lungs. I collected the samples of the regurgitated liquid for toxicological analysis. I also sent a blood sample for toxicological analysis.

Based upon my examination of Hillman's body, and my review of the toxicology report (copy attached), I have concluded that the decedent's death was immediately caused by asphyxiation due to aspiration of regurgitated stomach contents which likely was caused by alcohol and drug intoxication.

Sam Home
Sam Home, M.D.

LEAD COUNTY CORONER'S OFFICE

Toxicology Report

Report By: Jennifer Newsom, Toxicologist

Re: Hillman Case

Autopsy Date: August 9, C.Y.-2

I assisted in the autopsy on Perry Hillman. The results of that autopsy are as follows:

1. The blood sample analysis showed a blood alcohol concentration of .12% (or 1.2 grams of alcohol per 100 milliliters of blood). It also showed presence of seconal at 14 ppm (parts per million) and codeine at 4 ppm (parts per million).

2. A microscopic analysis of the sample stomach contents showed presence of chrystalline secobarbital sodium (seconal) and codeine.

*Jennifer Newsom*_____
Jennifer Newsom
Toxicologist
Lead County Coroner's Office

Certificate of Death
STATE OF GOLDEN

NAME OF THE DECEASED
Perry Hillman

ESTIMATED TIME OF DEATH
7:00 P.M., 8/8/C.Y.-2

SURVIVORS
Cameron Hillman

PRIMARY CAUSE OF DEATH
Asphyxiation

SECONDARY CAUSE OF DEATH
Intoxication

DUE TO (LIST ALL)

The secondary cause of death was intoxication by alcohol and barbituates (seconal) causing regurgitation.

I certify that the foregoing is true and correct.

Sam Home
Sam Home, M.D.

Witness Statement of Jessica Timberwolf

Date: January 28, C.Y.-1

My name is Jessica Timberwolf and I am the widow of Perry Hillman. I am a personal shopper at high-end retail stores. I specialize in shopping for designer clothes. Perry and I had been married almost a year when he suddenly died.

Perry and I did not have a typical relationship. I was twenty-five years younger than Perry. We met at a party four years ago and within a couple of weeks I was moving into Perry's home. We had a few things in common. Both of us liked to drink and have a good time. We both also liked celebrity "factoids." For example, we both found it hysterical that Fatty Arbuckle was accused of crushing a woman to death. Though Perry and I loved each other, we had our fair share of shouting matches, especially after a few drinks, but they never got physical.

In December, C.Y.-3, Perry and I took a trip to Las Vegas to celebrate the New Year. We stayed at the Desert Shamrock Suites. On the fourth day of our weeklong trip, Perry bent down to tie his shoe in the middle of the casino. While down on one knee, he pulled a small box from his pocket. He opened the box and presented me with an engagement ring. He asked me to marry him and I said that I would. We were married that evening in the hotel's chapel by an Elvis impersonator. Perry and I decided to keep the marriage a secret because neither he nor I wanted to upset Cameron. Perry knew that Cameron would be furious if he/she found out about the marriage, and I didn't want him/her to have another reason to hate me. Cameron and I didn't get along. He/she didn't like that I was so much younger than Perry, and he/she hated that Perry and I lived together. Perry and I were both afraid of Cameron's reaction if he/she found out we got hitched in Vegas.

Unfortunately, Perry and I were not meant to be together. Simply put, the age gap between us was starting to become a strain on our relationship. Also, we constantly disagreed over starting a family. I wanted to have a child, while Perry was vehemently against it. He already had one child, and had no desire to raise another. Furthermore, ever since we had gotten married, Perry refused to let me go out socially without him and became increasingly possessive. In July, C.Y.-2, I was contemplating leaving Perry. I felt smothered in the relationship and that I couldn't live the life that I wanted. One evening, I suggested to Perry that we "take a break." He got angry and threatened to hurt me, saying that if he couldn't have me, nobody could. Then, a few nights later, I told Perry I thought it would be a good idea if I moved out for awhile. Perry again had a violent reaction. He lunged towards me, lost his balance and fell against a bookcase, breaking his jaw. I took him to the hospital to have his jaw set. The doctor explained to me that the pain medication prescribed to Perry could make him queasy, and that if he had to throw-up, either Perry or I would have to cut the bands holding his jaw in place so that he wouldn't choke on the vomit. Perry told me to hold on to the scissors the doctor gave us to cut the bands. Perry wasn't sure if he would be able to cut the bands if he needed to because the pain-killers made him feel woozy.

By August 6, C.Y.-2, I was more determined than ever to get away from Perry. At this point I genuinely feared for my safety and planned to leave Perry as soon as he recovered a bit more. The pain medication made him belligerent and I was increasingly afraid to be around him, but I wanted to wait until his jaw healed a little more. Because Perry's jaw had been fastened shut to promote healing, I had to prepare liquid meals for him.

On August 7, C.Y. -2, I again told Perry that I wanted out of the marriage. He became angry and upset, but he couldn't yell very well because his jaw was wired shut. He managed to mumble that he could not go on without me. I felt bad for him and I told him I would stay until the next morning. I fixed him his meal that evening because Casey, the housekeeper, wasn't there.

The morning of August 8, C.Y. -2, I left while Perry was sleeping. I went to stay with a friend who lives out of state. I had no intention of ever returning to Lead County. I didn't think I could handle being in the same county, let alone city, with Perry.

I was stunned when I got a call from Cameron that Perry had died. Even though I didn't want to be married to him anymore, I still loved Perry. I can't help but feel a little responsible for Perry choking. I mean, if I had been there, I might have been able to cut the rubber bands in time.

Technically Perry and I are still married. I never finished the paperwork to file for divorce. I guess I still hoped that Perry and I would be able to work it out, that he would realize how he was treating me and would turn back into the wonderful guy I married.

I know that Cameron and I have never really gotten along, but I can't believe he/she could think I could ever harm his/her father.

I have reviewed my witness statement. This is a complete and accurate account.

Jessica Timberwolf
Jessica Timberwolf

Witness Statement of Dr. Skyler Welby

Date: February 15, C.Y.-1

My name is Skyler Welby, M.D. I received my medical degree from Golden State University and completed my post-graduate residency training in pathology at UCLA-Harbor General Hospital.

On January 22, C.Y.-1, I was retained by Mutual Life Insurance to review the autopsy report for Perry Hillman. I was told that Hillman was insured under a Mutual Life Insurance policy and that a claim had been filed by the named beneficiary under that policy. I was also told that, as is typical, the policy contained an exclusion precluding payment of benefits when death results from suicide.

The autopsy report indicates that the decedent died of asphyxiation caused when the decedent aspirated his own vomit. The report also reveals that the decedent had a blood alcohol level of .12%, which is greater than the alcohol concentration mandating classification as "legally drunk" in the State of Golden. In addition, there was codeine and there was a high level of secobarbital sodium (seconal) in the decedent's blood as well as in the contents of the decedent's stomach.

Based upon this report, it is my opinion that the decedent's death was a suicide. The presence of blood alcohol, but no detected alcohol in decedent's stomach contents, indicated that he had taken his last drink long enough for it to have passed completely from his stomach; typically this would occur in three hours. Furthermore, the fact that seconal was found both in his stomach contents and in his bloodstream indicates that the seconal had been more recently ingested. While it is impossible to precisely determine how many seconal tablets decedent had ingested, based upon the level of seconal found in his bloodstream, I would estimate that he had ingested 10-14 tablets, which is easily enough to cause death.

Death by barbiturate poisoning (seconal is a barbiturate) often – though certainly not always – results when the decedent ingests a sufficient quantity to cause unconsciousness and then his body attempts to rid itself of the intoxicants by regurgitating the contents of the stomach. In the case of an individual who is rendered unconscious by barbiturates, the state of unconsciousness is often so deep that the individual is not awakened by the regurgitation, and thus aspirates – and is asphyxiated by – the contents of the stomach. In my opinion that is precisely what occurred in Perry Hillman's case.

In my opinion, the amount of seconal ingested by Hillman indicates that it was deliberately ingested. The normal dose would be one tablet, so it is difficult to imagine that he would have accidentally ingested 10-14 tablets. It is also unlikely that he could have unwittingly been given an overdose. While it is true that he would have had to ingest the tablets in crushed form, since he could not open his jaw, it appears from the chemist's report, which I have reviewed, that the tablets were crushed and mixed into his liquid meal. The quantity of tablets was such that the taste of the liquid meal would have been affected and he likely would have detected a difference had the seconal been "slipped" into his drink by someone else.

I concede that alcohol can dull one's sense of taste, as can codeine which was also detected in Hillman's blood analysis. But it is my view that the taste of the beverage would have been sufficiently affected that it would be hard for him not to have noticed something strange. Since he had apparently finished the entire drink, I must assume that he was not surprised by any unusual taste to his drink.

I have reviewed my witness statement. This is a complete and accurate account.

S. Welby
             Skyler Welby, M.D.

RESUME

Skyler Welby, M.D.

Educational Background
- Residency, Pathology, UCLA-Harbor General Hospital (C.Y.-26 – C.Y.-23)

- MD, Golden State University (C.Y.-32)

- BS, Chemistry, with honors, University of Golden (C.Y.-36)

Experience
- Professor of Medicine
  Golden State University School of Medicine
  Chair of Pathology Department
  Lead, Golden (C.Y.-12 – present)

- Chief, Department of Pathology
  Silverado University Hospital
  Silverado, Golden (C.Y.-17 – C.Y.-12)

Professional Associations
- American Medical Association
- Golden Medical Society
- American Pathology Society

Publications

- Welby, S. Mechanism of hypoxia-induced alteration of canine isolated basilar artery. *Intensive Care Medical Journal* C.Y.-10;34:733-750.

- Welby, S. Diagnosis of endometrial carcinoma by endoscopic ultrasound-guided fine needle aspiration biopsy. *J Pathology* C.Y.-8;2:519-545.

- Conner, R., Welby, S. Primary inflammatory fibrosarcoma of the cerebral arteriolar tone in rats. *Path Lab Med* C.Y.-2;148:812-830.

LOVE ME TENDER WEDDING CHAPEL

Certificate of Marriage

This is to certify that <u>Perry Hillman</u>

And <u>Jessica Timberwolf</u>

Have united in Marriage on the <u>29th</u> day of <u>December</u>.

In the Year of <u>C.Y.-3</u>.

At <u>Las Vegas, Nevada</u>.

Minister <u>J. Wilson</u>
Witness <u>Rod Ingle</u>
Witness <u>Stella Burns</u>

Mutual Life Insurance Company

+9302 Westbrook Avenue
Silverado, Golden 93816

February 20, C.Y.-1

Re: Perry Hillman

To Whom It May Concern:

My name is T. Whittaker Stone and I am the claims officer for the Mutual Life Insurance Company. Perry Hillman was an insured under life insurance policy number 17-14785 issued by Mutual Life Insurance on September 23, C.Y.-5. That policy, under which Hillman's life was insured for one million dollars, contained a standard suicide exclusion in effect for the first five years following issuance of the policy. I have attached a photocopy of the provision in Hillman's contract.

On August 19, C.Y.-2, Cameron Hillman, the sole beneficiary under the terms of Perry Hillman's life insurance policy, submitted a claim for benefits under that policy. On September 25, C.Y.-2, I mailed Cameron Hillman a letter indicating that, because Perry Hillman's death resulted from suicide during the period of exclusion, the only benefits that would be paid under the policy were benefits equal to one-half of the premiums paid prior to the date of decedent's death, which amounted to $8,575.00.

Very truly yours,

T. Whittaker Stone

T. Whittaker Stone

Mutual Life Insurance Company

49302 Westbrook Avenue
Silverado, Golden 93816

Level Term Series III
Life Insurance Policy
Policy No. 17-14785

*   *   *   *   *

SUICIDE EXCLUSION

If the Insured, Perry Hillman, while sane or insane, commits suicide during the first five (5)

years the policy is in force, the only benefits payable will be an amount equal to one-half of

all premiums paid prior to the date of death. The five year period begins on the Effective

Date of the policy, to-wit, September 23, C.Y.-5.

*   *   *   *   *

Mutual Life Insurance Company

49302 Westbrook Avenue
Silverado, Golden 93816

Cameron Hillman
1525 Donna Drive
Silverado, Golden 91304

September 25, C.Y.-2

Re: Life Insurance Policy No. 17-14785

I have reviewed the death certificate filed for Perry Hillman and have concluded that Perry Hillman's death was caused by circumstances which are excluded from coverage by the terms of the above-referenced policy (suicide). Accordingly, under the terms of the policy, the sole obligation of the Company is payment of one-half the amount of all premiums paid prior to death. As three annual premium payments had been received by the Company prior to Mr. Hillman's death, the total amount of benefits due under the policy is eight thousand five hundred seventy-five dollars.

A check in the amount of eight thousand five hundred seventy-five dollars will be issued to you upon return of a copy of this letter, acknowledging your acceptance of the benefits as payment in full under Life Insurance Policy No. 17-14785.

Sincerely,

T Whittaker Stone
_____

I acknowledge the aforementioned terms and agree to accept payment of $8,575.00 as payment in full of benefits due under Life Insurance policy No. 17-14785.

_____
Cameron Hillman

Jury Instructions

Members of the jury, you have now heard all the evidence and the closing argument of the attorneys. It is my duty to instruct you on the law that applies to this case. You will have a copy of my instructions with you when you go to the jury room to deliberate.

I will now tell you the law that you must follow to reach your verdict. You must follow that law exactly as I give it to you, even if you disagree with it. If the attorneys have said anything different about what the law means, you must follow what I say. In reaching your verdict, you must not speculate about what I think your verdict should be from something I may have said or done.

Pay careful attention to all the instructions that I give you. All the instructions are important because together they state the law that you will use in this case. You must consider all of the instructions together. You must decide this case based only on the law and the evidence.

A witness is a person who has knowledge related to this case. You will have to decide whether you believe each witness and how important each witness's testimony is to the case. You may believe all, part, or none of a witness's testimony. In deciding whether to believe a witness's testimony, you may consider, among other factors, the following:

1.   How well did the witness see, hear, or otherwise sense what he or she described in court?

2.   How well did the witness remember and describe what happened?

3.   How did the witness look, act, and speak while testifying?

4.   Did the witness have any reason to say something that was not true? Did the witness show any bias or prejudice? Did the witness have a personal relationship with any of the parties involved in the case? Does the witness have a personal stake in how this case is decided?

5.   What was the witness's attitude toward this case or about giving testimony?

Sometimes a witness may say something that is not consistent with something else he or she said. Sometimes different witnesses will give different versions of what happened. People often forget things or make mistakes in what they remember. Also, two people may see the same event, but remember it differently. You may consider these differences, but do not decide that testimony is untrue just because it differs from other testimony.

However, if you decide that a witness has deliberately testified untruthfully about something important, you may choose not to believe anything that witness said. On the other hand, if you think the witness testified untruthfully about some things but told the truth about others, you may accept the part you think is true and ignore the rest.

You must not be biased in favor of or against any witness because of his or her race, sex, religion, occupation, sexual orientation or national origin.

Plaintiff has the burden in this case to prove each element of his claim by a preponderance of the evidence. The term "preponderance of the evidence" means the greater weight and degree of credible evidence admitted in this case. Simply put, Plaintiff must prove it is more likely than not that each element of his claim is true.

Plaintiff claims that Mutual Life Insurance Company breached its duties under its life insurance policy when it notified Plaintiff that it would not pay full benefits on the life insurance policy in which Perry Hillman is the named insured.

Your verdict should be for Plaintiff if you find that there are no viable affirmative defenses and you also find that:

1. Defendant issued its policy of life insurance to Perry Hillman; and

2. The policy was in force on Perry Hillman's date of death; and

3. Plaintiff was then the beneficiary of the policy.

Defendant does not dispute the essential elements of the claim, but rather contends as an affirmative defense that Perry Hillman's death was a suicide and, therefore, it is relieved of its duty to pay full benefits under the policy. Defendant has the burden to prove the affirmative defense by a preponderance of the evidence. If you decide that Plaintiff has proven all elements of his/her claim by a preponderance of the evidence, and Defendant has not proved an affirmative defense, then you must find for Plaintiff.

Your foreperson shall preside over your deliberations. All jurors should participate in all deliberations and vote on each issue. The votes of ten or more jurors are required to reach a verdict. The verdict must be in writing and the verdict form has been prepared for you. It is as follows:

[READ VERDICT FORM]

In just a few moments, you will be taken to the jury room by the bailiff. The first thing you should do is elect a foreperson who will preside over your deliberations like the chairperson of a meeting. It is the foreperson's job to sign and date the verdict form when all of you have agreed on a verdict in this case and to bring the verdict back to the courtroom when you return.

In closing, let me remind you that it is important that you follow the law spelled out in these instructions in deciding your verdicts. There are no other laws that apply to this case.

**IN THE CIRCUIT COURT OF THE THIRTEENTH JUDICIAL DISTRICT
IN AND FOR LEAD COUNTY, STATE OF GOLDEN
CIVIL DIVISION**

CAMERON HILLMAN	)	
	)	
v.	)	Case No. CV 49-3023
	)	
MUTUAL LIFE	)	VERDICT FORM
INSURANCE CO.	)	

We, the Jury, answer the questions submitted to us as follows:

Do you find, by a preponderance of the evidence, that Mutual Life Insurance Company owes benefits of $1,000,000 under Life Insurance Policy No. 17-14785 to Cameron Hillman?

ANSWER: Yes _____ No _____

Dated this _____ day of _____, 20___.

_____
Foreperson

Chapter 10

State of Golden

v.

Richard D. Buck

(murder)

IN THE CIRCUIT COURT OF THE THIRTEENTH JUDICIAL DISTRICT

IN AND FOR LEAD COUNTY, STATE OF GOLDEN

CRIMINAL DIVISION

STATE OF GOLDEN	)	
	)	
v.	)	Case No. CR 99-403
	)	
RICHARD D. BUCK,	)	
Defendant.	)	

IN THE CIRCUIT COURT OF THE THIRTEENTH JUDICIAL DISTRICT

IN AND FOR LEAD COUNTY, STATE OF GOLDEN

CRIMINAL DIVISION

The 9th day of January, C.Y.

STATE OF GOLDEN	)	**Felony Information**
	)	
v.	)	Case No. CR 99-403
	)	
RICHARD D. BUCK,	)	
Defendant.	)	
	)	

Comes now the undersigned and states that on or about October 6, C.Y.-2, in

Silverado, Lead County, State of Golden, a felony, in violation of section 187 of the

Golden Penal Code, was committed by the above defendant, who at the time and place

last aforesaid, did willfully and with malice aforethought murder Rebecca Buck.

Jen D. Lee
Jen D. Lee
District Attorney, Lead County

Witness List

Witnesses for the State:

1. Investigator Terry Cutler * * *

2. Lara Merckle * *

Witnesses for Defendant:

1. Richard Buck *

2. Brooke Charmin * *

Each side must call both witnesses listed for their respective party.

* This witness must be a male.

* * This witness must be a female.

* * * This witness may be either gender.

Stipulations

1. Federal Rules of Criminal Procedure and Federal Rules of Evidence apply.

2. Each witness, except for Defendant, who gave a statement reviewed the officer's report of his or her statement and signed the statement verifying that it was accurate.

3. All exhibits in the file are authentic and, unless otherwise noted, are the original of that document.

4. Other than what appears in the witness statements, there is nothing exceptional or unusual about the background of any of the witnesses that would bolster or detract from their credibility.

5. All dates are denoted by C.Y. (current year) and C.Y.-1 indicating, for example, that the date is the current year minus one.

6. All pretrial motions shall be oral.

7. No party may "invent" witnesses or evidence not specifically mentioned in this problem.

8. "Beyond the record" is not a proper objection. Rather, attorneys shall use cross-examination as a means of challenging a witness whose testimony strays beyond the facts contained in the witness's statement.

9. It is stipulated the Brooke Charmin's birthday is October 6, C.Y.-23.

10. Section 187 of the Golden Penal Code provides: "Murder is the unlawful killing of a human being with malice aforethought."

11. The parties stipulate to the admissibility of Criminologist Edwin Falker's opinions, but not the correctness of such opinions.

12. The parties stipulate that Rebecca Buck's blood type is AB negative.

13. The prosecution and defense may call only the two witnesses listed on their respective witness list. Each party may call additional witnesses by deposition or witness statement. Any such testimony is subject to objections pursuant to the Federal Rules of Evidence. If a witness is called by deposition or witness statement, the opposing party may cross-examine that witness by deposition or witness statement. The parties have agreed to waive Confrontational Clause objections for only these witnesses.

SILVERADO POLICE DEPARTMENT

Report Type: INITIAL REPORT

Report by: Investigator Terry Cutler *(initialed: TC)*

Date: 10/6/C.Y.-2

I was contacted by dispatch to meet Officer Baines at the residence located at 13208 Coldbrook, Silverado. I responded to the location at 6:50 a.m. Officer Baines and I walked through the living room of the residence, which appeared to have been vandalized. Baines then directed me to his squad car where Richard Buck was seated. Baines informed me that Buck, a resident of the house, is a lieutenant with the Lead County Sheriff's Department. Lt. Buck resides in the residence with his wife, Rebecca. Lt. Buck appeared agitated and distraught. I introduced myself to Buck and asked him to tell me what had transpired. He informed me that he returned home approximately 25 minutes ago and found his house torn apart and his wife missing. I asked him if he had attempted to call any family or friends to inquire as to his wife's whereabouts. He informed me that he called his wife's sister, Lara Merckle, and she didn't know of Rebecca's whereabouts. He didn't call anyone else "because if anybody would know where she was at, it would be her sister." He then called the police. He said, based on the condition of his house, he "knows something bad has happened to Rebecca."

I directed Officer Baines to get the names and numbers of family and friends from Lt. Buck and to begin making calls. I then re-entered the residence for a closer inspection. In the living room, several chairs and a coffee table were overturned, and a large fish aquarium had been smashed. Water, glass and dead fish were strewn across the carpet. On the carpet, near the door leading to the garage, there was a stain approximately 4"x 8" which appeared to be blood. Whatever had transpired in the residence appeared to have been confined to the living room, as I could detect no disturbance elsewhere in the house. In the attached two car garage, there was one vehicle, a C.Y.-1 Jaguar. Nothing appears to have been upset in the garage.

I ordered a full forensics examination of the residence, including the garage.

I returned to the front of the house where Lt. Buck was still seated in the front seat of Officer Baines' patrol vehicle. He told me the Jaguar was his vehicle and that his wife drove a CY-5 Honda Accord.

As I was about to re-enter the residence, my attention was directed to a woman, who approached Buck and began screaming and swinging her arms wildly at him as he sat with the car door open. She was screaming, "You did it you bastard. You killed her, just like you said you would." The woman, identified as Lara Merckle, Rebecca Buck's younger sister, was restrained by a patrol officer. I ordered that she be placed in my vehicle where I could speak with her. "Attachment A" to this report is her statement to me. I concluded the interview with Merckle and returned to Buck's location.

Buck appeared to be angry and concerned about Lara Merckle and said, "That sister has always had it in for me. I love Rebecca. That crazy sister of hers just doesn't understand our relationship."

I asked Buck to remain in the vehicle until I could leave from the scene and then he and I could have a further discussion at the station. Buck expressed anger and asked if he was in custody. I informed him that he was not. He told me that I shouldn't be bothering with him and that I should get out there and find his wife. He exited the vehicle and walked away from my location and went and stood in the front yard of his residence.

"ATTACHMENT A TO INITIAL REPORT"

WITNESS STATEMENT: LARA MERCKLE

DATE: 10/6/C.Y.-2

Rebecca Buck, who I call Beca, is my sister. Beca and Richard Buck have been married three years. Richard continually abused Beca both physically and verbally. They constantly had screaming matches which ended with both of them hitting one another. I have witnessed such incidents on a number of occasions. The most recent incident was last week at the Buck residence. During that incident, when Richard returned home, he berated Beca because he said the house looked like a pigsty. Beca yelled something back at him and Richard grabbed both her arms and squeezed so hard that there were bruises there within minutes. Richard only let go when I grabbed him by the arm and screamed at him.

Richard is an abusive tomcat. I warned her before she married that animal that he was a bully and a womanizer, but she wouldn't listen. She was so unhappy with all of the abuse. She once told me that she knew he was never going to stop abusing her. She said that she wished there was an escape, but she knew there wasn't because he would find her wherever she went. And now look what's happened. He's killed her, I know he has.

Officer Cutler informed me that Richard was the one who called the police and that there was no evidence that anything had happened to Beca. But Officer Cutler does not know who he was dealing with. It is like Scott Peterson, the guy who killed his pregnant wife and tried to hide the body. Once, right in front of me, Richard told Beca that the only reason that idiot Peterson didn't get away with it was because he didn't do a good enough job getting rid of the body. I know that Beca's dead and

Richard killed her.

Reviewed and verified by: *Laura Merckle*

Laura Merckle

SILVERADO POLICE DEPARTMENT

Report Type: SUPPLEMENTAL REPORT

Report by: Investigator Terry Cutler *(initialed: TC)*

Date: 10/7/C.Y.-2

At 8:50 a.m. on the above date, Lt. Buck called me and said he had reconsidered and would discuss his wife's disappearance with me. We agreed to meet in my office in 20 minutes.

At 9:15 a.m. Lt. Buck and I sat in my office. I informed him that he was not a suspect and not in custody. Buck informed me that he is a 15-year lieutenant with the Lead County Sheriff's Department. He is second in command at the East County Sheriff's substation. Buck said he had just come off a 10-hour shift when he returned home yesterday morning. He had last seen his wife on the afternoon of October 5th. He reported that he and his wife have been married three years and that while they had the usual ups and downs, they were happily married.

I asked Buck about the accusations that Lara Merckle had made at the scene. He told me that Merckle had it in for him and would go out of her way to hurt him and spread lies about him. I asked Buck specifically about the altercation from last week that Merckle spoke of and he denied that it was serious. I specifically confronted him with the reference to the Scott Peterson case. He denied making any such reference.

I inquired of Buck whether any ideas as to his wife's whereabouts had occurred to him since we spoke at the scene. He indicated that he had called several of her "tennis friends" and they did not know of her whereabouts. Once again, he reiterated that his wife's closest confidant was her sister, Lara Merckle. Buck said he had no idea where Rebecca might be or what had happened to her. Throughout the interview he appeared distraught and anxious.

I asked Buck about his activities on his 10-hour shift. He told me that he hadn't left the station until his shift was over at 5:00 a.m. on October 6th.

Buck expressed concern that he was being questioned like a suspect and urged me to move the investigation to a more fruitful area. He again expressed concern that he believed something bad has happened to his wife.

I agreed to keep him apprised of the investigation and the interview was terminated.

SILVERADO POLICE DEPARTMENT

Report Type: SUPPLEMENTAL REPORT AND WITNESS STATEMENT

Report by: Investigator Terry Cutler *(initialed: TC)*

Date: 10/8/C.Y.-2

At 11:30 a.m. on the above date, I went to Lara Merckle's residence to further interview her about the disappearance of her sister, Rebecca Buck. I asked Merckle about the last time she spoke to her sister. "Attachment A" to this report is her statement.

"ATTACHMENT A TO SUPPLEMENTAL REPORT"

SUPPLEMENTAL WITNESS STATEMENT: LARA MERCKLE

DATE: 10/8/C.Y.-2

The last time I spoke with my sister Beca was about 12:30 a.m. the morning she disappeared. It was a typical call. Beca vented about how much she hated her husband and how miserable she was. Toward the end of the call, Beca told me that she's always believed that she could never divorce her husband because he would never let her. Beca stated she was looking forward to the cruise we were going to take because it gave her an opportunity to get away from the miserable SOB for a week. Beca then said she couldn't take it anymore and that she was going to divorce Richard when she got back from the cruise. Beca wanted to keep her decision quiet because she didn't want Richard to find out until she was ready to tell him. She was afraid of what he might do.

Reviewed and verified by: *Laura Merckle*
                                     Laura Merckle

LEAD COUNTY
OFFICE OF FORENSIC SERVICES

Report by: Edwin Falker, Criminologist

Report Date: 10/8/C.Y.-2

On October 6, C.Y.-2, I conducted an examination of the Buck residence located at 13208 Coldbrook, Silverado, pursuant to a request by Inv. Cutler of the Silverado Police Department.

What appeared to be a 4"x 8" bloodstain was located on the carpet approximately 6 feet from the door connecting to the garage. There was also what appeared to be a blood smear (approximately 2"x 4") at the base of the connecting door on the interior side of the door (see attached Diagrams #1 and #2). I collected samples from both locations for analysis at the forensics lab.

Edwin Falker
Edwin Falker

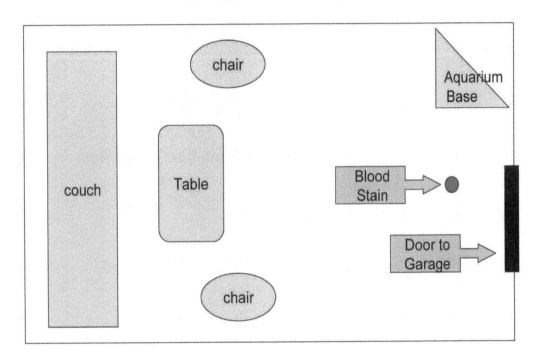

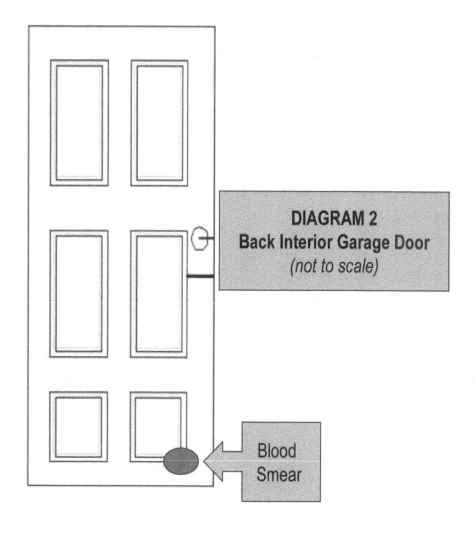

DIAGRAM 2
Back Interior Garage Door
(not to scale)

Blood
Smear

SILVERADO POLICE DEPARTMENT

Report Type: SUPPLEMENTAL REPORT

Report by: Investigator Terry Cutler *(initialed: TC)*

Date: 10/10/C.Y.-2

As of 4:35 p.m. this date, neither Rebecca Buck nor her vehicle have been located. Every law enforcement agency in the state has been notified and supplied with photos and relevant information. The news media has been alerted and local and regional news outlets have published Mrs. Buck's photograph.

I called Commander Cody from the Sherriff's Office and learned that Sgt. Diva was on duty during the dusk to dawn shift of October 5th/6th. I contacted Sgt. Diva at his home. He told me that Lt. Buck left the station for an unspecified time during the "early morning hours" and returned to the station about 4:45 a.m. I asked Diva if he could be more specific as to what time Lt. Buck had left, but he was unable to recall. Attached is Sgt. Diva's statement.

Attachment to Report
Statement of Sergeant Diva

My name is Sergeant D. Diva. I work at the Lead County Sherriff's department.

I was on duty during the dusk to dawn shift of October 5/6, C.Y. -2. I saw Lieutenant

Buck leave the sheriff's station during the early morning hours and return to the station

about 4:45 a.m. I am unable to recall the exact time when Lieutenant Buck left the

station.

Reviewed and verified by: _D. Diva_____
                                  D. Diva

SILVERADO POLICE DEPARTMENT

Report Type: SUPPLEMENTAL REPORT AND WITNESS STATEMENT

Report by: Investigator Terry Cutler *(initialed: TC)*

Date: 10/11/C.Y.-2

At approximately 3:00 p.m. this date, I met with Lara Merckle at her suggestion. She said she had more information about her sister's disappearance. "Attachment A" to this report is her statement.

Merckle showed me cruise tickets for the cruise that Rebecca Buck and her were scheduled to go on. Copies of these tickets are attached to this report as "Attachment B."

At the conclusion of the interview, I suggested to Merckle that perhaps her sister was tired of being abused and simply ran away from her life. Merckle became angry at such a suggestion and denied her sister would do such a thing.

A true and accurate map of the areas relevant to this investigation is attached to this report as "Attachment C." On the map, I indicated the relevant distances.

"ATTACHMENT A"

SUPPLEMENTAL WITNESS STATEMENT: LARA MERCKLE

DATE: 10/11/C.Y.-2

I know that Richard Buck was having an affair with another woman. I have never trusted Richard from the beginning, and knew something was not right. Because of my suspicion, I followed Richard on a number of occasions. On several occasions prior to October 5-6, Richard would leave work during his shift and drive to an apartment in downtown Silverado, about 6 miles from the Sheriff's East County substation. I would wait in my car outside of the apartment until Richard came out with a woman wearing a bathrobe. As Richard left, the two would kiss and then Richard would head back to the Sheriff's station.

I didn't know who this other woman was until this morning. I was suspicious about this woman playing a role in my sister's disappearance, so I drove to the apartment to confront the woman. I learned the woman's name was Brooke Charmin. Charmin refused to let me into her apartment, and when I confronted her about the affair, Charmin denied it. I explained to Charmin that Beca had disappeared on the morning of the 6th. Upon hearing this, Charmin said, "Oh my God, what has he done?" I demanded to know what this comment meant, but Charmin refused to explain and slammed the door in my face.

I don't know if my sister knew about any affair. Beca had never talked to me about any affair. But my sister was smart. I think she probably suspected something was going on.

I know that my sister did not just leave because we were scheduled to go on a cruise in a couple of weeks. Beca was really excited about the trip, and couldn't stop talking about it.

Reviewed and verified by: *Laura Merckle*
                                     Laura Merckle

"ATTACHMENT B"

CruiseLineExpress BOARDING PASS

NAME	CABIN#	DINING ROOM
REBECCA BUCK	849	SAPPHIRE
LARA MERCKLE	849	SAPPHIRE

DESTINATION	DEPARTURE	RETURN
HONOLULU, HAWAII	10/22/C.Y.-2	11/03/C.Y.-2
	10/22/C.Y.-2	11/03/C.Y.-2

"ATTACHMENT C"

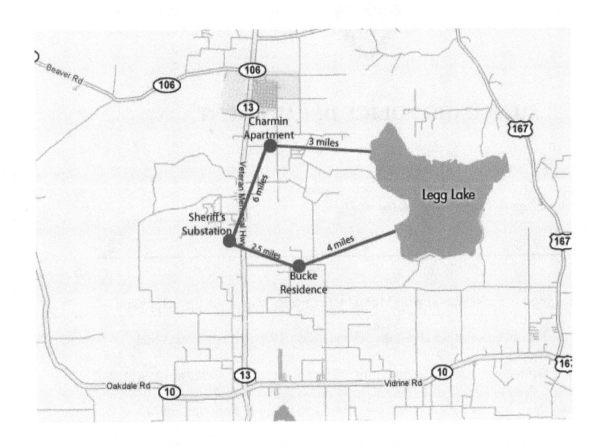

SILVERADO POLICE DEPARTMENT

Report Type: SUPPLEMENTAL REPORT

Report by: Investigator Terry Cutler *(initialed: TC)*

Date: 10/12/C.Y.-2

Following my conversation with Merckle, I contacted Buck via his cell phone and asked if we could talk further about the investigation. We agreed to meet that evening at the Denny's on Kimber at 6:00 p.m. When I arrived, he was already seated. I told him that there were some questions concerning an absence from the station on October 6th. He told me that he thought the discussion was going to be about finding Rebecca, not about a fruitless fishing expedition.

I asked Buck if he had left the station during his shift the morning his wife disappeared. He became angry and told me he didn't appreciate being called a liar.

I then told Buck about my recent conversation with Lara Merckle. Buck didn't say anything, but simply put his head in his hands. Buck then admitted to me that he had left the station to go to his girlfriend's apartment. He stated he hadn't told me before because it really made him look bad. I asked Buck if his wife knew about the girlfriend. He said he wasn't sure, but he had a suspicion that his wife had recently figured it out. Buck offered that October 6th was his girlfriend's birthday, and that he had bought her ruby earrings and went to her apartment to give them to her. Buck looked in his wallet and found a receipt for the earrings, a copy of which is attached to this report as "Attachment A."

Buck then told me that he had been a terrible husband to his wife, but that he would never have killed her. Buck explained that he had aspirations of becoming Sheriff. He told me that someone doesn't get elected Sheriff unless they at least have the appearance of a happy home. He told me that things weren't great between him and his wife, but that they needed to stay together for both their sakes. According to Buck, if they got divorced, he would have no chance of becoming Sheriff. Buck then related that his wife had threatened to leave on one occasion. Buck said he responded by telling her that he really needed her here, and that he would never let her leave. Buck said that those were just words said in anger, and he just wanted to show her how important it was to him that she stand by his side.

"ATTACHMENT A"

Jacqueline's Fine Jewelry
4930 Winston Street
Silverado, GO 93029

14k Gold Ruby Earrings		$108.95
	Sub total	$108.95
	Tax	$ 8.99
	Total	$117.94

Method of payment: Cash

_____
Sales Associate: Susan

SAVE RECEIPT FOR RETURN

SILVERADO POLICE DEPARTMENT

Report Type: SUPPLEMENTAL REPORT AND WITNESS STATEMENT OF
BROOKE CHARMIN

Report by: Investigator Terry Cutler *(initialed: TC)*

Date: 10/13/C.Y.-2

I contacted Brooke Charmin at her apartment located at 403 Main Street at 8:00

a.m. Charmin invited me in and asked if I was inquiring about Richard Buck. I asked

her about her relationship with Buck. "Attachment 1" to this report is her statement.

"ATTACHMENT 1"

WITNESS STATEMENT: BROOKE CHARMIN

DATE: 10/13/C.Y.-2

I have been having an affair with Richard Buck since last summer. We would usually get together twice a week and have dinner at my house. The relationship was very discrete. Richard is a sweet and caring man who was trapped in a meaningless marriage.

Sometimes Richard discussed the possibility of leaving his wife, but he appeared reluctant to leave her because he thought it might hurt his career.

I saw Richard the early morning hours of October 6th. Richard arrived at my apartment about 1:00 a.m. and left about 3:30 a.m. I am certain of that date because it was my birthday, and we were celebrating.

Richard would not have done anything to his wife because he was so damned concerned about his career. He is an easygoing, thoughtful guy who would never resort to any violence.

I have never had a confrontation with Lara Merckle. I have never met Lara Merckle, nor did a person with that name ever visit me at my apartment.

Reviewed and verified by: *Brooke Charmin*
                                          Brooke Charmin

LEAD COUNTY
OFFICE OF FORENSIC SERVICES

Report by: Edwin Falker, Criminologist

Report Date: 10/16/C.Y.-2

      I conducted analysis on the two blood samples taken from the Buck residence on October 6, C.Y.-2.

      Analysis revealed that the blood from both locations is AB Negative. AB Negative is shared by only one percent of the population.

      I obtained the medical records of Rebecca Buck which records indicated her blood was also AB Negative.

      To date, there has been no request for a DNA analysis to confirm that the blood found originated with Rebecca Buck.

Edwin Falker
Edwin Falker

SILVERADO POLICE DEPARTMENT

Report Type: SUPPLEMENTAL REPORT

Report by: Investigator Terry Cutler *(initialed: TC)*

Date: 12/2/C.Y.-2

The investigation into the disappearance of Rebecca Buck has developed no new avenues of investigation. Interviews with Lara Merckle, Mrs. Buck's sister, indicate that Rebecca Buck has not contacted her. Merckle is convinced that if Rebecca Buck were alive, her sister would have contacted her.

Given the circumstances of Rebecca Buck's disappearance, her blood in the house, Buck's threats days before Rebecca Buck's disappearance, his infidelity and his dubious alibi, I submitted the case to the Lead County District Attorney for prosecution of Richard Buck for the murder of his wife.

On December 1, CY-2, D.D.A. Abbot rejected the case for prosecution.

SILVERADO POLICE DEPARTMENT

Report Type: SUPPLEMENTAL REPORT AND WITNESS STATEMENT

Report by: Investigator Terry Cutler *(initialed: TC)*

Date: 9/20/C.Y.-1

I responded to Legg Lake, a man-made lake located in Legg Park in Silverado, in response to a report that three boys discovered a car submerged in approximately fifteen to twenty feet of water. The car, a Honda Accord, year C.Y.-5, was registered to Richard and Rebecca Buck.

The lake is located in a gorge. The southwestern end where the vehicle was found is surrounded by thirty to forty foot cliffs. The cliffs are accessible via a service road in the park. The lake is approximately four miles from the Buck residence.

I ordered a forensics team to the site. They determined that the car had been submerged for at least 8 months. They did not locate any blood stains in the car or trunk. It was reported to me from forensics that even if blood had been left in the car, the long-term exposure to water would have "compromised, if not completely eroded" all evidence of blood. A cameo necklace was found in the trunk. "Attachment A" to this report is Frank Falla's statement. Mr. Falla was head of the forensics team.

I examined the vehicle and found it to be intact. There appeared to be no external damage and the interior was intact, including the sound system and hubcaps. The car did not appear to have been vandalized.

I contacted Lara Merckle and asked her to meet me at the station where she identified the necklace found in her sister's Honda as belonging to her sister. "Attachment B" to this report is her witness statement.

"ATTACHMENT A"

Statement of Frank Falla

My name is Frank Falla. I work in the forensics unit at the Silverado Police Department. At Investigator Cutler's request, I gathered a forensics team and we reported to Legg Lake on 9/20/C.Y.-1 to investigate a Honda Accord found at the site. I reported our findings to Investigator Cutler. The car had been submerged in the water for at least eight months. No blood stains were found in the trunk of the car, however, because of the long-term exposure to water, if there had been any evidence of blood it would have been compromised, if not completely eroded. A cameo necklace was found in the trunk.

Reviewed and verified by: *Frank Falla*
                                                            Frank Falla

"ATTACHMENT B"

WITNESS STATEMENT: LARA MERCKLE

DATE: 9/20/C.Y.-1

Officer Cutler contacted me and asked me to meet him at the police station where he showed me a cameo necklace. The cameo necklace belonged to my sister. It was a family heirloom that my mother gave to Beca. My sister wore the necklace constantly. It was very special to her. I noticed that some of the links on the necklace chain are stretched and broken, which makes me think the necklace was torn off of Beca's neck.

Reviewed and verified by: *Laura Merckle*
                         Laura Merckle

**LEAD COUNTY
OFFICE OF FORENSIC SERVICES**

Report by: Edwin Falker, Criminologist

Report Date: 9/24/C.Y.-1

On September 21, C.Y.-1, Inv. Cutler requested a DNA analysis of hair removed from a brush taken from the Buck residence on October 6, C.Y.-2 be done to determine if the hair came from the same source as the blood collected from the Buck residence on October 6, C.Y.-2.

With a degree of certainty of .9987, it is my conclusion that said blood and said hair came from the same donor.

Edwin Falker
Edwin Falker

Jury Instructions

Members of the jury, I thank you for your attention during this trial. Please pay attention to the instructions I am about to give you.

In this case, Defendant is accused of murder in the first degree. Every person who unlawfully kills a human being with malice aforethought is guilty of the crime of murder in violation of Golden Penal Code section 187. To prove the crime of murder the State must prove the following elements beyond a reasonable doubt:

1.   A human being was killed;

2.   The killing was unlawful; and

3.   The killing was done with malice aforethought.

"Malice" may be either express or implied. Malice is express when there is manifested an intention unlawfully to kill a human being. Malice is implied when:

1.   The killing resulted from an intentional act;

2.   The natural consequences of the act are dangerous to human life; and

3.   The act was deliberately performed with knowledge of the danger to, and with conscious disregard for, human life.

When it is shown that a killing resulted from the intentional doing of an act with express or implied malice, no other mental state need be shown to establish the mental state of malice aforethought. The mental state constituting malice aforethought does not necessarily require any ill will or hatred of the person killed. The word "aforethought" does not imply deliberation or the lapse of considerable time. It only means that the required mental state must precede rather than follow the act.

Richard Buck has entered a plea of not guilty. This means you must presume or believe that Richard Buck is not guilty unless and until the evidence convinces you otherwise. This presumption stays with Richard Buck as to each material allegation in the indictment through each stage of the trial until it has been overcome by the evidence to the exclusion of and beyond a reasonable doubt.

To overcome the Defendant's presumption of innocence, the State has the burden of proving the following two elements:

1. The crime with which the Defendant is charged was committed.

2. The Defendant is the person who committed the crime.

Defendant is not required to prove anything.

Whenever the words "reasonable doubt" are used, you must consider the following: A reasonable doubt is not a mere possible doubt, because everything relating to human affairs is open to some possible or imaginary doubt. It is that state of the case which, after the entire comparison and consideration of all the evidence, leaves the minds of the jurors in that condition that they cannot say they feel an abiding conviction of the truth of the charge.

It is to the evidence introduced during this trial, and to it alone, that you are to look for that proof. A reasonable doubt as to the guilt of Defendant may arise from the evidence, a conflict in the evidence, or a lack of evidence. If you have a reasonable doubt, you should find Defendant not guilty. If you have no reasonable doubt, you should find Defendant guilty.

You must decide this case based only on the law and the evidence. It is up to you to decide what evidence is reliable. You should use your common sense in deciding which evidence is reliable and which evidence should not be relied upon in considering your verdict. You may find some of the evidence not reliable or less reliable than other evidence.

A witness is a person who has knowledge related to this case. You will have to decide whether you believe each witness and how important each witness's testimony is to the case. You may believe all, part, or none of a witness's testimony. In deciding whether to believe a witness's testimony, you may consider, among other factors, the following:

1. Did the witness seem to have an opportunity to see and know the things about which the witness testified?

2. Did the witness seem to have an accurate memory?

3. Was the witness honest and straightforward in answering the attorneys' questions?

4. Did the witness have some interest in how the case should be decided?

5. Does the witness's testimony agree with the other testimony and other evidence in this case?

6. Has the witness been offered or received any money, preferred treatment, or other benefit in order to get the witness to testify?

7. Had any pressure or threat been used against the witness that affected the truth of the witness's testimony?

8. Did the witness at some other time make a statement that is inconsistent with the testimony he or she gave in court?

9. Was it proved that the witness had been convicted of a crime?

You may rely upon your own conclusions about the witnesses. A juror may believe or disbelieve all or any part of the evidence or the testimony of any witness.

Defendant in this case has become a witness. You should apply the same rules to consideration of his testimony that you apply to the testimony of the other witnesses.

There are some general rules that apply to your deliberations. You must follow these rules in order to return a lawful verdict:

1.   You must follow the law as it is set out in these instructions. If you fail to follow the law, your verdict will be a miscarriage of justice.

2.   This case must be decided only upon the evidence that you have heard from the answers of the witnesses and have seen in the form of exhibits and these instructions.

3.   This case must not be decided for or against anyone because you feel sorry for anyone or are angry at anyone.

4.   Remember the lawyers are not on trial. Your feelings about them should not influence your decision in this case.

5.   Your duty is to determine if Defendant has been proven guilty or not. It is the judge's job to determine the proper sentence if Defendant is found guilty.

6.   Whatever verdict you render must be unanimous; that is, each juror must agree to the same verdict. The verdict must be the verdict of each juror as well as of the jury as a whole.

7.   It is entirely proper for a lawyer to talk to a witness about what testimony the witness would give if called to the courtroom. The witness should not be discredited for talking to a lawyer about his or her testimony.

8.   Your verdict should not be influenced by feelings of prejudice, bias, or sympathy. Your verdict must be based on the evidence and the law contained in these instructions.

Deciding a proper verdict is exclusively your job. I cannot participate in that decision in any way. Please disregard anything I may have said or done that made you think I preferred one verdict over another.

Only one verdict may be returned as to the crime charged. The verdict must be in writing and the verdict form has been prepared for you. It is as follows:

[READ VERDICT FORM]

In just a few moments, you will be taken to the jury room by the bailiff. The first thing you should do is elect a foreperson who will preside over your deliberations like the chairperson of a meeting. It is the foreperson's job to sign and date the verdict form when all of you have agreed on a verdict in this case and to bring the verdict back to the courtroom when you return.

In closing, let me remind you that it is important that you follow the law spelled out in these instructions in deciding your verdicts. Even if you do not like the laws, you must apply them. There are no other laws that apply to this case.

IN THE CIRCUIT COURT OF THE THIRTEENTH JUDICIAL CIRCUIT

IN AND FOR LEAD COUNTY, STATE OF GOLDEN

CRIMINAL DIVISION

STATE OF GOLDEN	)
	)
v.	) Case No. CR 99-403
	)
RICHARD D. BUCK,	)
Defendant.	)
	)

VERDICT

As to the charge of murder in the first degree, in violation of Golden Penal Code section 187, we, the jury, find the Defendant, Richard Buck:

_____   Guilty

_____   Not Guilty

So say we all.

_____
Foreperson of the Jury

_____
Date

Chapter 11

William Striver and Frances Gomez

v.

Rancho Fire Department

(employment discrimination)

IN THE CIRCUIT COURT OF THE
THIRTEENTH JUDICIAL CIRCUIT
IN AND FOR LEAD COUNTY, STATE OF GOLDEN
CIVIL DIVISION

WILLIAM STRIVER AND FRANCES   )
GOMEZ,   )
)
     Plaintiffs,   )
)
v.   )   Golden No. 10634[1]
)
RANCHO FIRE DEPARTMENT,   )
)
     Defendant.   )
)
_____)

---

[1] Modified from a case file originally prepared by The American Bar Association Section

of Labor & Employment Law, Copyright © 2009.

**IN THE CIRCUIT COURT OF THE
THIRTEENTH JUDICIAL CIRCUIT
IN AND FOR LEAD COUNTY, STATE OF GOLDEN
CIVIL DIVISION**

WILLIAM STRIVER AND FRANCES GOMEZ,	)))	Golden No. 10634
Plaintiffs,	))	COMPLAINT FOR DAMAGES
v.	)))	
RANCHO FIRE DEPARTMENT,	))	Jury Trial Demanded
Defendant.	))))	

PLAINTIFFS WILLIAM STRIVER ("STRIVER") AND FRANCES GOMEZ ("GOMEZ") as individuals and husband and wife, complain and allege as follows:

1. The Court has personal jurisdiction over Defendant Rancho Fire Department (hereinafter referred to as "RFD") because it is a resident of and/or doing business in the State of Golden.

2. Venue is proper in this County because Defendant RFD resides and/or does business in this County.

3. Striver has been employed by Defendant RFD since C.Y.-22 and has held the rank of engineer for the past 15 years. He is and has been since C.Y.-6 assigned to Station 31. Gomez has been a firefighter with RFD since C.Y.-6, she was stationed at Station 36 until July 18 C.Y.-2 when she was transferred to Station 31.

4. Defendant RFD is a Department of the City of Rancho which has a population of 160,000. Defendant RFD operates 8 fire stations in Rancho.

5. The sworn personnel at Defendant RFD work one of three shifts, A, B, or C. The shifts are arranged in a "platoon schedule" because Defendant RFD covers 24 hours of every day of the year.

6. In C.Y.-6, Striver and Gomez saw each other as they both responded to a general alarm fire. They met several times subsequently and ultimately started dating in April, C.Y.-3. At that time, Striver was still assigned to Station 31 and Gomez was assigned to Station 36. Both worked the A shift. The relationship between Striver and Gomez culminated in their marriage on July 4, C.Y.-2.

7. Within two weeks of their marriage, Defendant RFD informed Plaintiffs in a memorandum that Defendant RFD was transferring Gomez to the B shift based on Defendant RFD's anti-nepotism policy, even though Striver and Gomez worked at separate stations. As a result of being assigned to different shifts, they only have 9 days a month in which they are together, as opposed to 18 before the transfer.

8. Upon information and belief, Plaintiffs allege that it was highly unlikely that they would cross paths on response calls, that an engineer does not supervise, evaluate, or control the work of a firefighter, that the anti-nepotism policy should not have been applied to them, and that Defendant RFD discriminated against them based on their marital status. Plaintiffs further allege that working on the same shift did not affect the Department's morale since Plaintiffs were boarded at different stations.

9. Striver and Gomez filed a charge of discrimination against Defendant RFD for violating Golden Government Code section 12940(a) alleging marital status

discrimination. Plaintiffs received a right to sue letter from the Golden Department of

Fair Employment and Housing.

PRAYER FOR RELIEF

WHEREFORE, Striver and Gomez pray for judgment against Defendant as

follows:

1. That Plaintiffs be re-assigned to work the same shift;

2. Damages in an amount to be proved at trial;

3. Reasonable attorney's fees;

4. Cost of suit; and

5. For such other and further relief as the Court deems just and proper.

DATED: November 4, C.Y.-2

Respectfully submitted,

Gregory D. Marks

GREGORY D. MARKS
816 Congress Ave., Suite 1700
San Juan, State of Golden 90263
Attorney for Plaintiff

**IN THE CIRCUIT COURT OF THE
THIRTEENTH JUDICIAL CIRCUIT
IN AND FOR LEAD COUNTY, STATE OF GOLDEN
CIVIL DIVISION**

WILLIAM STRIVER AND FRANCES GOMEZ,	)))	
Plaintiffs,	))	
v.	))	Golden No. 10634
RANCHO FIRE DEPARTMENT,	)))	DEFENDANT'S ANSWER TO COMPLAINT FOR DAMAGES
Defendant.	)))	
_____	)	

DEFENDANT RANCHO FIRE DEPARTMENT hereby answers the Complaint by admitting, denying and affirmatively alleging as follows:

1. Answering Paragraphs 1-5, Defendant RFD admits the allegations contained in said paragraphs.

2. Answering Paragraph 6, Defendant RFD lacks sufficient information to respond and on said ground denies each and every allegation contained in said paragraph.

3. Answering Paragraph 7, Defendant RFD admits that Frances was transferred to the B shift and denies each and every other allegation contained in said paragraph.

4. Answering Paragraph 8, Defendant RFD denies each and every allegation contained in said paragraph.

5. Answering Paragraph 9, Defendant RFD admits the allegations contained in said paragraph.

AFFIRMATIVE DEFENSE

6. As a separate affirmative defense to the Complaint, Defendant RFD alleges that at all times relevant hereto, it was permitted to reasonably regulate for reasons of supervision, safety, security or morale, the assignment of working spouses in the same department, division or facility and that Defendant RFD acted in full compliance with all applicable federal, state and local laws.

WHEREFORE, Defendant prays for judgment as follows:

1. That the Complaint be dismissed in its entirety;

2. That judgment be granted to Defendant;

3. For costs of suit; and

4. For such other further relief as the Court may deem just and proper.

DATED: December 30, C.Y.-2

Danielle Bride
_____
DANIELLE BRIDE
4545 Main St.
San Juan, State of Golden 90264
Attorney for Defendant

Witness List

Witnesses for Plaintiffs:

    1. William "Bill" Striver *

    2. Frances Gomez * *

Witnesses for Defendant:

    1. Sam Hatch * * *

    2. Pat C. Gundum * * *

Each side must call both witnesses listed for their respective side in any order.

    *   This witness must be a male.

    * *   This witness must be a female.

    * * *   This witness may be either gender.

This is a bifurcated trial on the issue of liability only.

Stipulations

1. Federal Rules of Evidence apply.

2. Each witness who gave a deposition did agree under oath at the outset of his/her deposition to give a full and complete description of what occurred and to correct the deposition for inaccuracies and completeness before signing the deposition.

3. All witnesses called to testify who have in statements identified tangible evidence, can, if asked, identify the same at trial.

4. All exhibits in the file are authentic and, unless otherwise noted, are the original of that document.

5. All depositions were signed under oath.

6. Other than what appears in the witness statements or depositions, there is nothing exceptional or unusual about the background of any of the witnesses that would bolster or detract from their credibility.

7. All dates are denoted by C.Y. (current year) and C.Y.-1 indicating, for example, that the date is the current year minus one.

8. All pretrial motions shall be oral.

9. No party may "invent" witnesses or evidence not specifically mentioned in this problem.

10. "Beyond the record" is not a proper objection. Rather, attorneys shall use cross-examination as a means of challenging a witness whose testimony strays beyond the facts contained in the witness' statement or deposition.

11. The law is accurately set forth in the jury instructions.

12. The plaintiff and defendant may call only the two witnesses listed on their respective
witness list. Each party may call an additional witness by deposition or witness
statement. Any such testimony is subject to objections pursuant to the Federal Rules
of Evidence. If a witness is called by deposition or witness statement, the opposing
party may cross-examine that witness by deposition or witness statement.

Deposition of William "Bill" Striver
Date: March 1, C.Y.-1

Q: Bill, when did you first join the Rancho Fire Department?

A: It was November of C.Y.-22.

Q: And what positions have you held with the department?

A: Firefighter and engineer.

Q: When did you become an engineer?

A: I don't know the exact date, C.Y.-16, I guess.

Q: What are the basic duties of a firefighter?

A: When we're in the station, we're responsible for maintaining the station, cleaning it. On fire scenes, we each have specific jobs.

Q: And you've been an engineer for 16 years; can you tell me what an engineer does?

A: An engineer is responsible for the apparatuses, to make sure that they're in good operating condition under the rules set forth by the department. When you're on an engine company, you're responsible for pumping at a fire, which means you pump the water to the hose lines to the firefighters. If you're on a ladder truck you're responsible for all the duties on a ladder truck, which would be putting up the aerial. When you're not in any of those capacities, you're under the supervision of the captain. You follow his orders and you go in and fight the fire or whatever task is given.

Q: Now, who evaluates your performance?

A: The captain does.

Q: Who evaluates the performance of a firefighter?

A: The captain.

Q: Typically, in a station what personnel would one expect to find?

A: In a 24-hour shift, we have ten people consisting of two captains, a truck and an engine captain, two engineers which are either on a truck or engine. We'll have four firefighters, two on each truck and engine and then two paramedic firefighters that operate on the rescue ambulance.

Q: Let me stop you right there. You mentioned a truck and an engine. Explain how those are different.

A: No problem. An engine is the primary vehicle for transporting water. It consists of a water tank and pumps. There are, of course, a few ladders and hose lines but like I said it is essentially a water transporting and pumping vehicle.

Q: Okay, and how does that differ from a truck?

A: A truck doesn't have a water tank or pumps. A truck is generally bigger than an engine and transports most of the fire personnel, most of the ladders and all the rest of the equipment we use.

Q: Thanks for clearing that up. Now, let me back up. We were talking about station personnel and so on. Who is in command of the station?

A: The captain is.

Q: When you go out on your truck, tell me what people would be on the truck.

A: The captain, engineer and two firefighters.

Q: And who is in command of the truck?

A: The captain's in command of the truck.

Q: At the scene of a fire who's in command of the personnel?

A: The captain is.

Q: Does the engineer direct or order the firefighter with respect to performance of his or her duties?

A: No.

Q: Have you found yourself involved in fire suppression services where other engine companies were present as well?

A: Yes. There's the tiered response for every call depending on what it is.

Q: When you say "tiered response," can you explain that?

A: Tiered response is – let's say there's a house fire, you would get three engines and a truck from one station, and two trucks from another station. So the tiered dispatch system is just based on what the call is, how big the building is, et cetera.

Q: If there are multiple stations responding to let's say a fire, how many captains would one expect to find at the scene?

A: One per incident.

Q: How many times have you responded to fires where there were multiple stations responding?

A: Too many to count.

Q: With respect to those experiences, have you ever found yourself in a position as an engineer directing the services of a firefighter from another company?

A: Not in a supervisor's position, I never have. We have such a high level of training that everybody knows their responsibility and they act accordingly.

Q: Who would be conducting the supervision in that situation?

A: The captain or battalion chief.

Q: When would one expect to find a battalion chief at a fire scene?

A: Any time there are multiple engines, trucks, et cetera, at the incident.

Q: Let's turn to a more personal matter. When did you first meet Frances?

A: I first met her at a fire in C.Y.-6.

Q: Prior to your marriage, how long did you and Frances go together?

A: About a year.

Q: When you first started dating Frances, what shifts did you both work?

A: We both worked on the "A" shift, but at different stations, I was at 31 and she was at 36.

Q: Explain how the shifts work.

A: Each shift is 24 hours. We start at 7:00 in the morning and go to 7:00 in the morning the next day. The way the schedule goes, if you're on the "A" shift, you work – you're on one shift 24 hours, you're off 24 hours. You're on again for 24 hours, you're off. And then you're on again for 24 hours and then off four days after that. All three shifts work that schedule and that's how it covers every day of the year. I just happened to bring the current March schedule. So you can see how it works.

Q: Let's go ahead and have the schedule you've produced be a part of your deposition. I'm going to mark that Attachment "A." As a result of working on the same shift, how many days off per month did you and Frances have together?

A: Approximately 20. Well, 18 to 20 depending on how many days in the month. Plus, it could be less if we work overtime or trade shifts with someone.

Q: At what point was Frances transferred to a different shift?

A: Well, we got married on July 4, C.Y. -2. Then on July 18, the department issued a memo saying that relatives couldn't work on the same shift anymore, she had to change shifts and was reassigned to the "B" shift the next week.

Q: As a result of Frances being re-assigned to a different shift, how many days per month do you have together?

A: When our shifts were moved, it went down to nine to ten days off depending on the amount of days in the month. But the whole thing is just ridiculous because there is actually more of a chance of crossing paths than before when we were both on "A" shift assigned to different stations.

Q: Can you explain that?

A: The station she was assigned to before was not the primary station that we would respond with the most. Now, in the current situation, she often works at those stations that we do respond with all the time. Right now she is even assigned to the same station that I'm at but on a different shift. So in the morning – and it's happened, we have been allowed to work on that shift together at the same station on different apparatuses for, you know, a period of time. And the possibility for that happening naturally, because of her working on the opposite shift of me, it could happen any day. Because if we come in and take over for somebody, you know, we can end up in the same situation, being on the same call with each other, even on the same apparatus.

Q: So the chances are greater of you two interfacing now that you are on separate shifts than when you were on the same shift?

A: Definitely.

Q: Did you know a firefighter named Robert Rialto?

A: Yes.

Q: Do you know how Bob Rialto died?

A: Yes. I was there.

Q: Please tell us what happened.

A: It happened about ten years ago. We had responded to a blaze at a warehouse and one of our guys had become trapped in the building. Bob ignored the danger to his own life and ran into the blaze and tried to save our comrade.

Q: Was the comrade Bob tried to save someone he knew very well?

A: Yes, it was his brother, Keith Rialto.

Q: Was it standard procedure for a firefighter to risk his life to enter a burning building to rescue another firefighter?

A: No.

Q: What is the procedure in that situation?

A: No procedure; you can't have a set of rules for every situation.

Q: When a firefighter is trapped, does the captain decide how the situation should be handled?

A: Yes.

Q: Did the captain order Bob Rialto to enter the burning warehouse to try to rescue his brother?

A: No.

Q: I thought you said the captain was in charge?

A: In that situation the captain could not give the order because Keith Rialto was the captain and he was trapped in the fire.

Q: Didn't anyone else assume command when the captain was not present?

A: Yes. Bob was the next ranking person on the scene.

Q: So he gave himself the order to enter?

A: That's one way to look at it.

Q: Why didn't any of the other firefighters enter the building?

A: Captain Rialto had ordered everyone back because of the threat of the roof caving in.

Q: Everyone present obeyed that order?

A: Everyone except Bob, but once he assumed command he had the right to decide for himself what to do.

Q: Have you ever been made an acting captain?

A: In the past, I have. Maybe four or five times.

Q: Is it standard within the city that engineers are called upon to be acting captains on occasion?

A: No, that wasn't the circumstances. The circumstances are, if you're interested in being promoted into that position, they give you the opportunity to act. It's never to – as an engineer, I've never been asked to be an acting captain to take his place.

Q: Have you ever given direction to firefighters as an engineer?

A: Direction as an engineer? No.

Q: As an engineer, told them what to do?

A: No.

Q: Never been in that circumstance. Are you aware of any other engineers that have had the responsibility for telling firefighters to take action?

A: Not in a supervisory role.

Q: I believe you described the department as not being very receptive that you had a married relationship with another firefighter. Would that be accurate?

A: Correct.

Q: What is your understanding of why the department wouldn't want a husband and wife to work in the same station during the same hours?

A: To back up, I really don't know. I mean, other than that the department has never dealt with this before.

Q: Do you believe that if you saw your wife injured, you'd react more than if you saw another firefighter injured?

A: No, because we're – it's like a brother and sisterhood of people. There's no difference in reaction. We are that close together that we react the same, we help each other the same.

Q: So there's no difference in the emotional attachment you have to your wife than to the other employees you work with?

A: Not to the other firefighters.

I have reviewed this transcript. This is a complete and accurate account.

Bill Striver

William "Bill" Striver

Attachment "A"

March C.Y.-1						
S	**M**	**T**	**W**	**Th**	**F**	**S**
	1 A – on B – off C – off	2 A – off B – on C – off	3 A – on B – off C – off	4 A – off B – off C – on	5 A – on B – off C – off	6 A – off B – off C – on
7 A – off B – on C – off	8 A – off B – off C – on	9 A – off B – on C – off	10 A – on B – off C – off	11 A – off B – on C – off	12 A – on B – off C – off	13 A – off B – off C – on
14 A – on B – off C – off	15 A – off B – off C – on	16 A – off B – on C – off	17 A – off B – off C – on	18 A – off B – on C – off	19 A – on B – off C – off	20 A – off B – on C – off
21 A – on B – off C – off	22 A – off B – off C – on	23 A – on B – off C – off	24 A – off B – off C – on	25 A – off B – on C – off	26 A – off B – off C – on	27 A – off B – on C – off
28 A – on B – off C – off	29 A – off B – on C – off	30 A – on B – off C – off	31 A – off B – off C – on			

Deposition of Frances Gomez
Date: March 1, C.Y.-1

Q: How long have you been employed by the Rancho Fire Department?

A: I was hired on June 24th, C.Y.-6.

Q: When did you and Bill commence a dating relationship?

A: We began dating at about the end of March, beginning of April, C.Y.-3.

Q: Now, during your dating relationship up until your marriage, did anybody from the department ever tell you that your relationship with Bill created a conflict?

A: No, never.

Q: Did anybody ever tell you that there was a problem associated with the efficiency of supervision?

A: No, never. He's not a supervisor.

Q: Did anybody ever advise you that there was a morale problem?

A: No, never.

Q: Did anybody ever tell you during that period that there was a safety concern with respect to you and Bill?

A: No, never. Bill and I both have always maintained a very professional attitude.

Q: Now, from your perspective, what problems have you experienced as a result of being separated on different shifts from Bill?

A: Honestly, I don't know where to begin. At work, not only is it stressful just being there, but it's obviously emotionally draining because the energy that needs to be set aside for all of the issues that have been brought on by the separation that have to be dealt with daily, both in the work environment and off duty. It's on your mind every time you go to work and every time you go home. It just seems like we're being – or I am being disciplined for something. That I did something wrong. I got married. And they make me feel like, you know, it's some kind of punishment or something. They're enforcing a policy that does not apply to my situation, to our situation. They are very selective on what policies they truly enforce and who they enforce them with. That's why I feel that we're being discriminated against. Because if we never got married and just moved in together, they would not have done any of this. And they say the same policy doesn't apply for brother-in-laws and brothers in this department. It is clearly in front of them and they are just continuing to actively enforce it on us and nobody else. And you know, it's caused us to seek marital counseling just to try to hold together what we have. Because they put a wedge in between our personal life and our work.

Q: Do you know of any other relatives who are working on the same shift?

A: Yes. Brett and Shaun Gibson, they're brothers and they both work on the "C" shift.

Q: What stations do Brett and Shaun Gibson work at?

A: Right now Brett works at 31 and Shaun works at 33. I went in and spoke with Chief Hatch and told him/her "right now Brett Gibson and his brother, Shaun Gibson, are both working on the "C" shift." And he/she did absolutely nothing about it.

Q: You indicated that if you and Bill work on the same shift but at a different station the anti-nepotism policy would not apply. Tell me why you think that.

A: I can't say it enough. Bill is not a supervisor. He does not supervise me.

Q: Isn't there the possibility that if acting as captain in a situation where multiple stations are responding, he *could* be your supervisor?

A: That is extremely unlikely.

Q: When you were transferred from the "A" shift to the "B" shift, did that have any impact on you with respect to overtime?

A: Well, in a sense no, because there's a lot more vacancies for firefighters to actually have overtime, but I'm still limited because we're only able to see each other when "C" shift is on. Those are our days off together. So instead of being able to work, let's say, 20 overtimes a month, which would be the case if we were on the same schedule, I can only really sign up for "A" shift days, because if I was to work on the "C" shift, we would not be able to see each other, so in reality my ability to work overtime is reduced down to half. There's a lot of movement on my behalf because of staffing issues now.

Q: What do you mean by "movement"?

A: Take today for example, we're both on duty and I'm currently assigned to station 31 "B." If Bill has the opportunity to sign up for overtime and there is no engineer vacancy on schedule "B," except for 31 "B," what they will do is, rather than displace an engineer at his current assignment, they will pull me out of my station and put me into another station where there was a vacancy with a firefighter and flip flop the overtime firefighter and myself who is currently assigned to the station.

Q: If you were to compare the number of times that your path has crossed with Bill's since you were separated into the "B" shift contrasted with when both you and Bill were working on "A" shift together, what would that look like?

A: Now that we're assigned to different shifts, nearly every time I had been signed up, there had been a vacancy at his station. And when I sign up, I've been given the opportunity to get the overtime, but I can't work the "A" shift because that is when my husband is there. So, you know, we have to keep moving other staffing around to move somebody into station 31 and move me out to a different station. And when they do that – there's been a few times where they actually tell us to get overtime at a slower station and due to whatever schedule there may be, because at that station they opt to take the overtime. And when they actually make the movement of me going to another station to pull me out of station 31, people have been put in station 31 and it cancels their overtime and now somebody's forced into that overtime.

Q: Is there a greater opportunity for you and Bill to interact now that you're working on the "B" shift than when you and he were on the "A" shift and you were working at separate stations?

A: Yes.

Q: Can you explain that?

A: There's an opportunity where, you know, we work at a station nearly next to each other over – I should say the next district over. And when that happens, we run into each other on calls. The assignment which consists of three engines, two trucks, a battalion chief, and rescue ambulance for certain districts, we run into each other. And the overtime, there's that situation in general. We're located at the same station right now and if somebody needs to hold over or come in early for somebody, or whatever the situation may be, then we're directly working together with each other at the same station, versus where if we were just assigned to the "A" shift at different stations, we both report to duty, we go absolutely separate ways. We report under different supervisors and there is no conflict. Before, I'd go days without ever seeing Bill. But now, you know, we're running into each other constantly, all the time.

Q: You told us they offered you the "B" and "C" shift, how did you react to that?

A: Knowing how a 24-hour schedule works and what it's like to already be on a 24-hour schedule, it's really easy to do the math. That I would now nearly not see my husband. And the response to that was – just in my mind, disappointing because of the effect that it was going to have in my life. And I tried to express that to them, that this was clearly not the answer to whatever they were trying to enforce, and that the policy doesn't apply because he's not a supervisor.

Q: What was the reason you were told that you were being moved to different shifts?

A: Because of the anti-nepotism policy; because Bill was a supervisor.

Q: Is that the reason that you were being moved?

A: And because it was uncharted territory in the fire department.

Q: The work schedule that you requested to work would be the same whether it's "A," "B," or "C"?

A: Correct.

Q: In effect, if you work that same schedule, that would mean that you would have the same days off, is that correct?

A: Correct.

Q: Which double the number of days that you currently have off together?

A: That's correct.

I have reviewed this transcript. This is a complete and accurate account.

Frances Gomez
Frances Gomez

Deposition of Deputy Chief Pat C. Gundum
Date: March 9, C.Y.-1

Q: In an instance in which a fire captain was either injured on a call or unavailable to do his duties, who would take command pursuant to the department's chain of command?

A: Pursuant to the chain of command, it would be the engineer.

Q: And is that based on your experience with the department in your 26 years here?

A: Yes.

Q: Now, can you describe what an acting position is?

A: An acting position is a position in which a person of a lower rank is temporarily assigned, but they're charged with the same responsibilities as a person that would normally be there in that capacity. Usually a person is assigned to an acting position when they are interested in promotion and have passed the examination for the higher rank.

Q: What is the Rancho Fire Department's policy on married people working together?

A: Married people who are working together are assigned to opposite shifts.

Q: Is that fire department policy or a city policy?

A: That's based on the spirit and the intent of the city policy.

Q: When you learned that the two grievants were married did you make a determination whether the city policy was being violated?

A: At some point in time, yes.

Q: And what conclusion did you come to?

A: That the anti-nepotism policy required that people who were married must work on separate shifts to minimize the possibility of any conflicts.

Q: Who made the final decision of what action, if any, would be taken regarding the working assignments of the two plaintiffs?

A: I did.

Q: You did. Did you do that after conferring with the fire chief?

A: No.

Q: What decision did you come to?

A: I came to the decision that since they met the definition of relatives, that I would assign them the same way I have to assign other relatives on the job based upon the change we made concerning the department's policy after consultation with the H.R. department and the city.

Q: And do you know approximately the date that change occurred?

A: Approximately July 18, C.Y.-2.

Q: And were department members informed of this change?

A: Yes. They were informed in person, with a conversation with the fire chief, pretty much one-on-one, as well as written correspondence, a memo.

Q: Who had the one-on-one conversations with the chief?

A: I believe the chief met with the majority of the individuals impacted.

Q: Did the change come about as a result of the issues raised by the Plaintiffs?

A: Ultimately, yes.

Q: Now, let's take a look at the city's policy. It's identified as "department command." And let me take you to Roman Numeral III, which is rank. And Roman Numeral III represents the order of rank from the highest rank to the lowest rank. Correct?

A: Yes.

Q: Now, let's start with the fire captain. Does he have any responsibility to supervise employees?

A: Yes.

Q: And what type of supervisory responsibilities does the captain have?

A: The fire captain is responsible for an entire work crew usually consisting of a driver and two firefighters. He also has the responsibility to train, evaluate and discipline those personnel on an ongoing basis, and he or she serves as the officer in charge of the fire station environment.

Q: How often does a fire captain evaluate his subordinates?

A: It's a continuous and ongoing process and there are annual evaluations.

Q: Does the captain prepare evaluations for engineers, firefighters and paramedics?

A: Yes.

Q: You also indicated that part of the responsibility of the captain is to discipline. Can you explain to me what kind of authority the captain has relative to the imposition of discipline?

A: He or she has the authority to take, first of all, immediate corrective action when deemed necessary. And for more involved matters, he or she would commence the progressive discipline process for doing some ongoing issues surrounding primarily work-related matters, things of that nature.

Q: Now, an engineer is not engaged in any performance evaluations of a firefighter or paramedic, correct?

A: I don't know that I agree with that statement.

Q: An engineer does not have the authority, absent approval or direction from the captain, to tell a firefighter or a paramedic what to do, correct?

A: That's not a true statement.

Q: So when a captain is present, a firefighter is not under the direction or supervision of an engineer, correct?

A: Right. When the captain is physically present, yes.

Q: An engineer cannot direct a firefighter or paramedic as to what he or she should do when there's a captain present, correct?

A: Correct.

Q: Now, an engineer is not charged with the environment of the fire station, is he?

A: No.

Q: Let me ask you this, with Frances Gomez being assigned to one station and Bill Striver functioning as an engineer at another station, the two of them have no inter-working relationship, do they?

A: Yes, they would on major emergencies.

Q: On major emergencies?

A: Yes. Any time more than one fire engine is dispatched, the potential is there.

Q: So in a major emergency there's a potential for spouses to be together or relatives to be together. Is that what you're telling me?

A: Yes.

Q: Absent a major emergency with Bill Striver working one station and Frances Gomez working in another station, they do not have a working relationship, do they?

A: No, they wouldn't.

Q: Now, the city's policy, which is the clarification of the city's department anti-nepotism policy, came out as a result of this case, correct?

A: Yes, but the department policy has been in place for several years now, ever since a tragedy involving two brothers who died in a fire.

Q: You are referring to the deaths of Keith and Robert Rialto?

A: Yes. It was clear from what happened with the Rialtos that no amount of training could overcome the emotions toward loved ones trapped in the fire. And that is why we adopted the anti-nepotism policy.

Q: Let's return to the anti-nepotism policy for a moment. As you understand the policy, Chief, what is its purpose?

A: The purpose of this policy is to avoid conflicts as they might relate to safety, fiscal responsibility, and morale within the city work force.

Q: When you say "conflicts," what do you mean by that, Chief?

A: I mean that two people who have a close relationship could create a conflict, particularly if one is supervising the other or is made to evaluate or otherwise impact that person's employment, it likely would create a conflict of interest.

Q: So one of the major responsibilities or purposes of the policy is to avoid conflict of interest in which one relative is placed in a position of supervising or of evaluating the performance of another, right?

A: Yes.

Q: And you would agree with me, would you not, that in this case, William Striver does not supervise and has never supervised Frances Gomez?

A: Yes.

Q: And you would also agree with me that Bill Striver has never been called upon to engage in any performance evaluation of Frances Gomez?

A: Yes.

Q: And you would agree with me that Bill Striver does not control the terms and conditions of Frances Gomez's conditions of employment, correct?

A: Yes.

Q: Now, you mentioned safety as a consideration for the anti-nepotism policy, what did you mean by that?

A: Well, I meant that when two closely aligned employees are working together, there's a concern for the compromise of safety whether it be for their fellow firefighters or the public at large.

Q: You also mentioned fiscal responsibility, what did you mean by that?

A: Well, there's occasion for it to be an adverse impact financially due to leave of absence on the part of employees. As an example, if one spouse is home ill and the other spouse takes off to take care of that spouse, both spouses are being compensated – paid while off sick, in addition to two additional people I have to call back and pay time-and-a-half. Two people times time-and-half, plus the two spouses, means that I'm paying five people because one person is actually sick. That's not good, sound fiscal management.

Q: What did you mean when you said that there was a morale factor?

A: I think the morale factor started this to begin with, the whole issue. It started in the rumor mill, if you will. I was contacted by Battalion Chief Hatch concerning someone who came to him/her, who he/she didn't identify, that had some concern or was feeling uncomfortable with the situation pertaining to the two plaintiffs. That's what I mean by the morale issue. It kind of started with rumors flowing out of the department.

Q: And is the anti-nepotism policy predicated upon responding to rumors?

A: No.

Q: Why do you say no?

A: Because the point was not to respond to rumors, but to best ensure safety for workers and the public.

I have reviewed this transcript. This is a complete and accurate account.

Pat C. Gundum
Pat C. Gundum

Deposition of Fire Department Chief Sam Hatch
Date: March 11, C.Y.-1

Q: Chief Hatch, does the Rancho Fire Department have rules and regulations pertaining to firefighters and/or engineers who marry one another?

A: If you read the department rules, they contain a section and that paragraph says: "it is the policy of the city that relatives of city officers or employees shall not be hired, promoted or transferred into positions in which one relative may supervise directly or indirectly any other relative."

Q: Did this cover Mr. Striver and Ms. Gomez?

A: Mr. Striver is an engineer. In appropriate circumstances, he takes command when a captain isn't available. In effect, he would be a supervisor in appropriate circumstances if Ms. Gomez worked directly in the same unit.

Q: Why would Striver and Gomez ever work together?

A: In Rancho, it is not uncommon or unusual for multiple stations to respond to the same fire. In those instances, Ms. Gomez could come under him if she was working under his supervision as an engineer.

Q: What is the rationale for that policy?

A: The city's policy has many reasons. One of which is to provide for the safety of its citizens, not just for the firefighters.

Q: Does the department believe that relationships between its personnel have an impact on safety?

A: Yes, particularly in a marital situation. The city does not put employees in a situation where they make decisions that could be influenced by a relationship, particularly involving a spouse.

Q: Chief, there has been a claim that the department violated the law, in particular the Fair Employment Practices Act. Was the department aware of that act in its dealing with Striver and Gomez?

A: Yes. We are dedicated to full compliance with the law. However, the code, specifically addresses only one discriminatory issue and that is marital status. It says right here: "nothing in this part relating to discrimination on account of marital status shall do either of the following: A) affect the right of an employer to reasonably regulate, for reasons of supervision, safety, security, or morale, the working of spouses in the same department, division or facility, consistent with the rules and regulations adopted by the commission."

Q: Is the department prohibited from assigning a firefighter to a shift based upon marital status?

A: Within a city or department you can assign them to areas where there's no direct supervision or the possibility of supervision of that employee, so that you never have a reporting situation that can occur or the possibility of that reporting situation to occur. When the plaintiffs got married, under the rules and regulations and under the law as it currently stands, the department had to take action. The city, in response to that, removed the possibility of supervision in emergency type situations and assigned the junior of the two people to a different work schedule.

Q: As a result of the reassignment did Ms. Gomez suffer any injury?

A: There was no loss of pay or loss of rank. There was no loss of overtime either. Both Striver and Gomez had the same chance as always and as other personnel to take overtime. For their own reasons they may have decided not to, but that was not because we limited either of them from working overtime.

Q: From the city's perspective, what is this case really about?

A: The key is the city has the right, to ensure that we provide services to the city, to ensure that we have the proper people doing it and to ensure there is no potential for conflict in doing those services. Common sense and logic tells you that a husband and wife combination is not something you put into an emergency situation. The reasons are: supervision, safety, security, and morale.

Q: Did you have discussions with the city personnel people before this situation with Mr. Striver and Ms. Gomez?

A: Yes.

Q: Who was present during the discussions you had with the personnel department?

A: It was the HR director, counsel and me.

Q: Do you recall was Chief Gundum present during any of those discussions?

A: Maybe he/she was involved in a telephone conversation, I believe, at the other end of the discussion.

Q: What was the purpose of those discussions?

A: The purpose of the discussions were to review the city policy, and quite frankly, to let me know whether I was in violation of the city policy in the manner in which I was applying – or the department was applying the policy in the field.

Q: Did you learn in what way might you be violating the policy?

A: Understanding I had only been with Rancho for two years, it came to light the fire department had been typically interpreting this policy to mean that over the course of the 120 shifts a year as a regular assignment, that people or members of the department that were considered to be relatives were not allowed to work the same shift at the same station. Then I was told conversely, that anytime you have relatives working on the same shift, even at different stations, that you were in violation of the policy.

Q: How did you go about fixing that policy?

A: I identified that there were six members within the department that fell under the definition of relative. I decided that rather than come out immediately with a memorandum, without any type of explanation of what the department was doing with regard to enforcing the policy, that I would take a week and catch these members on shift to talk them through what occurred with regards to the city's policy, what occurred with regard to the fire department not following the city policy. And that at the conclusion of my meeting with each of them, that effective immediately thereafter that we would start enforcing the city policy department-wide.

Q: Outside of these meetings, did you inform the department of your decision?

A: Once I met with the six members that were affected, I sent a memorandum on how the department was going to begin effectively enforcing that policy.

Q: I am showing you a memo you authored dated July 27, C.Y.-2, do you recognize that document?

A: I do.

Q: And is that the document you just referred to?

A: It is.

Q: And that was issued to each and every member of department?

A: It was.

Q: To your knowledge, has that policy been enforced since it was put into effect?

A: To the best of my knowledge it has.

Q: And how many employees are in the department?

A: We have a total department complement of the 176 and I believe 159 are sworn firefighter staff.

Q: And other than this policy, is there a reason why you wouldn't want people assigned to the same shift?

A: One of the reasons is that the department, as well as the city, by policy doesn't want to give the impression of a special relationship or special working relationship that relatives might bring to the situation. Additionally, because of the emergency services that we operate under, the policy specifically talks about not having a working relationship. Whether it's through training exercise, whether it's through emergency scene response, and the like, that type of a special relationship could occur.

Q: What would be the impact of that special relationship?

A: When they say blood is thicker than water, the reality is that if you have a relative that is in duress or dire need that you would be – have a propensity, I believe, to want to take care of that person foremost before any of your other duties took place.

Q: Are you aware that there are two brothers, Brett and Shaun Gibson, who are currently working on the same shift.

A: Yes.

Q: Isn't that in violation of your anti-nepotism policy?

A: No because, you see, the Gibson brothers are both firefighters so there is no supervisory potential there so it's a completely different situation.

Q: During your tenure as chief, is the policy here inconsistent anywhere else that you've worked as a chief?

A: In the other jurisdictions where I have served there have been similar restrictions on relatives working together.

I have reviewed this transcript. This is a complete and accurate account.

S. Hatch
_____
Sam Hatch

EXHIBIT 1

MANUAL OF PERSONNEL RULES, PRACTICES, AND PROCEDURES FOR CITY OF RANCHO	SECTION: 1.00 Personal Conduct and Standards of Employment SUBJECT: 1.25 Anti-Nepotism Policy

SUPERSEDES: August 15, C.Y.-16	NEW EFFECTIVE DATE: June 3, C.Y.-14	PAGE 1 OF 1
APPROVED BY CITY MANAGER:		

I.   It is the policy of the City that relatives of City officers or employees shall not be hired, promoted, or transferred into positions in which one relative may supervise, directly or indirectly, any other relative, or work in a capacity which would allow an employee to evaluate or control the terms, conditions or performance circumstances of employment of a relative. Relatives of City officers or employees, or members of the City Council or members of any City Board or Commission shall not be employed in any position in which the employment of such relative has the potential for adversely impacting the safety, security, morale, or efficiency of supervision of other employees, or in which there may be created a potential conflict of interest.

II. A "relative" shall be defined as a son, daughter, brother, sister, parent, grandparent or spouse. Half-relatives, step-relatives and in-laws are included in these restrictions.

III. This policy governs the future hiring, promotion or transfer of relatives only. The department head shall be responsible to ensure that work assignments are made so as to avoid conflicts of interest or violation of this policy. If no conflict of interest exists because employees have no working relationship, supervisory or evaluative control over one another, no action shall be necessary. If conflict exists, such action may include reassignment to another position, work location or work shift within the department. If such reassignment or other alternative is not available within the department, the Human Resources Department will be contacted to identify other possible alternatives within other City departments.

The employee is responsible for immediately notifying the department head of an impending marriage or an impending acquired relationship with another employee within the same department.

EXHIBIT 2

Administrative Procedures of the Rancho Fire Department

	Section:	4000
	File:	4003
DEPARTMENT COMMAND	Rev. Date:	March 19, C.Y.-7
	Date:	April 30, C.Y.-7
	Approved:	

I.   POLICY
   A.   The administrative control of the Rancho Fire Department is placed under the fire chief, who shall manage, control and direct the activities and personnel of the Fire Department.

II.   PROCEDURE
   A.   In the absence of the fire chief, the duties of the fire chief shall be assumed in the following sequence, unless otherwise specified by the fire chief:
      1.   Deputy Fire Chief
      2.   Fire Battalion Chief

III.   RANK
   A.   The order of rank for sworn personnel in the Fire Department shall be as follows:
      1.   Fire Chief
      2.   Deputy Fire Chief
      3.   Fire Battalion Chief
      4.   Fire Captain
      5.   Fire Engineers
      6.   Firefighters, Paramedics

EXHIBIT 3

Rules and Regulations of the Rancho Fire Department

POSITION RESPONSIBILITIES	**Section:**	**1000**
	File:	**1003**
	Rev. Date:	**April 23, C.Y.-9**
	Date:	
	Approved:	

*   *   *   *   *

V.   CAPTAINS

   A.   Authority

      1.   Captains shall have absolute command and control of their respective companies while on duty.

   B.   Duties

      1.   Captains shall enforce all departmental rules, regulations and procedures: safety procedures, station rules, apparatus maintenance, cleanliness of quarters and apparatus and everything pertaining to the efficient operation and condition of their companies and personnel under their command.

   C.   Powers

      1.   Captains shall preserve order and discipline in and about the company quarters and at fires.
      2.   They may detail any and all members under their command to any duty consistent with the efficient operation of their company.

   D.   Department Communications

      1.   Captain shall send or cause to be sent all official communications through proper channels with appropriate comments, remarks or recommendations.

E.   Attendance at Incidents

1.   Captains shall answer all alarms of incidents in their district or as dispatched when on duty unless otherwise instructed. If there are multiple stations responding, then one captain may report per incident.
2.   The first regular officer of an engine or truck company to arrive at an incident shall be in charge of such incident until the arrival of a superior officer and the assumption of command. When an acting officer is in charge of the first engine or truck company to arrive at an incident, he/she shall turn over command to the first regular officer to arrive at such incident who will assume command until the arrival and assumption of command of a superior officer.

F.   Response to Incidents

1.   Captains shall be held responsible for the proper response of the apparatus and personnel under their command at all alarms and incidents.
2.   Captains shall, upon receipt of any alarm, carefully check location on map to ascertain proper response thereto, location of hydrants or any additional information necessary for quick and efficient response.

G.   Reports

1.   Captains shall promptly and officially make written reports as required through regular channels on the appropriate forms as provided, giving full details.
2.   Captains shall make monthly written reports on specified forms covering the activities of the company directly under their command and shall forward same to their Captain II.

H.   Other Duties

1.   Captains shall perform such other duties as their superiors may prescribe consistent with the performance of the duties of their position.

VI.   ENGINEERS AND OTHER DRIVERS

A.   Authority

1.   Apparatus shall be in charge of firefighters with the rating of engineer. Engineers shall be responsible for the cleanliness and operating efficiency of the apparatus to which they are assigned while in quarters and to the proper and safe operation in driving the apparatus to and from incidents and while working at incidents.

B.   Duties

1.   Engineers shall be responsible for the proper operation of their apparatus at fires, to ensure that proper engine pressure is given to ensure proper nozzle pressure under any and all conditions.

2.   Engineers shall, when taking over the apparatus from the member of the opposite shift, check batteries, lights and such other equipment as may be necessary to assure themselves that the machine is in readiness for instant response.

3.   Engineers shall be subject to such other duties outside their regular line of work as may be prescribed by their superior officers. They shall be governed by all general rules and regulations affecting firefighters.

VII.   FIREFIGHTERS/FIREFIGHTER-PARAMEDICS

A.   Definition

1.   A firefighter or firefighter/paramedic is a duly appointed employee of the Fire Department for the purpose of fire suppression, emergency medical service and other related duties, who has been hired through regular procedure by the City of Rancho.

B.   Duties

1.   Firefighters shall respond to all alarms with their respective companies, perform the duties specifically detailed to them in a safe manner, obey all rules and regulations of the department, and perform such other duties in connection with the department as their superior officers may require.

EXHIBIT 4

MEMORANDUM

DATE: July 27, C.Y.-2

TO: All Fire Department Personnel

FROM: S. Hatch, Chief

RE: Clarification of City/Department Anti-Nepotism Policy

It has recently been brought to my attention that Fire Department administration has not been following the City's/Department's Anti-Nepotism Policy with regard to work assignments.

In the past, Department administration and staff have incorrectly interpreted this policy as applying only to regular work assignments at the employees' assigned station without regard to position coverage, force hires, and shift trades. As a result of this discrepancy being brought to Fire administration's attention, effective July 18, C.Y.-2, the Department began applying the City's/Department's Anti-Nepotism Policy to *all* assignments, including regular work assignments, position coverage, force hires, shift trades and other such assignments that may exist.

The only exception to the Anti-Nepotism Policy that may cause relatives to be assigned to the same shift (but not to the same station), is a large-scale incident or catastrophe wherein a major recall of Fire Department personnel has occurred.

Jury Instructions

Members of the jury, you have now heard all the evidence and the closing argument of the attorneys. It is my duty to instruct you on the law that applies to this case. You will have a copy of my instructions with you when you go to the jury room to deliberate.

I will now tell you the law that you must follow to reach your verdict. You must follow that law exactly as I give it to you, even if you disagree with it. If the attorneys have said anything different about what the law means, you must follow what I say. In reaching your verdict, you must not speculate about what I think your verdict should be from something I may have said or done.

Pay careful attention to all the instructions that I give you. All the instructions are important because together they state the law that you will use in this case. You must consider all of the instructions together. You must decide this case based only on the law and the evidence.

This is a civil case brought by Plaintiffs, William Striver and Frances Gomez, against Defendant, Rancho Fire Department ("RFD"). Plaintiffs were employed by RFD. Plaintiffs bring their suit under the Golden Fair Employment Practices Act, Golden Code section 12940, which prohibits discrimination based upon marital status. This section provides in relevant part:

> It shall be an unlawful employment practice, unless based upon a bona fide occupational qualification, or, except where based upon applicable security regulations established by the United States or the State of Golden: (a) For an employer, because of the race, religious creed, color, national origin, ancestry, physical disability, mental disability, medical condition, marital status, sex, age, or sexual orientation of any person, to refuse to hire or employ the person or to refuse to select the person for a training program leading to

employment, or to bar or to discharge the person from employment or from a training program leading to employment, or to discriminate against the person in compensation or in terms, conditions, or privileges of employment . . . . (3) Nothing in this part relating to discrimination on account of marital status shall . . . (A) Affect the right of an employer to reasonably regulate, for reasons of supervision, safety, security, or morale, the working of spouses in the same department, division, or facility, consistent with the rules and regulations adopted by the commission.

Plaintiffs have the burden in this case to prove their claim by a preponderance of the evidence. The term "preponderance of the evidence" means the greater weight and degree of credible evidence admitted in this case. Simply put, Plaintiffs must prove it is more likely than not that their claim is true.

Defendant RFD contends that Plaintiffs are covered by the City's anti-nepotism policy because Mr. Striver might be in situations where he would be supervising or controlling the work of Ms. Gomez. Defendant RFD contends that while Plaintiffs' marital status played a role in Defendant RFD's decision to transfer Ms. Gomez, Defendant RFD acted because Plaintiffs' close relationship violates the anti-nepotism policy, which raises public safety concerns.

Under Golden law it is unlawful employment practice for an employer, because of marital status to discriminate against a person in compensation or in terms, conditions, or privileges of employment because of marital status. To prevail on a claim of discrimination, Plaintiffs bear the burden of proving by a preponderance of the evidence that their marital status played a motivating role in, or contributed to, Defendant RFD's decision.

Under Golden law, the prohibition of discrimination on account of marital status does not supersede the right of an employer to reasonably regulate, for reasons of supervision, safety, security, or morale, the assignment of working spouses in the same department, division, or facility.

Defendant RFD may show its policy is reasonably necessary to supervision, safety, security, or morale and is thus a bona fide occupational qualification in either one of two ways: Defendant RFD may show that there is a factual basis for believing that all or substantially all persons excluded by its policy would be unable to perform safely and effectively because of their marital relationship; or Defendant RFD may show that it is impossible or impractical to determine whether Defendant RFD has a reasonable basis for believing that Plaintiffs should not be able to perform on the same shift as a firefighter and engineer. You may consider more than simply Plaintiffs' ability to perform the tasks of the firefighter and engineer jobs. You may also consider the effect that allowing Plaintiffs to serve would have on the achievement of Defendant RFD's objectives relating to safety, supervision, security or morale because of its effect on its other employees, its command structure, its training programs, or any other reason relating to Defendant RFD's operations.

You should be mindful that, although the law prohibits discrimination based upon marital status, the law does not require an employer to extend any special or favorable treatment to employees because of their marital status. You must not second guess Defendant RFD's decision or permit any sympathy for Plaintiffs to lead you to substitute your own judgment for that of Defendant RFD, even though you personally may not favor the action taken and would have acted differently under the circumstances.

Therefore, if you find that Plaintiffs were transferred to different shifts because of their marital status, you must find for Plaintiffs, unless you find that it was reasonably necessary for reasons of supervision, safety, security or morale.

A witness is a person who has knowledge related to this case. You will have to decide whether you believe each witness and how important each witness's testimony is to the case. You may believe all, part, or none of a witness's testimony. In deciding whether to believe a witness's testimony, you may consider, among other factors, the following:

1.   How well did the witness see, hear, or otherwise sense what he or she described in court?

2.   How well did the witness remember and describe what happened?

3.   How did the witness look, act, and speak while testifying?

4.   Did the witness have any reason to say something that was not true? Did the witness show any bias or prejudice? Did the witness have a personal relationship with any of the parties involved in the case? Does the witness have a personal stake in how this case is decided?

5.   What was the witness's attitude toward this case or about giving testimony?

Sometimes a witness may say something that is not consistent with something else he or she said. Sometimes different witnesses will give different versions of what happened. People often forget things or make mistakes in what they remember. Also, two people may see the same event, but remember it differently. You may consider these differences, but do not decide that testimony is untrue just because it differs from other testimony.

However, if you decide that a witness has deliberately testified untruthfully about something important, you may choose not to believe anything that witness said. On the other hand, if you think the witness testified untruthfully about some things but told the truth about others, you may accept the part you think is true and ignore the rest.

Your foreperson shall preside over your deliberations. All jurors should participate in all deliberations and vote on each issue. The votes of ten or more jurors are required to reach a verdict. The verdict must be in writing and the verdict form has been prepared for you. It is as follows:

[READ VERDICT FORM]

In just a few moments, you will be taken to the jury room by the bailiff. The first thing you should do is elect a foreperson who will preside over your deliberations like the chairperson of a meeting. It is the foreperson's job to sign and date the verdict form when all of you have agreed on a verdict in this case and to bring the verdict back to the courtroom when you return.

In closing, let me remind you that it is important that you follow the law spelled out in these instructions in deciding your verdicts. There are no other laws that apply to this case.

**IN THE CIRCUIT COURT OF THE
THIRTEENTH JUDICIAL CIRCUIT
IN AND FOR LEAD COUNTY, STATE OF GOLDEN
CIVIL DIVISION**

WILLIAM STRIVER AND FRANCES   )
GOMEZ,   )
)
    Plaintiffs,   )
)
v.   )   Golden No. 10634
)
RANCHO FIRE DEPARTMENT,   )
)
    Defendant.   )
)
_____)

Verdict

We, the jury, find that Defendant, Rancho Fire Department, did (____)/did not

(____) unlawfully discriminate against Plaintiffs, William Striver and Frances Gomez,

on account of their marital status.

Date   Foreperson

State of Golden

v.

Jake Chambers

(sexual assault)

IN THE CIRCUIT COURT OF THE THIRTEENTH JUDICIAL CIRCUIT

IN AND FOR LEAD COUNTY, STATE OF GOLDEN

CRIMINAL DIVISION

STATE OF GOLDEN	)	
	)	
v.	)	CASE NO: CR 93-343
	)	
JAKE CHAMBERS,	)	
Defendant.	)	
	)	

IN THE CIRCUIT COURT OF THE THIRTEENTH JUDICIAL CIRCUIT

IN AND FOR LEAD COUNTY, STATE OF GOLDEN

CRIMINAL DIVISION

STATE OF GOLDEN	)	**Felony Information**
	)	
v.	)	CASE NO: CR 93-343
	)	
JAKE CHAMBERS,	)	
Defendant.	)	
	)	

Comes now the undersigned and states that on or about June 11, C.Y.-1, in Silverado, Lead County, State of Golden, a felony, in violation of section 3121 of the Golden Penal Code, was committed by the above defendant, who at the time and place last aforesaid, sexually assaulted Susanna Walker.

Judy D. Martinez
Judy D. Martinez
District Attorney, Lead County

Witness List

Witnesses for the State:

1. Susanna Walker * *

2. Detective Nic Lusk * * *

Witnesses for Defendant:

1. Jake Chambers *

2. Eddie Dean *

Each side must call both witnesses listed for their respective party in any order.

* This witness must be a male.

* * This witness must be a female.

* * * This witness may be either gender.

Stipulations

1. Federal Rules of Criminal Procedure and Federal Rules of Evidence apply.

2. Each witness, except for Defendant, who gave a statement or interview reviewed the officer's report of his or her statement or interview and signed the statement or interview verifying that it was accurate and complete.

3. All exhibits in the file are authentic and, unless otherwise noted, are the original of that document.

4. Other than what appears in the witness statements, interviews, and witness testimony, there is nothing exceptional or unusual about the background of any of the witnesses that would bolster or detract from their credibility.

5. All dates are denoted by C.Y. (current year) and C.Y.-1 indicating, for example, that the date is the current year minus one.

6. All pretrial motions shall be oral.

7. No party may "invent" witnesses or evidence not specifically mentioned in this problem.

8. "Beyond the record" is not a proper objection. Rather, attorneys shall use cross-examination as a means of challenging a witness whose testimony strays beyond the facts contained in the witness's statement, interview, or prior testimony.

9. It is stipulated that Cindy Walker is unavailable as a witness in this matter. It is further stipulated that counsel for both sides had an opportunity to develop this witness's testimony during the preliminary hearing. Either party may offer her testimony in accordance with the Federal Rules of Evidence.

10. It is stipulated that Defendant pled guilty to sexual assault upon a minor, a felony, in CY-2, and that he was placed upon probation for a period of three years following his conviction.

11. In a pretrial hearing the court has ruled that the statement given by Defendant on June 14, CY-1, was given after a voluntary, knowing, and intelligent waiver of his Miranda rights, and that it may be used at trial.

12. Section 3121 of the Golden Penal Code provides: "A person commits sexual assault when the person engages in sexual intercourse with a complainant:

　　1.　By forcible compulsion;

　　2.　By threat of forcible compulsion that would prevent resistance by a person of reasonable resolution; or

　　3.　Who is unconscious."

13. The prosecution and defense may call only the two witnesses listed on their respective witness list. Each party may call additional witnesses by deposition or witness statement. Any such testimony is subject to objections pursuant to the Federal Rules of Evidence. If a witness is called by deposition or witness statement, the opposing party may cross-examine that witness by deposition or witness statement. The parties have agreed to waive Confrontational Clause objections for only these witnesses.

Lead County Sheriff's Department

Report Type: Incident Report

Report by: Detective Nic Lusk, Badge Number P9278 *(initialed NL)*

Position/Department: Lead County Sheriff's Department, Investigator, Sex Crimes Division

Date: June 21, C.Y. -1

Incident: Alleged sexual assault of Susanna Walker by Jake Chambers on June 11, C.Y. −1.

Involvement by officer: Susanna Walker, DOB C.Y. -21, came into the station Wednesday, June 14, C.Y. −1, and reported that on June 11, she had been raped at her boyfriend's apartment by his roommate and that her boyfriend had shown up during the rape and had beaten her because he thought she was cheating on him.

She reported that while she was waiting for boyfriend Dean, roommate Chambers pushed her into his bedroom, ripped off her tank top and raped her. She reported that Dean then beat her because he believed she was having consensual sex with Chambers.

I examined her bruising. She had a large bruise on the left side of her face. The inside of her mouth appeared to have a cut. She also had another cut on the right side of her face. Her stomach had a large bruise that appeared horizontal across her stomach.

On June 16, C.Y. -1, I reinterviewed Walker. (See transcript of interview.)

Initial Investigation: I spoke with Jake Chambers at his apartment on the afternoon of June 14, C.Y. −1. Eddie Dean was not present. Chambers gave consent to search their apartment. In the hallway connecting the bedrooms there was a table that looked broken. The screen door at the front door was torn. In Chambers' bedroom, we found what appeared to be a blue woman's tank top similar to the one the victim had described she was wearing at the time of the incident. The tank top was torn. The bed was pushed against two walls and the tank top was found in the far corner next to the wall. I photographed the tank top and collected it as evidence. (See "Attachments 1 and 2" to this Report.) [In a follow-up interview, Walker confirmed that the tank top was hers.] We searched the apartment for a bikini top and bottom, but did not find either. In a trash container in the kitchen I noted multiple empty beer containers and a wilted bouquet of flowers in a vase. I photographed the contents of the trashcan and collected the bouquet as evidence. (See "Attachment 3" to this Report.)

We took Chambers to the station and I questioned him about what had happened. Chambers told me he had consensual sex with Walker and then Dean showed up. He explained that Walker hastily dressed and left his bedroom. He then heard Walker and Dean fighting. Chambers said he went to see what was going on and that he and Dean then got into a fight after Walker left. I examined Chambers for injuries and he had a bite on his lower left arm and some small cuts on his upper arms.

Other Important Information: No warrant was obtained, consent for a look around the house was given, no Miranda waiver card from Chambers. Arrest was made on June 19, C.Y. –1.

Attachment "1"

Attachment "2"

Attachment "3"

Lead County Sheriff's Department

Report Type: Follow-up Interview of Susanna Walker

Interviewer: Detective Nic Lusk *(initialed NL)*

Date of Interview: June 16, C.Y. -1

Q: Ms. Walker, I have interviewed Mr. Chambers and Mr. Dean about what happened on June 11 and now I have some additional questions for you.

A: I guess so.

Q: Okay, tell me again why you were at their apartment that day.

A: Like I already told you, Jake is the roommate of my former boyfriend, Eddie Dean. Eddie and I had made plans to go to the beach, but when I got to their apartment Eddie wasn't there. Jake told me that Eddie had a call to pick his mother up at the airport and would be back in about an hour.

Q: What time did you arrive at their apartment?

A: Right around noon, maybe a little after.

Q: What did you do when you learned Dean wasn't there?

A: I was irritated that he hadn't called and told me he would be late but I didn't want to drive all the way back to my house, so I decided to stay there and wait for him. Jake offered me a beer, so I sat down on the couch and had a beer with him.

Q: Was Jake drinking when you got there?

A: Yeah, he was pretty drunk.

Q: How did you know?

A: The coffee table was covered with empties and he was acting really loopy. Plus, later when he got close to me in his bedroom I could smell it on his breath.

Q: Okay, we will get to what happened in the bedroom in a little bit. So, you sat down on the couch and had a beer. What happened next?

A: He made some comment about how cute I looked, which I kind of laughed off. I had a tank top and a pair of shorts on over my bathing suit. I really didn't think too much of his comment because he was always saying stuff like that. We just talked for a little bit and drank our beers.

Q: How many drinks did you have?

A: One.

Q: Were you drunk?

A: Maybe I was a little buzzed, because I had not eaten anything, but I wasn't drunk.

Q: What happened next?

A: We sat around talking for a while, just hanging out.

Q: Then what?

A: Well, he had just bought a new guitar and he asked me if I wanted to see it. I followed him towards his room to check it out, but I didn't go inside. I just stood in the doorway and listened while he played a couple of songs.

Q: Did anything happen while he was playing the guitar?

A: No, I just stood there and listened while he played.

Q: Where were you standing?

A: I was standing in the doorway. I didn't go in his room at all.

Q: What happened after he was done playing?

A: He came over and began to kiss me.

Q: What did you do?

A: I pushed him away and told him that I did not think that we should be doing this. Then he said, "Why not? You told me that you were interested in me before."

Q: Go on.

A: I told him that was old history.

Q: What happened next?

A: He tried to kiss me again. I pushed him away and tried to walk back towards the living room. As I turned around he grabbed my arm and pulled me to the bed. Then, he jumped on me and held me down.

Q: Were you two arguing? Was anything being said?

A: I had said something to him about being a creep when I tried to go towards the living room. Everything had gone so fast I guess I didn't really say anything, except maybe scream a little. After he threw me on the bed and was holding me down, he slapped me in the face hard and said something about how he had wanted to hurt me since that night in the club.

Q: What happened then?

A: I tried to fight him off, but he's a big guy.

Q: What happened next?

A: He ripped off my shirt. Not ripped it off like over my head, but literally ripped it off. My bikini top came with it. Then, he began pulling down my shorts and bikini bottoms. I tried to stop him, but I couldn't. I tried kicking and screaming, but Jake slapped me in the face and told me to stay still. I tried to bite and claw my way out from under him even harder. But then he hit me really hard in the side and knocked the wind out of me. It hurt so bad, but I knew there was nothing that I could do, so I just laid there and cried while he raped me.

Q: How long did it take for all this to occur?

A: I don't know.

Q: Then what happened?

A: Well, right after he finished but was still laying on me I heard the front door slam. I guess he must have heard it too because he jumped off me and ran into the bathroom.

Q: What did you do after he got off you?

A: By that time I was hysterical. I jumped off the bed and pulled on my shorts. I couldn't find my top, so I grabbed one of his shirts and tried to cover myself a little. Then, I ran for the door. I got out the door and into the hallway. Eddie was coming down the hallway and before I even got the chance to say anything, he said, "I can't believe this" and hit me across the face. After that everything was pretty much a blur. Eddie was screaming at me. He grabbed me by the arm and dragged me down the hallway to the door. Then, he picked me up and threw me out the door. He threw me so hard that I smashed through the screen door and hit the railing across the hall.

Q: Then what happened?

A: I covered myself up as best I could and ran to the car.

Q: Why did it take you so long to report this?

A: I couldn't get myself to leave the house for a couple of days. I didn't want anyone to see my face. I was really embarrassed and didn't want anyone to know what had happened, especially my family.

Q: Why were you so afraid to tell your family?

A: I really did not want my parents to find out. My family is deeply religious, and I'm Catholic.

Q: What made you finally decide to go to the police?

A: My sister, Cindy.

Q: Tell me about that.

A: I usually see her a couple of times a week. But after I was attacked I avoided her calls and called in sick to work. I guess Cindy finally figured that something was wrong because she came to my apartment a couple of days ago and when she saw my face she demanded to know what had happened. I told her everything and she brought me here.

Q: Where do you live?

A: I live at 7720 Wellesley in Silverado.

Q: Where do you work?

A: I work at the Hafeman-Bilz advertising firm as a traffic coordinator.

Q: How long have you known Jake Chambers?

A: Since around May C.Y. –2.

Q: How did you meet one another?

A: It was after I had moved to Silverado from St. Louis about two years ago. A friend and co-worker of mine, Christy Negler, and I went to a club called the Recoco. We were having a couple of drinks at the bar when we were approached by Jake and Eddie.

Q: What happened?

A: Well, like I said, I was at the bar with Christy when they approached and offered to buy us a drink. We hung with them, talking and dancing. We ended up going over to their apartment afterward to hang out. We eventually split off into couples. I went with Eddie into his room, while Jake and Christy stayed out in the living room. Eddie and I had only been back in his room for about a half hour or so when I heard Christy yelling. Eddie and I came into the living room and Christy was yelling at Jake. We ended up getting her a cab and she went home.

Q: Do you know why she was yelling at Jake?

A: She told me that he had come on to her really hard, putting his hands all over her. She was really upset. She never told me exactly what happened that night, but she would never go clubbing with me again if she knew that Jake was going to be there.

Q: So that night she left and you stayed at their apartment?

A: Yes.

Q: Anything else happen that night?

A: Not really. I stayed with Eddie that night and Jake made some crack to me in the morning, but that was it.

Q: What did Jake say?

A: He said something to me about Christy being a prude and that he wished she were more like me. I didn't really know him that well, so I didn't think too much of it. I guess it creeped me out a little bit, but I never mentioned it to Eddie.

Q: Can you tell me about your relationship with Eddie?

A: Sure. Eddie and I have been together since that night until Jake raped me. He was really nice. I really liked him, but he took the relationship much more seriously than I did.

Q: What do you mean when you say that he took the relationship more seriously?

A: I am pretty young and I like to have fun. I just really didn't think of him on a permanent basis. I never hooked up with other guys or anything, but I wasn't exactly looking for a ring on my finger, either. I guess since Eddie is a little older he thought about that stuff more than I did. I guess my nonchalance about the relationship upset him because he started getting really overprotective.

Q: How was he overprotective?

A: It started off pretty mild with comments about the way I was dressed when we would go out. He would tell me that I looked too available, stuff like that. We were constantly arguing about me flirting with guys and he accused me of cheating on him. There were a couple times that he actually came out on the dance floor when I was at a club, grabbed me and pulled me off the floor by my arm.

Q: Can you tell me what it was that angered him so much?

A: I can't say exactly, but I guess it was because he has jealousy problems. I like to go to clubs and dance. Jake and Eddie would rather sit at the bar and get wasted, so I would leave them at the bar and go dance. When you are at a club dancing, naturally guys are going to come up and dance with you. I never saw a problem with it. He also heard some rumors that I had cheated on him. I tried to tell him that they were lies, but I guess the rumors only fueled his insecurity.

Q: Did you ever cheat on him?

A: No. I guess I had a few innocent kisses from guys at a club, but nothing more than that.

Q: Was he ever physically abusive?

A: Besides what happened after Jake raped me, he had never hit me or anything like that. The few times he pulled me off the dance floor was about as physical as it got.

Q: Did any of this effect your relationship with him?

A: Yeah. I kind of stopped hanging out with him for a little while. I mean, we still went out from time to time, but if I wanted to go out to a club it was usually with my girlfriends and not with Eddie.

Q: But you stayed with him?

A: Yeah. Despite his over protectiveness, I still liked the guy. Later in the relationship things were pretty much on and off, but when it was on it was fine.

Q: Okay, I want to ask you about your relationship with Jake Chambers prior to the alleged rape. Were you two friends?

A: I guess you could have called us friends. I didn't really like him at first because of the whole incident with Christy, but after that we got along pretty well. We were cool with each other when Eddie and I weren't having problems. But if Eddie and I were fighting, then Jake was usually a jerk to me. I knew he told some stuff to Eddie about me that wasn't true, so I guess that was a problem I had with him. I didn't really hold it against him though, because it was just stuff he had heard and relayed to Eddie, so I figured he was just being a friend.

Q: Is it fair to say that you two were only friends because of you and Eddie's relationship?

A: I guess so. We never hung out with each other, just the two of us. There was one occasion when I was out and I ran into him at a bar. That did not end well.

Q: Can you tell me about it?

A: I was with a couple of my friends and I was ordering a drink when someone slapped me on the butt. I turned around furious, but there was Jake smiling, so we had a little chuckle about it. We had a few drinks together and danced some. I guess we were kind of flirting with each other. I said something about how it was funny because I had initially been interested in him rather than Eddie. He asked me what I was talking about and I told him that Christy and I had played rock, paper, scissors in the bathroom at the Recoco that night and she had won so I let her pursue him and I went after Eddie. After I told him that he began to get really forward with me. He put his hands all over me and tried to kiss me. I had to push him away from me several times and when he would not stop I slapped him in the face pretty hard. He stormed off and must have called Eddie, because Eddie showed up about half an hour later. We got into a really big fight over the whole thing and didn't talk for a couple of weeks.

Q: When did that occur?

A: I guess it was about 2 months before the rape, so sometime in April.

Q: How did you and Jake get along after that?

A: It was pretty strained.

Q: But you didn't leave the apartment on the day you were assaulted when you found out Eddie wasn't there.

A: I guess that was a big mistake. But that didn't give him the right to do what he did.

Q: Do you have anything to add?

A: The whole thing is really sad and ironic.

Q: What do you mean ironic?

A: When I got there that day, I had flowers for Eddie. I was going to tell him how much I cared for him.

Q: You had flowers when you arrived at the apartment?

A: Yeah, it was a spring bouquet in a glass vase.

Q: What did you do with them when you got there?

A: I put it on the coffee table so it would be the first thing Eddie saw when he walked in.

Q: Anything else I need to know about?

A: Not that I can think of.

Interview terminated at 14:05 hours.

Reviewed and verified by: *Susanna Walker*
                             Susanna Walker

Lead County Sheriff's Department

Report Type: Interrogation of Jake Chambers

Interviewer: Detective Nic Lusk *(initialed NL)*

Date of Interview: June 14, C.Y. -1

Q: Good afternoon Mr. Chambers, could you please state your name and current address for the record?

A: Jake Chambers. I live at 1020 Prospect, Apartment C in Silverado, Golden State.

Q: Mr. Chambers, before we get started I need to read you your rights. Okay?

A: Okay.

Q: You have the right to remain silent. If you give up that right, anything you say can and will be used against you in a court of law. You have the right to an attorney and to have an attorney present during questioning. If you cannot afford an attorney, one will be provided to you at no cost. During any questioning, you may decide at any time to exercise these rights, not answer any questions, or make any statements. Do you understand the rights I have just read to you?

A: Yeah, I guess so.

Q: Do you wish to speak with me?

A: I don't know what choice I have. I guess so. This is about Susanna, isn't it?

Q: Mr. Chambers, how old are you?

A: I am twenty-six years old.

Q: What is your occupation?

A: I am pursuing a career as an actor. I work as a waiter to get by when I don't have any acting gigs. Currently, I work at Nonna's Piazzo, an Italian restaurant in the hills.

Q: When did you meet Susanna Walker?

A: I met her about two years ago at a club.

Q: Can you elaborate on the night you two first met?

A: Sure. Eddie and I went to Recoco and noticed her and one of her friends. We went over and bought them a couple of drinks. We hung out until the place closed and then went back to our house later that evening. Eddie liked her, so I hung out with her friend. I guess you could say that I was playing wingman for him. At our house, Eddie and Susanna went back to his room and Susanna's friend and I were out in the living room.

Q: Did anything happen between you and the friend?

A: We kissed for a little while in the living room and ended up getting in a fight about something. She started yelling at me and ended up leaving.

Q: Did Susanna go with her?

A: No. I thought that it was kind of weird, because they called a cab for her and she left, but Susanna stayed.

Q: Okay, I would like to focus your attention on June 11, C.Y. -1. How did you begin that day?

A: I woke up pretty late and was a little hung over from the night before. Eddie took off, so I began to pick up the mess from the night before.

Q: You say the house was messy. Can you describe it for me?

A: Like I said, we had a little party the night before, so there were beer bottles on the table, the ashtrays were full, stuff like that. I know Susanna is claiming I was drunk, but the bottles on the table were from the night before.

Q: Were you drinking that day?

A: No. I was way too hung over. You know, I feel weird talking about this. I know you are trying to nail me, man. Maybe I should get a lawyer.

Q: Listen, you waived your rights and agreed to talk about this, now let's talk. What time did Susanna show up?

A: What the hell? I didn't do anything criminal. Okay, I'll tell you it was right after Eddie had left, so I guess it would have been probably around noon.

Q: What happened when she got to the apartment?

A: I was just sitting there in a pair of shorts watching TV when she knocked on the door. I told her that Eddie had gone to the airport, but she didn't seem to care. She sat down next to me on the couch and started watching TV.

Q: What was she wearing?

A: She had on a bikini top and shorts over her bottoms.

Q: Was she wearing a tank top over her bikini top or any sort of shirt?

A: I know Susanna is claiming that she was wearing a shirt that I had ripped off, but all she had on when she came over that day was the bikini top and some shorts over the bottoms.

Q: We found a torn blue tank top behind your bed. Do you know where it came from?

A: I have no idea. Like I said, we had a party the night before, so our place was pretty trashed.

Q: Okay, what happened after she sat down?

A: We talked for a while, and then she got up and said that she had to go to the bathroom. It had only been about a minute when I heard her yell something about me playing a tune for her on my new guitar, so I went back to my bedroom to see what she was talking about.

Q: Had either of you had anything to drink prior to you going back into the bedroom?

A: I think she may have grabbed a beer from the fridge, but like I said I was too hung over.

Q: What happened once you got back to your bedroom?

A: When I got to my door, I saw her standing there naked with just my guitar covering her body. Her bikini was on the floor. I asked her what she was doing and she said something like, "I think you know what I am doing." She put the guitar down, came up to me and started kissing me. She pushed me on the bed and closed the door. Everything had happened so fast I really didn't stop to consider what was going on. If I had just been thinking straight, this whole thing could have been avoided.

Q: What do you mean if you had been thinking straight?

A: I guess that I was caught up in the moment. I would never do anything to hurt Eddie. We have been best friends since we were kids. I would not throw that away for any girl, especially not someone like her.

Q: What happened after you two were on the bed?

A: Before I knew it, she had taken off my shorts and we were having sex. It all happened really fast. I didn't even have time to think about what was going on.

Q: How long did this go on?

A: I guess the whole interaction from the time I came to the bedroom door till the time I heard the front door was probably about 10 minutes.

Q: So you two were interrupted by the sound of the front door?

A: Yeah, we were on my bed and then I heard the front door slam. I knew it was Eddie and that is when the reality of the whole situation rushed back into my head.

Q: What did you do when you heard the door?

A: I pushed her off me, grabbed my shorts and went into my bathroom.

Q: Then what happened?

A: The next thing I heard was Eddie yelling and a crash from the hallway. I heard Susanna crying and yelling that she was sorry, but that ended a moment later when I heard the front door slam. I went out into the hallway to see what was going on and before I knew it Eddie jumped me and was coming after me. I have never seen him that angry; he was like a raving lunatic. We wrestled around for a little bit, but eventually I had him pinned down. He scratched me several times and bit my forearm. But other than that neither of us was hurt. After he calmed down a bit, I let him up and he charged out the door.

Q: He left the apartment?

A: Yes.

Q: When did Eddie come back?

A: He came back later that night and I explained to him what had happened. He was pretty upset and was actually worried about Susanna. I didn't see what he had done, but he said that he had hit her pretty hard. He said he was thinking about going to the cops. I couldn't believe that he felt bad for her after all he had been through with her.

Q: What do you mean by that?

A: I tried telling him several times to get rid of her and now he felt bad after she had seduced his best friend. She was always flirting with guys and even came on to me one other time. I have heard about her partying and sleeping with the bouncers and bartenders at some of the clubs she went to. I tried to tell Eddie about it, but he would never listen. He was so in love with her that he was just blind.

Q: Can you give me any reason why Susanna would make all this up?

A: I know that this is probably not proper, but she is nothing but a tramp and she doesn't want her parents finding out about it. She knew about my sexual assault case and she is trying to clear her name with her parents and with Eddie by dragging me into this and making me look like the bad guy. I heard that she is claiming to have been a virgin. That is ridiculous, although we don't hang out in the same circles, I could give you the names of about ten people that would tell you otherwise.

Q: Let's talk about your sexual assault case. As I recall, that was about a year before all this happened, is that right?

A: That's all behind me now.

Q: What do you mean?

A: I pled to sex with a minor and got three years probation.

Q: I had a chance to pull up the reports on that case. The girl was 17 and claimed she was forcibly raped, isn't that right?

A: Yeah, but that's not what happened. I thought she was old enough and she was certainly willing.

Q: In looking through the arrest report she claims she was raped right in your bedroom.

A: It didn't happen then and it didn't happen this time.

Q: I understand what you are saying. Is there anything else I need to know about this?

A: I've said my piece.

Interview terminated at 14:15 hours.

Lead County Sheriff's Department

Report Type: Interview of Eddie Dean

Interviewer: Detective Nic Lusk *(initialed NL)*

Date of Interview: June 17, C.Y. -1

Q: Mr. Dean, can you please state your name and current address for the record?

A: My name is Eddie Dean. I live at 1020 Prospect, Apartment C here in Silverado.

Q: And how old are you?

A: I am twenty-six.

Q: Are you employed?

A: I work at Blakely-Morris as a financial consultant.

Q: Can you tell me about your relationship with Susanna Walker?

A: Susanna and I had been going out for about a year before I caught her and Jake together. We had been dating pretty steadily since I met her at the Recoco. Our relationship was pretty bumpy because she was always flirting with guys when we went out and I knew that she had cheated on me several times.

Q: How did you know that she was cheating on you?

A: Jake and I were friends with several bartenders and bouncers at some of the clubs we went to and it seemed like every time I went out someone was telling me that Susanna had been there dancing and hanging out with some other guy. Plus, she never acted like she had a boyfriend.

Q: Why did you continue to date her?

A: I don't know why I kept going back to her, I guess it was because I loved her and believed her whenever she told me that nothing had happened. I sure wish I had not been so naive. It would have saved me a lot of trouble.

Q: Was your relationship with her sexual?

A: Yeah, I slept with her the first night we met. It's crazy that she is claiming that she was a virgin. She told me that I was her first, but I strongly doubt that.

Q: Why would she claim to be a virgin?

A: She doesn't want her parents to find out about her. She may go to church every Sunday, but trust me, she is no saint.

Q: Before the incident with Jake, had you ever hit her or abused her?

A: She made me pretty mad on several occasions, but I had never hurt her until that day.

Q: Can you tell us what happened on Sunday, June 11, C.Y. -1?

A: I felt lousy that morning because Jake and I had been up partying pretty late the night before. We had been drinking at a club and then brought it home and didn't finish until pretty late. The next morning about 11:00 I called Susanna and asked if she wanted to hang out at the beach that afternoon. But about noon my mom called and I had to go and pick her up at the airport.

Q: Did you see Jake before you left?

A: Yes, he was getting up just as I was leaving. He said that he felt pretty awful. I asked him if he wanted to go the beach with Susanna and me, but he said he would probably stay home and clean up.

Q: So you left and went to the airport, then what?

A: I called Susanna and left a message telling her not to come over until around three because I was going to be late. My mom called when I was about halfway to the airport and said that her ride had shown up, so she didn't need me to come. So I turned around and went home. I tried to call Susanna on her cell, but there was no answer.

Q: What happened when you got back home?

A: When I got there I noticed that Susanna's car was there. I went up to the apartment, and when I opened the door I didn't see either of them. I heard a rustling noise coming from Jake's room. I headed down the hall and when I was almost to his door, Susanna came out with nothing on but her shorts.

Q: Then what?

A: I exploded. It pretty much confirmed everything I had heard about her. I felt like an idiot for believing her when she denied all of it. I couldn't control myself. I hit her and threw her out the door. I slammed the door and then went after Jake, who was out in the hallway by then. I tackled him and we wrestled around a little bit, but Jake is bigger and he pinned me down. He held on to me for a while and finally I calmed down a bit.

Q: Were you surprised to see her with Jake?

A: Not really. She had hit on him one night when they had run into each other at a club. He had told me that she was all over him that night. We got into a big fight over the whole thing.

Q: Did it appear that she had been assaulted when you saw her?

A: I know that she claims to have been raped, but it sure didn't look like it to me. If she had been crying or hurt I couldn't tell it by the look on her face when she saw me. She looked like someone who had just been caught, not like a victim.

Q: Did she have any bruises or any blood on her face?

A: No, I didn't see anything like that.

Q: Did you and Susanna talk after that day?

A: She called me a couple of days later and left messages, asking me to forgive her. I would have saved them if I knew it would have helped Jake, but at the time I was upset and I erased them right after I listened to them. I never expected her to accuse Jake of raping her.

Q: Tell me about your relationship with Jake.

A: He is my best friend. We have been buddies since the first grade.

Q: What about after the incident with Susanna?

A: I was pretty upset with him for a couple of weeks afterwards, but I decided that Susanna was not worth sacrificing my best friend. He told me what had happened when I got back home that night. How she had come on to him and he had not been thinking straight. I really have no reason not to believe him, especially knowing how Susanna is. I should have seen it coming, I guess.

Q: Do you know Jake to be aggressive with women in general?

A: Well, Jake doesn't need to try with girls, they come to him. Jake and I pretty much hang out all the time and rarely does he approach women. It's not that he is shy, he just doesn't have to, they throw themselves at him. To answer your question, I have never seen him be aggressive with a woman.

Q: What about the night you and Susanna met each other? There has been some talk about him being overly aggressive with Susanna's friend that night.

A: That girl? That is nothing but more of Susanna's manipulative ways to bolster her claim. As I remember that night, Jake and that girl got into it over politics or something about abortion. She was pretty mad at him, but it was not because he hit on her. Jake just isn't that desperate.

Interview terminated at 15:30 hours.

Reviewed and verified by:___*Eddie Dean*_____
                                            Eddie Dean

IN THE CIRCUIT COURT OF THE THIRTEENTH JUDICIAL CIRCUIT

IN AND FOR LEAD COUNTY, STATE OF GOLDEN

CRIMINAL DIVISION

TRANSCRIPT OF PRELIMINARY HEARING TESTIMONY

WITNESS: CINDY WALKER

BEFORE THE HONORABLE SARA JOHNSON

APPEARANCES:

PAT FREIGHT FROM THE DISTRICT ATTORNEY'S OFFICE OF LEAD COUNTY, REPRESENTING THE STATE OF GOLDEN

MITCHELL KART, ESQ., REPRESENTING JAKE CHAMBERS

DATE: JUNE 20, C.Y.-1

Q: Good morning, Ms. Walker. My name is Pat Freight. I work for the Lead County District Attorney's office. Can you please state your name for the record?

A: My name is Cindy Walker.

Q: Ms. Walker, are you related to Susanna Walker?

A: Yes, she is my sister.

Q: I need to ask you some questions about your knowledge of the events involving your sister on June 11, C.Y.-1, okay?

A: Of course. I want to do anything I can to see that the man who did this to her is punished.

Q: First, let's start with you describing the nature of your relationship with Susanna.

A: She is my baby sister. I'm eight years older than her and we've always been very close. I'm very protective of her.

Q: I take it you see her often?

A: At least twice a week.

Q: What did you know of her relationship with Eddie Dean?

A: They had been dating on and off for I think better than a year. I thought she was too young for him, but she liked him.

Q: Do you know Eddie Dean's roommate, Jake Chambers?

A: I met him once or twice. A real piece of work. I've known his type all my adult life. He's a low-life, a predator.

Q: Why do you say that?

A: Listen, any woman who's been out there dating knows exactly what I'm talking about. He thinks he's a ladies man and when he doesn't get what he wants he just takes it.

Q: Susanna says you went to her apartment after the assault. I'd like to talk about that. Do you recall what day that was?

A: It was a Wednesday, the 14th, I think.

Q: Why did you go?

A: She wasn't answering her phone and she wasn't at work. I was concerned. So I went to her apartment.

Q: Tell me about that.

A: She was a basket case, both physically and emotionally. When she saw it was me she grabbed on to me and sobbed. When I was finally able to understand her – she blurted out that she was so ashamed because she had been attacked.

Q: Did she say who attacked her?

A: Eddie's roommate – Jake.

Q: Did she give you any specifics of the attack?

A: Just that she had gone to their apartment to tell Eddie how much she cared about him. She even took him flowers. She had come by my house earlier that day and we cut some flowers and she made an arrangement for Eddie. She was pretty pumped up about seeing him.

Q: Did she give any details about what happened once she got there?

A: She said that Jake was his usual awful self and attacked her and then when Eddie got there he went into a rage and beat on her. I hope you put both those guys in jail.

COURT: Mr. Kart, any cross-examination of this witness?

A [by Mr. Kart]: None at this time.

COURT: Thank you, Ms. Walker. You may be excused.

Jury Instructions

Members of the jury, I thank you for your attention during this trial. Please pay attention to the instructions I am about to give you.

In this case, Jake Chambers is accused of sexual assault in violation of section 3121 of the Golden Penal Code. To prove the crime sexual assault, the State must prove the following two elements beyond a reasonable doubt:

1.   Jake Chambers committed an act upon Susanna Walker in which the sexual organ of Jake Chambers penetrated the vagina of Susanna Walker.

2.   The act was committed by forcible compulsion. "Forcible compulsion" means compulsion by use of physical force or emotional or psychological force, either express or implied.

Jake Chambers has entered a plea of not guilty. This means you must presume or believe that Jake Chambers is innocent. This presumption stays with Jake Chambers as to each material allegation in the indictment through each stage of the trial until it has been overcome by the evidence to the exclusion of and beyond a reasonable doubt.

To overcome Defendant's presumption of innocence, the State has the burden of proving the following two elements:

1.   The crime with which Defendant is charged was committed.

2.   Defendant is the person who committed the crime.

Defendant is not required to prove anything.

Whenever the words "reasonable doubt" are used, you must consider the following: A reasonable doubt is not a mere possible doubt, because everything relating to human affairs is open to some possible or imaginary doubt. It is that state of the case which, after the entire comparison and consideration of all the evidence, leaves the minds of the jurors in that condition that they cannot say they feel an abiding conviction of the truth of the charge.

It is to the evidence introduced during this trial, and to it alone, that you are to look for that proof. A reasonable doubt as to the guilt of Defendant may arise from the evidence, a conflict in the evidence, or a lack of evidence. If you have a reasonable doubt, you should find Defendant not guilty. If you have no reasonable doubt, you should find Defendant guilty.

You must decide this case based only on the law and the evidence. It is up to you to decide what evidence is reliable. You should use your common sense in deciding which evidence is reliable and which evidence should not be relied upon in considering your verdict. You may find some of the evidence not reliable or less reliable than other evidence.

A witness is a person who has knowledge related to this case. You will have to decide whether you believe each witness and how important each witness's testimony is to the case. You may believe all, part, or none of a witness's testimony. In deciding whether to believe a witness's testimony, you may consider, among other factors, the following:

1.   Did the witness seem to have an opportunity to see and know the things about which the witness testified?

2.   Did the witness seem to have an accurate memory?

3.   Was the witness honest and straightforward in answering the attorneys' questions?

4. Did the witness have some interest in how the case should be decided?

5. Does the witness's testimony agree with the other testimony and other evidence in this case?

6. Has the witness been offered or received any money, preferred treatment, or other benefit in order to get the witness to testify?

7. Had any pressure or threat been used against the witness that affected the truth of the witness's testimony?

8. Did the witness at some other time make a statement that is inconsistent with the testimony he or she gave in court?

9. Was it proved that the witness had been convicted of a crime?

You may rely upon your own conclusions about the witnesses. A juror may believe or disbelieve all or any part of the evidence or the testimony of any witness.

Defendant in this case has become a witness. You should apply the same rules to consideration of his testimony that you apply to the testimony of the other witnesses.

There are some general rules that apply to your deliberations. You must follow these rules in order to return a lawful verdict:

1. You must follow the law as it is set out in these instructions. If you fail to follow the law, your verdict will be a miscarriage of justice.

2. This case must be decided only upon the evidence that you have heard from the answers of the witnesses and have seen in the form of exhibits and these instructions.

3. This case must not be decided for or against anyone because you feel sorry for anyone or are angry at anyone.

4.   Remember the lawyers are not on trial. Your feelings about them should not influence your decision in this case.

5.   Your duty is to determine if Defendant has been proven guilty or not. It is the judge's job to determine the proper sentence if Defendant is found guilty.

6.   Whatever verdict you render must be unanimous; that is, each juror must agree to the same verdict. The verdict must be the verdict of each juror, as well as of the jury as a whole.

7.   It is entirely proper for a lawyer to talk to a witness about what testimony the witness would give if called to the courtroom. The witness should not be discredited for talking to a lawyer about his or her testimony.

8.   Your verdict should not be influenced by feelings of prejudice, bias, or sympathy. Your verdict must be based on the evidence and the law contained in these instructions.

Deciding a proper verdict is exclusively your job. I cannot participate in that decision in any way. Please disregard anything I may have said or done that made you think I preferred one verdict over another.

Only one verdict may be returned as to the crime charged. The verdict must be in writing and the verdict form has been prepared for you. It is as follows:

[READ VERDICT FORM]

In just a few moments, you will be taken to the jury room by the bailiff. The first thing you should do is elect a foreperson who will preside over your deliberations like the chairperson of a meeting. It is the foreperson's job to sign and date the verdict form when all of you have agreed on a verdict in this case and to bring the verdict back to the courtroom when you return.

In closing, let me remind you that it is important that you follow the law spelled out in these instructions in deciding your verdicts. Even if you do not like the laws, you must apply them. There are no other laws that apply to this case.

IN THE CIRCUIT COURT OF THE THIRTEENTH JUDICIAL CIRCUIT

IN AND FOR LEAD COUNTY, STATE OF GOLDEN

CRIMINAL DIVISION

STATE OF GOLDEN	)	
	)	
v.	)	CASE NO: CR 93-343
	)	
JAKE CHAMBERS,	)	
Defendant.	)	
	)	

VERDICT

As to the charge of sexual assault in violation of section 3121 of the Golden Penal

Code, we, the jury, find Defendant, Jake Chambers:

_____   Guilty

_____   Not Guilty

So say we all.

_____

Foreperson of the Jury

_____

Date